Home

Encounters: Experience and Anthropological Knowledge

ISSN: 1746–8175

Series Editor: John Borneman

The *Encounters* series examines the issues that affect all anthropologists in the field. These short collections of essays describe and analyze the surprise and interest of the fieldwork encounter, on topics such as money, violence, food and sex. The series aims to show that anthropological knowledge is based in experience, bringing into the public realm useful and thought-provoking areas for discussion that previously anthropologists have been reluctant or unable to highlight.

Previously published in this series:

Children: Ethnographic Encounters, edited by Catherine Allerton
Crowds: Ethnographic Encounters, edited by Megan Steffen
Food: Ethnographic Encounters, edited by Leo Coleman
Money: Ethnographic Encounters, edited by Stefan Senders and Allison Truitt
Sex: Ethnographic Encounters, edited by Richard Joseph Martin and Dieter Haller
Violence: Ethnographic Encounters, edited by Parvis Ghassem-Facha

Home

Ethnographic Encounters

Edited by
Johannes Lenhard and Farhan Samanani

BLOOMSBURY ACADEMIC
LONDON • NEW YORK • OXFORD • NEW DELHI • SYDNEY

BLOOMSBURY ACADEMIC
Bloomsbury Publishing Plc
50 Bedford Square, London, WC1B 3DP, UK
1385 Broadway, New York, NY 10018, USA

BLOOMSBURY, BLOOMSBURY ACADEMIC and the Diana logo are trademarks of
Bloomsbury Publishing Plc

First published in Great Britain 2020

Series design: Raven Design
Cover photo by Olya/Voloshka on Unsplash

Library of Congress Control Number: 2019949109

ISBN: HB: 978-1-3501-1594-1
ePDF: 978-1-3501-1595-8
eBook: 978-1-3501-1596-5

Series: Encounters: Experience and Anthropological Knowledge

Typeset by Deanta Global Publishing Services, Chennai, India
Printed and bound in Great Britain

To find out more about our authors and books visit www.bloomsbury.com
and sign up for our newsletters.

Contents

Acknowledgements

This publication has been a long time in the making, unfolding across a changing set of contributors, two publishers (as one was bought up) and numerous drafts. Our contributors have our deepest gratitude and admiration, not only for sticking with this project through the long process of publication, but for providing a rich and provocative set of chapters, which we have been proud to edit.

We also want to thank the Cambridge Anthropology department for funding and hosting the workshop that provided the initial spark for this project, in 2014. Mattei Candea, Harri Englund and John Borneman provided valuable insight as discussants, while William Vega, Xiaoqian Liu, Thalia Gigerenzer, Tobias Hauserman, Peter Lugosi, Christiana Strava and Apostolos Andrikopoulos gave stimulating presentations. Within the department, we also want to say thanks to our supervisors at the time Sian Lazar and James Laidlaw for their support with drafts of our contributions.

Our funders, the German Cusanuswerk and the Gates Cambridge Foundation respectively, also deserve a big thank you for making the underlying research for this collection possible. A word of thank you also to the great team at Bloomsbury, and to particularly Lucy and Miriam, for supporting us throughout the editing process.

Behind each chapter in this volume stands a sprawling community of kin, friends and interlocutors, who have helped give shape to the ideas within. For each of us, as researchers, these communities have been a vital part of our homes within the world, nurturing, supporting and challenging us, making our work possible. Between eleven contributors, there are far too many names to list here. But our deepest thanks go to all of our partners in making home.

Contributors

Adam Bobbette is a postdoctoral fellow in the New Earth Histories programme, University of New South Wales.

Susannah Crockford is postdoctoral researcher at Ghent University, Belgium, in a European Research Council funded project on narrative in the Anthropocene. Previously, she completed a PhD in anthropology at the London School of Economics in 2017. The research for her contribution was supported by an Economic and Social Research Council Doctoral Studentship.

Martin Fuller is a researcher in the Department of Sociology at the Technical University of Berlin. His research interests include contemporary art and cities, activities of housing and the production of space, and the sociology of pleasure.

Mathew Gagné is a PhD candidate in Anthropology at the University of Toronto. His research explores gay sex in the digital age and how new media has impacted intimacy and queer male sociopolitical life in Beirut. His work has been published in the *Journal of Middle East Women's Studies*, *Middle East Journal of Culture and Communication*, *Kohl: A Journal for Body and Gender Research*, and Jadaliyya.com.

Stephen Gudeman graduated from Harvard and Cambridge. His first research was in Latin America, where he studied family organization, economy, religion and godparenthood in relation to the house. He drew on these interests some years later when jointly overseeing a comparative project in Eastern Europe sponsored by the Max Planck Institute in Germany. He has written extensively about his fieldwork and been concerned to build an anthropological and comparative view of economy.

Faten Khazaei has recently completed her PhD in Sociology at the University of Neuchâtel, Switzerland. Her PhD was funded by the Swiss National Science Foundation and her dissertation is entitled *Manufacturing Difference: Double Standard in Institutional Responses to Intimate Partner Violence (IPV)*. It investigates how IPV is named, framed and addressed differently for Swiss citizens and migrants. She also teaches courses in gender studies at the University of Geneva. Her research interests focus on gender, culture, violence and institutions. Her most recent published article is 'Grounds for Dialogue: Intersectionality and Superdiversity' (2018).

Johannes Lenhard is Centre Coordinator of the Max Planck Cambridge Centre for Ethics, Economy and Social Change. While his postdoctoral project looks at the ethical projects of venture capital investors, he before that spent seven years trying to understand the life projects of homeless people in London and Paris.

Max Ott studied architecture and has worked as a project and freelance architect. From 2011–16 he was a research associate at the Chair of Urban Design and Regional Planning at the Technical University of Munich and in 2017 and 2018 he was a guest lecturer at the University of Applied Sciences Munich. He is an associate member of the interdisciplinary research group Urban Ethics, funded by the German Research Foundation (DFG).

Sascha Roth earned his PhD in anthropology from Halle University with a thesis on people's housing and home-making efforts as well as informal practices in the context of the state's housing regime in Soviet and contemporary Baku. His areas of interest are postsocialism, politics of representation, housing, architecture, anthropology of the state, kinship, ideologies and utopias. Currently he is scientific coordinator at the Max Planck Institute for Social Anthropology. He wants to say special thanks to the Max Planck Institute for Social Anthropology in Halle/Saale, the International Max Planck Research School on the Anthropology, Archaeology and History of Eurasia (IMPRS ANARCHIE), and the Graduate School Society and Culture in Motion for funding his PhD project.

Farhan Samanani is a postdoctoral research fellow at the Max Planck Institute for the Study of Religious and Ethnic Diversity, and an Honorary Research Associate at the University of Oxford. He is interested in how communities and shared forms of value are shaped across lines of difference. Farhan is driven to produce research that helps build and spark social change, and to do so he works with a range of nonprofit, government and community groups. His work focuses on the contemporary UK, and especially on London.

Nikita Simpson is a PhD candidate in Anthropology at the London School of Economics. She has recently returned from fieldwork in the foothills of the

North Indian Himalayas, where she studied women's mental distress in the context of rapid politico-economic change. Nikita also works closely on social and digital approaches to mental health challenges with the SHM Foundation, and has previously worked at the World Health Organization in Health Promotion. She wants to say many thanks to Alpa Shah and Laura Bear for their ongoing guidance; to Johannes Lenhard, Archie Henderson and Rani Sachdev for reviewing earlier versions of this piece; and mostly to all those who made up her home in the Himalayas.

Ann-Christin Wagner is a lecturer in Anthropology of Development at the University of Edinburgh. For her doctoral studies, Ann did fourteen months of ethnographic fieldwork with Syrian refugees in northern Jordan in 2016/17. In 2019, she conducted research with Syrian and Congolese youth in Uganda and Jordan as a research fellow on a pilot study on adolescent refugees' reproductive health (University of Edinburgh). Before her PhD, she worked with the International Organization for Migration in Geneva. She would like to thank Sophia Woodman for making me reconsider the role of mobility in making homes in exile and Ben White for introducing me to the work of Derek Robertson.

Melissa K. Wrapp is a PhD candidate in the Department of Anthropology at UC Irvine. Her dissertation explores the relationship between practices of experimentation in South African housing design and broader shifts in racialized property relations and activist practice post-apartheid. Wrapp's primary dissertation fieldwork in Cape Town was funded by the National Science Foundation Doctoral Dissertation Research Improvement Grant (Cultural Anthropology and Law & Social Sciences Programs, 2017–18) and a research grant from UC Irvine's Center for Global Peace and Conflict Studies. She would especially like to thank Chris, Dany, Matsobane and the entire Twalo family, without whom making home, and coming home, would not have been possible.

Preface

This provocative volume about the home pushes the boundaries of anthropological exploration. For more than three decades anthropologists have studied the house in different cultures. We know about houses in relation to kinship, the lineage and family. We have studied the place of the house in different economies, have shown how a house may be symbolically and religiously constructed, and have learned that houses are made from diverse materials in different environments.

The presentations in this book bid us to break that learning, for a house is not a home. The house has a variety of shapes, containers and social implications, but the home is equally diverse with its reverberations of privacy, secrecy, intrusions and hospitality. A focus on the home, with its many possible meanings, opens new spaces for our understanding of intimacy and distance, gender and embarrassment, community and its rejection, as well as the struggle for life and how we display ourselves to others.

Shifting our focus to the home also reveals the boundaries of sociality and locally accepted norms. It can disclose the difficult and ugly side of the sociality we build, and some of the terrors we seek to avoid.

The home inevitably seems to be a marker of gender difference from inside to outside. What happens, then, when queerness is not accepted as the foundation for building a home? Does queerness mean being homeless and without an accepted position in society, as one of the studies illustrates?

The home is often a marker of privacy, and a space to which others are not invited but voices penetrate thin walls and scarcely covered windows. What is being hidden in the home? Sexual intimacy? Family problems?

These distinctions and boundaries that help define the public and the private also affect the place of the anthropologist, for the anthropologist makes a home in the field, but that home may need to have different and porous boundaries as a site for anthropological encounters or perhaps be off-site, as several studies illustrate. When my wife, Roxane, and I lived in Panama, our one-room home was open to the many children she was studying and they, unlike their parents, often entered without shouting a greeting at the door, to the point that I was several times caught naked, unlike the children's elders, who dressed and undressed in their adjoining but windowless and enclosed sleeping room. Did my nudity affect my position with the children's elders or Roxane's position with the children?

If homes often mark family privacy this solitude may be inverted when physical fights in the family are played out not behind walls but in public spaces where others can watch. What does this social inversion, exemplified in pages that follow, mean for personal reputations?

Even as private spaces, homes are constituted in relation to public authority and laws. For Mandeville private vice became a public virtue, through the enactment of self-interest in the market. But Mandeville was looking at individuals. From the inverted perspective, public virtue may be deployed to counter private vice in the home through the intrusion of legal authorities when violence, especially gender related, tears a home apart, as examples in this volume demonstrate. When does the personal domain become public, and the public enter the private through the boundaries of the home?

Homes also are made within shared spaces and dense communities, which is especially true in apartment buildings, which several contributions to this volume consider. When Roxane and I lived for a year in Sweden, we quickly learned that accepted apartment behaviour may constrain home comportment. When we first moved in, I was not disposing of our garbage properly in the shared, outside bins. An inhabitant tracked down his ill-behaving neighbour, to my personal embarrassment, and entering our tiny kitchen showed me what I had to do in order not to transgress the shared outside space. Making a home in a community here became a mix of private and public behaviour to the point that intimate, private 'leavings' become public knowledge and a public vice. Variations of this negotiation and compromise between the public and private punctuate the studies in the pages that follow.

What about the homeless? Homeless people make a space, even if temporary, to which they return if only to sleep. Where do they fit in the social and political order, which often keeps them moving and homeless? Not surprisingly, their mental well-being is often as precarious as their physical. The homeless are located at the fringe of society, which averts its eyes from them. Just as distressing is the position of the recently evicted, who lack resources to keep a home. These situations return us to the question of the anthropologist's position. Where is the anthropologist's home, and how does the anthropologist make a home and feel at home in the field, a topic explored in a number of the studies?

Attention to the ways of home-making brings us to another dimension of occupying space: squatting. Is the homeless a squatter who has no rights to a space, or is the squatter different from the homeless? The squatter, like the homeless, may lack legal support and is constrained by the polity, yet the squatter or the homeless often seeks to 'improve' the space he occupies, which tracing back to the writing of John Locke, would give him rights to the land or its improvements. So, if the homeless 'make' a space at the margins of society, what is the difference between the homeless and the squatter?

Even when a space is legally purchased, marked by signs and minimally improved at the physical margins of a society, it may be treated by others as an open commons occupied only by the homeless and so available for despoliation. How do the homeless at the physical margins of society protect their position and appurtenances if not by physical violence, which can further endanger them?

Readers of this volume may think of their home as the major anchor in their lives. The disruptive studies in this volume question that assumption by showing how fragile the home and its place in society can be.

Stephen Gudeman

Introduction: Ethnography, dwelling and home-making

Johannes Lenhard and Farhan Samanani

Depending on how you view it, home changes its meaning. It can be made of bricks and mortar, possessions, feelings, stories or habits. It can be a fixed point in space, around which the stories of our lives centre, or it can be the name given to a range of practices, taking place across space and time, which animate these tales. It may be an ideal or a reality, or even a state of being. It is entangled in kinship and in social reproduction, but it may also come to underwrite social transformations. It may evoke warm feelings of belonging, the claustrophobia of a prison or the terror of violence. At home, we might forge relations of generosity and care, but the home can also be a marker of status and hierarchy. Within the home we welcome guests, and extend to them the expanses of hospitality, yet the self-same walls which shelter the guest also mark out and exclude the stranger.

Today, these myriad meanings have all been well documented by social scientists, from anthropologists to sociologists, historians and psychologists. Frequently they do not reconcile easily with one another, and more frequently still, particular investigations will content themselves with focusing on one particular notion of home. And yet, strikingly, we still also hold onto the idea of the home as a particular entity – as something singular and worthy of particular attention. This is a conviction most of us – in Anglophone countries at least – hold in our everyday lives. This belief is reflected in pop-philosophy and folk wisdom – which declares that 'home is where the heart is', and that 'there is no place like home' – as much as in our everyday routines – where you can witness a physical transformation, an untensing of the shoulders, or a marked change in expression, as we step through the threshold to mark the end of a busy day. Many of us would struggle to imagine our lives without the ideal and the physical presence of home. Academics, too, remain attached to the idea of home – as evidenced by the determination to approach the home as a distinct field of study.

In fact, for anthropologists in particular, the animated pursuit of home as a distinct domain of study is the product of relatively recent efforts. Previously the study of home was very often contained within adjacent domains of inquiry, such as kinship (Carsten and Hugh-Jones 1995). In other words, even as a growing body of ethnographic work has revealed the fundamental diversity of what home might entail, anthropologists have moved towards considering home as something important, even singular, in its own right. This same tension between singular and plural understandings of home marks other disciplines as well (Mallett 2004). To approach home as an ethnographer, then, is to have to contend with both these perspectives: one reflected in the empirical record, stressing heterogeneity and one woven both into everyday understandings and into theoretical ambitions, stressing commonality across this heterogeneity.

How we imagine home also has profound implications for how we conduct ethnography. Whether or not we intend to focus on the home as an object of inquiry, ethnographic fieldwork inescapably requires us to make a home in our field. The activities carried out in our own homes – eating and sleeping, relaxing and organizing – are often deeply necessary to our survival or well-being, and so we must find a way to recreate or translate these activities in the field. These are frequently highly relational activities, meaning that the act of making a home in the field is always negotiated alongside others. Even when we are doing ethnography 'at home', the question remains of how our own practices of home and dwelling might relate to the lives of our interlocutors. Our existing understandings of home inevitably become a part of such dialogues.

This volume and its contributions grapple individually and collectively with how we might understand the meaning of home, as ethnographers and through ethnography. Although its focus leans towards anthropology, the contributors here come from a range of disciplinary perspectives, and our hope is that this volume has something to offer for all of those who do ethnography, regardless of their disciplinary home. For those newer to ethnography, we hope the contributions here will provide an interesting and exciting range of glimpses into how ethnography is done, and all it can reveal. For researchers who practice ethnography themselves, we hope that this collection will furnish you with a range of useful critical reflections on the scope and limits of ethnography, and on the role of ethnographers in producing knowledge. For all, we hope it will expand your understanding of what home is and can be. Together, in this volume, we have four intertwined ambitions.

Firstly, we hope to contribute further to diversifying the meanings of home, by revealing articulations of home which take shape in unexpected places, through surprising practices or in the midst of complex negotiations. This volume approaches home not through ideal-typical dwellings, which sit at the heart of practices of social reproduction, but through some of its most marginal, creative, unstable or extreme articulations. Here, we look at homes built on the side of an active volcano, at practices of home-making when homeless on the street, while dealing with the ongoing vicissitudes of eviction, or when living as a multiply-displaced refugee. We think about the home not only as a site of belonging and comfort, but as a site where gendered hierarchies and violence are reproduced; where the lines between public and private are continually renegotiated rather than simply extended; and where dwelling is achieved through experimental practices, ranging from sex to ethnography itself.

In many instances, figures who dwell on the margins – from strangers, to refugees, to rough sleepers – are characterized as embodiments of unhomeliness. Their relevance to the study of home is often seen as a negative counter-image, which marks the limits of particular modalities of home, shoring up common ideals and practices, by providing an image of otherness against which they are constituted. This collection breaks with this characterization, revealing home and dwelling as something more diverse and creative, but also more fundamental to a wide range of human lives, marginal or not, than is often admitted.

Secondly, we aim to reflect on what it means to produce ethnographies of home, especially of homes that may seem unconventional. In particular, we are interested in questions around how the dwelling practices of ethnographers meet with those of our interlocutors, and of how the negotiations resulting from such meetings might play out. In doing so, we seek to join a growing conversation on what constitutes ethnographic method, and what constitutes ethnographic experience. Conventionally, ethnography is subject to a strange duality, where on the one hand, ethnographers are expected to immerse themselves in the flow of life in a given context (Geertz 1988). Yet, on the other hand, there are practices, such as sex, or subordination, which frequently seem off-limits to the ethnographer. There are also experiences, of hardship, hurt and fear, which jar with a romanticized vision of ethnographic immersion and which can risk being written out of the ethnographic record, when our disciplinary grammars do not easily allow them to be voiced (Pollard 2009; Clark and Grant 2015). This collection, then, aims to help expand these disciplinary grammars by reflecting on a diverse range of ethnographic practices which play with and challenge conventional approaches. In different ways, the chapters here approach the tension between heterogeneity and singularity, not only as a problem in conceptualizing home, but as a fundamental dilemma, requiring ongoing attention, within practices of ethnography.

Third, we hope to keep a firm focus on questions of power and inequality in the production of home. To be sure, many ethnographers are deeply sensitive to such questions. Yet insofar as there has been a move towards reaching for a singular understanding of home within anthropology and within other social sciences, such a move can risk displacing such questions, or making them a secondary matter, when set against the fundamental question of the singular meaning of home. Home is not the same for everyone and, as recent, resurgent anxieties in the media around refugees or the street-homeless reveal, access to home is not a given. People are at times violently prevented from being at home; they are at other times kept from making a new home in a new, safer environment. Power imbalances can also shape the way homes are structured, or influence how much work has to be put into home-making.

Finally, drawing these first three goals together, this volume asks how reconsidering the meaning of home might also lead us to reconsider the *ethics* – not just the practices – of doing ethnography. This introduction traces a path towards such an ethical reconsideration, before unpacking some of its implications. We start, in the next section, by reviewing how home has been characterized in the ethnographic record. This review provides readers with an overview of the ethnographic work on home, with a focus on anthropology. It also allows us to situate our own argument.

Across these diverse characterizations of home we identify a key distinction as to whether home is understood as an alienated or unalienated domain. Unalienated characterizations of home, whether they see home as a particular space, a set of practices or a general ideal, think of home as a domain where the self is deeply immersed in the world. Within such conceptions, home environments, ideals or practices closely reflect one's own sense of who one is. Home is wherever, or however, we 'feel at home'. Alienated characterizations, on the other hand, emphasize the tensions which arise between one's experience of self, or of the world, and one's experience of 'home'. Such alienation might emerge from the forms of conflict, hierarchy or exclusion which are often entangled within articulations of home. Yet unequal or not, all homes need to be reproduced. Families move, walls crumble and children need feeding. These practices of remaking home do not always entail simply reproducing a template. Rather, they may enable people to take a reflexive, critical perspective on their experiences of home, and remake home in novel, creative ways, drawing on a degree of creative alienation to do so.

Building on this review, we argue in the third section that although ethnographers are clearly attentive to the multiple forms home may take, ethnographic *methodologies* largely end up reproducing a singular idea of home as an unalienated domain. Based on this, they have developed an emphasis on techniques of *dwelling* in ethnography, where ethnographers are encouraged to immerse themselves in particular settings, soaking up knowledge and experience like a sponge. We trace the limitations of this method, when it comes to dealing with the dilemmas, dangers and entanglements of fieldwork and argue that in addition to methods of *dwelling* ethnographers ought to also adopt methods of *home-making*, where they approach the field as a site of collaborative creativity. On its own, either method can produce problematic challenges. However, we argue that when deployed in dialogue with one another, they have the potential to enrich ethnographic practice.

What is home?

The House: From reproduction to negotiation, conflict and creativity

When we think of home, it's likely that we imagine a particular building, in a particular place. In such visions, the materiality of the home plays a significant role in defining it. Perhaps we remember the odd colour of paint that we never got around to changing, the particular plush of the carpet, or the feeling of comfort when curling up on the worn couch. As Mallett (2004) argues, for many in the West, the idea of home is closely associated with that of the *house*, as a physical structure. As she notes, this association emerges from a broader ideological insistence that social reproduction and welfare are predominantly *private* affairs. In the 1990s, historians, architects and others began to trace how the two notions of house and home had become so closely linked, and what the implications of this linkage were (Bowlby et al. 1997; Dupuis and Thorns 1996; Madigan et al. 1990). Mallett traces how these critical investigations built on but also problematized earlier work which had focused on homes as material forms.

In anthropology, by contrast, for many generations there was little attention given to the house as a physical space, or indeed to homes at all. Early scholars such as Morgan (1981[1881]), writing on American aboriginal houses, or Malinowski, who defined the family as a group of kin tied to 'a definite physical space, a hearth and home' (quoted in Collier, Rosaldo and Yanagisako 1987), saw the physicality of the house as secondary. As Carsten and Hugh-Jones (1995) argue: the house was mostly seen as a partial container for the sorts of social relations, such as kinship, which were the primary focus of anthropology. Two seminal works by Bourdieu (1992[1970]) and by Levi-Strauss (1983) both clearly reflect this approach, but also mark the beginning of a turn away from it towards considering the materiality of the house.

In Bourdieu's famous essay on the Kabyle house, he traces how the layout and design of the house reflect a broader social and cosmological order, where corresponding distinctions of light/dark, public/private and male/female structure a broad range of social practices, values and meanings. In Bourdieu's account, the physical organization of the Kabyle house not only reflected this structured world view, but was also responsible for reproducing it. This argument would find full expression in his later theory of habitus, which he came to characterize as 'a system of predispositions inculcated by the material circumstances of life and by family upbringing' (Bourdieu 1976: 118). Nonetheless, for Bourdieu, while the materiality of the house was clearly important, his focus was not on the home as an institution, but rather on the overarching system of social relations which both preceded, shaped and existed beyond the house.

By contrast, Levi-Strauss presents a distinctive theory of the house, but focuses less on the materiality of it. Levi-Strauss develops his concept of the 'house society' as a way of thinking through kinship theory – and social relationships more generally – differently. He formulates an expansive definition of the house 'as a corporate body holding an estate made up of both material and immaterial wealth, which perpetuates itself through the transmission of its name, its goods and its titles down a real or imaginary line' (1983: 174). In what Levi-Strauss calls house-based societies, including Native American (Yurok, Kwakiutl) and medieval European societies, groups are formed and perpetuated by enfolding ideas of descent, residence, property ownership and alliances within the institution of the house – as both an idea and as a material building. Commenting on such (typically noble) family houses he writes: 'The whole function of [them] … implies a fusion of categories which are elsewhere held to be in correlation with and opposition to each other but are henceforth treated as inter-changeable: descent can substitute for affinity, and affinity for descent' (Levi-Strauss 1983: 187). This approach continued to see houses as 'containers'. However, in contrast to earlier approaches, *the act of containment itself* was highlighted as playing a critical role in sustaining the social processes it encompassed. This same focus on containment is taken up in this volume by

Sascha Roth, as lying at the heart of distinct but sometimes contending notions of familial and personal privacy in Azerbaijan.

Following on from these works, a number of others took up the idea of the home as an important social institution, enacted in a specific place and taking on a specific material form. Extending Levi-Strauss's own focus on marriage, Maurice Bloch (1993; 1995) traces how making a house and making a marriage are closely linked among the Zafimaniry in Madagascar. As the house becomes stronger – 'grows bones' – and into a hardwood construction over time, the relationship between the married couple becomes stronger. No longer separating out broader social processes and the home itself, Bloch instead argues that the house and the marriage are interdependent. Roth, again in his contribution here, notes a similar understanding of homes, in part, *as* marriages in Azerbaijan and in Turkic languages more generally.

Similarly, Stephen Gudeman (Gudeman and Hann 2015) has highlighted the role played by houses in producing a distinctive mode of economic organization, in his concept of the 'house economy'. Starting with his early work on Colombia, Gudeman argues, 'Material practices are organised through the house' (Gudeman and Rivera 1990: 2). While 'both the house and the corporation are means for accomplishing material tasks' the house economy is distinct in that it is 'smaller, is locally based and wholly or partly produces its own means of maintenance' (Gudeman and Rivera 1990: 10). This organization enables the house to pursue distinctive goals as well as distinctive modalities of mutuality and self-interest, in distinction from, but in dialogue with, those of the market. As such, Gudeman and his collaborators describe the house as the basic unit of economic life connected to others through bonds of exchange – while striving to be self-sufficient – and embedded in communities. Again, the role of the house itself in mediating these relations is key. Outside of capitalist modernity, Hart et al. (2010: 4) argue, 'For millennia, economy was conceived of in domestic terms as "household management"' – and understandings of work, labour and their productive potentials were often grounded in the home.

Carsten and Hugh-Jones (1995) build explicitly on Levi-Strauss's emphasis on the house's ability to draw different forms of relation together. They widen Levi-Strauss's scope of inquiry, and detach it from the specific typology of house (or non-house) societies, in order to interrogate in more general terms what sorts of relations come together within a house, and how we might understand houses holistically. In response, they argue that houses are created at the intersection of economic practices, kinship, reproduction and sustenance, political organization and symbolic categorization, and the body and physical infrastructure – and that houses work to mediate between each of these. As such, they conclude that 'the house [i]s a crucial practical and conceptual unit in the … organisation of widely different societies' (1995:5).

Alongside this move to understand how houses mediate relations, two other important perspectives emerged, with each of the three both drawing on and feeding into the others. The first of these was a turn towards paying closer attention towards the materiality of the house, which helped reveal the home as a site of creativity. The second focused on domestic labour and the role of women, and revealed the home as a site of contestation.

An early call to attend more seriously to the physicality of the home comes from Humphrey (1988), who notes that in those instances where homes are present in anthropological accounts they 'tend to be thought of as "case" of symbolism or cosmology rather than a subject in their own right' (1988: 16). Whether prescient, or trend-setting, Humphrey's brief intervention came around the start of a swell of attention given to home as a material form. Another seminal article by Miller (1998) challenged the idea of homes as simply an expression of a given cultural form, tracing instead how residents on a North London council estate decorated and renovated their council flats in ways which both reflected their class position and yet inflected this with a personal sense of identity and belonging. Focusing not on homes themselves, but on the possessions and practices of consumption that concentrate within their walls, Miller has continued to examine the importance of materiality for developing a sense of home (2009; 2001; 1998). He has come to argue that consumption is often an important act of social reproduction, care and self-shaping – all at once. As a result, the objects in one's home are simultaneously involved in ascribing the self into broader society, developing relationships of care, and inscribing a personal sense of biography, with the home itself serving as a focal point of each practice. Together, home, the possessions which fill it, and the memories which attach to both work to shore up our sense of identity and belonging against the tribulations we might face in the outside world (Miller 2001). The physical permanence of material objects, and their peculiar mode of assembly within the home, serve as durable sources of security (Petridou 2001). As such, for Miller (2009; 2001; 1998) and others (see also Gregson 2007; Dittmar 1992; Daniels and Andrews 2010; Cieraad 2006) home-making is directly linked to material practices such as shopping, arranging furniture in the rooms or narrating stories and memories of different objects.

Others too have traced the ways in which the materiality of the house, and the objects which circulate within it, not only reproduce and extend relations of care and kin, but work to inscribe households within wider society. In the introduction to their volume *House Life* Birdwell-Pheasant and Lawrence-Zúñiga (1999: 3) call for greater attention to the materiality of lived relations, arguing,

> Both households and families use houses more than as settings for activities of production and distribution or as consumer goods. They are also mechanisms of communication, which channel and regulate social interaction among family members and between separate households. ... The house defines a place that belongs to a particular set of people and also defines, through co-residence and shared usage, the set of people that belong to a particular place.

Carsten, too, has helped deepen an understanding of the materiality of kinship. In her study of Malay domestic life (Carsten 1997), she identifies the hearth as the centre of the house: it is the place where the family meets, where food is prepared, and where kinship is made through the transformation and sharing of substances. She argues: 'Hearths are obvious sources of physical sustenance, but they are also often the symbolic focus of the house, loaded with the imagery of the commensal unity of close kin. Houses are material shelters as well as ritual centres' (Carsten 2003: 55). By sharing food, kinship – for the Malay expressed in terms of being siblings – is forged or reinforced. Here, the physical and symbolic dimensions are not easily separated. Rather, as other authors have also argued, it is the physical enactment of kin relations, and their direct involvement in sustaining life through forms of care and nourishment, which gives them weight and reality, and invests them with memory and feeling (see Martens and Scott 2006; Pina-Cabral 1986). In conjunction with this focus on materiality, attention has also been placed on the home as a site of labour, and often of contestation. This turn has its roots in feminist debates over the status of domestic labour.

In 1966 Juliet Mitchell published an influential pamphlet tracing the tensions between socialist organizing, which focused on women's role in economic organizing, and feminist organizing, which turned to women's legal and social status. In response she argued there was a need to see these forms of marginality as closely connected (Mitchell 1984). In 1969, Margaret Benson, then an academic chemist, first made the now-familiar argument that housework was a form of labour, essential to making waged labour possible, which was unrecognized as such and thus went unrewarded. Following shortly after, Lise Vogel (1973) shifted the stress in Mitchell's and Benson's arguments. She acknowledged that such an arrangement permitted the exploitation and inferior social status of women, but also argued that because women were producing use values for consumption by themselves and their immediate relations, that housework remained a form of relatively unalienated labour. These early debates helped inform an understanding of home as both a site of exploitation and contestation, but also of belonging and social reproduction. So, for example, in her ethnography of a high-rise apartment in Karachi, Laura Ring (2006) traces how the inter-ethnic peace which prevails in the building, despite ongoing civil strife, is the product of the relentless work of women's domestic labours. In their everyday interactions, women work to build bonds between households and to managing both men's emotions and the local consequences of national events and narratives. Ironically, the success of these efforts can lead to the outcomes of these labours – friendship, care and peace – seem to some (including, initially, the ethnographer herself) as if they were simply a natural state, rather than a product of hard work.

Feminist depictions of domestic labour as alienated and/or appropriated value, draw on older Marxist ideas, whose wider applicability beyond Western industrial nations has generated significant debate within anthropology. In a famous critique, Marilyn Strathern (1988) argues that such characterizations of feminine labour are grounded in particularly Western notions of personhood and of self-ownership. In Melanesia, the labour women do in 'looking after' men, or in raising pigs that men take for ceremonial exchange is not alienated from their sense of self. Rather, bearing a relational notion of selfhood, Melanesian men, women and even pigs are all understood as 'made up' of other relations. The products of women's labour, including other bodies themselves (men, pigs) thus remain fundamentally associated with women themselves. Crucially, Strathern argues that in this context exploitation is still possible but that it occurs not through the alienation of labour – which is an inconceivable notion in a world of relationally constituted selves – but in instances where men engage in exchanges that run contrary to the sorts of relations women themselves work to cultivate. Strathern's work allows us to reimagine alienation beyond the narrower terms of the Marxist tradition, by recasting it as a matter of whether and how particular understandings of selfhood are reinforced or eroded within particular contexts and moments.

Careful attention to these tensions between exploitation and belonging, and between transformation and social reproduction, emerges in Lila Abu-Lughod's account of the lives of Awlad 'Ali Bedouin women (1990; 2016[1986]). Abu-Lughod traces how ostensibly oppressive norms of public male honour and private female modesty are creatively leveraged by women, who exert control over the domestic sphere in order to subvert male authority, practice their own forms of virtue, and cultivate forms of intimacy with other women that elide the public/private divide. These practices can often be deployed to creatively navigate constraining circumstances. For example, traditional practices of marriage involve elder relatives selecting a woman's betrothed, with little input from the bride herself, and with less regard given to the groom's finances, given that kin are anyway expected to provide additional economic support to the couple. However, chafing at the obligations this practice produces, and enchanted with the idea of a spouse with an independent income and access to alluring consumer goods, women resist such practices by asserting their own desirability. Through buying lingerie or make-up, they position themselves as desirable in a way that asserts a role for desire – both theirs and that of their husbands – in determining marriages. While such acts may involve resistance, they never break free from being implicated in power. In this case, the power of kin is diminished in part by granting a larger role to men and to consumer goods in shaping marriage. Such moves do not escape power but rather involve *negotiating* shifting power relations located within changing historical conditions. In this volume Susannah Crockford provides a similarly sensitive exploration of such tensions between belonging and exploitation, as they are mediated by the traditionally gendered ideals of home that survivalists in Arizona carry with them into their lives off-grid. Alongside Abu-Lughod, Crockford does not frame such ideals as teleologically exploitative, but presents them as a fraught field of power that all those in the field, including the ethnographer herself, strive to both negotiate and inhabit.

Lives within the home can be constrained by multiple, intersecting forms of power, from gendered hierarchies, to the biopolitical power of the state. Even under what may seem like desperate or desolate circumstances, however, home can provide a site of creative response (as well as a repository for hopes and dreams – see later discussion). This is illustrated in Clara Han's (2012) striking ethnography of slum households in Santiago, Chile, where she traces home as a site of 'active awaiting'. Living in a present where the possibilities for life are tightly constrained by debt, gang violence and the punitive force of the state, Han nonetheless traces how small interventions in the home – the pawning of a beloved music player, or the sheltering of a relative away from an abusive partner – create small spaces in which new, perhaps unknown possibilities might take root and grow. In this volume, by examining the story of one London resident after her eviction, the chapter by Farhan Samanani continues this exploration of how the possibilities for inhabiting both the present and future are so often tied up with the materiality of home, including everyday possessions such as mirrors and slow cookers.

Collectively, these developments in the anthropological understanding of home might be read in terms of a shift from seeing home as a locus of social reproduction to seeing home as a site of contestation and creativity. In Bourdieu and Levi-Strauss, home is understood in the first instance as a space where the existing social order is perpetuated. From this perspective there is a close fit between the material environment of the home, and the subjectivity of those who live in it – with each reproducing the other. In contrast, while later work has retained an interest in social reproduction, it has highlighted the home as a site of labour, creative practice, contestation and transformation. Here, the home does not simply reproduce subjects. Rather, the home is a site where multiple forms of power and complex biographical experiences collect. Within such spaces, individuals do not merely come to embody their home environment, but rather work to negotiate such environments in reflexive, creative ways. Borrowing the language of debates on domestic labour, traced briefly earlier, we might recognize the first of these perspectives, which emphasizes social reproduction, as framing the home as a relatively unalienated space, in that it stresses the close correspondence between home environments and subjectivity. By contrast, we might recognize the latter perspective as seeing the home also as the site of various forms of alienation, be these conflictual or creative.

Time and practice: Memories, imagination and the ideal home

If the depictions above can be seen as engaging with the *material* form of the house in various ways, a further set of perspectives engage with *representations and practices* of home. In terms of representations, the home is treated not simply as a symbol, but as a *space of imagination.* As Carsten and Hugh-Jones implicitly argue in their introduction, the home is anchored in past memory, while also being constantly remade in the present: it is firstly a 'social group … ritual construct which is related to ancestors, embodied in names, heirlooms and titles' and secondly an 'ordinary group of people concerned with their day-to-day affairs, sharing consumption and living in the shared space of a domestic dwelling' (Carsten and Hugh-Jones 1995: 45). Caroline Humphrey (2005), in her analysis of Soviet shared houses and apartment blocks, takes us one step further, into the imagination and hence the future. In the city of Magnitogorsk, where workers' dwellings were often built around a central, public living space, workers would frequently adapt the space according to their routines and imaginations, rather than necessarily following Soviet ideals: 'Comforts of everyday domestic practices (*byt*) gradually invaded the austere spaces of even the exemplary Soviet Nakomfin apartment house' (2005: 40). The infrastructure and built environment interacted with the 'imaginative and projective inner feelings of the people' (2005) – together they were 'mutually constitutive of fantasy' (2005: 43), for instance in carving out private spaces where quiet conversations could take place. And, as Martin Fuller reveals in this volume, such practices of inhabitation which open up future imaginaries can take place even before a physical home exists – as he explores in his ethnography of a community-designed housing block in contemporary Berlin.

As an imaginative space, homes are never static – they are often grounded in memories and the past and are often – inspired by imaginations, dreams and ideals – taken into the present and the future. The home stretches out across time. In their review of the literature on homelessness and home, Kellett and Moore (2003) position it as in-between personal and collective-cultural memory and desire: 'Certain aspects of home seemingly shape and motivate homeless people's experience and behaviour … and the desire for [it] acts as a powerful personal and cultural objective' (2003: 8, 124). Likewise, for people in situations of displacement, Brun and Fabos (2015) argue that 'understandings of home are often based on the past: people long for the home they lost' (2015: 7). Doná (2015: 69) describes this nostalgia as the 'memories of, longing for, and imaginations of homes that are idealised', anchored in a specific collection of sanitized past experiences. Home might therefore also be understood as a place that carries what Kenyon (1999) calls a right to return, as a place of origin (Birdwell-Pheasant and Lawrence-Zúñiga 1999), or as a place we depart from and have a desire to return to (Hobsbawm 1991). At the same time, these memories and ideals are inescapably shaped in ongoing dialogue with certain sets of norms and practices associated with the 'ideal' home, as imagined within particular ideologies (Mallett 2004). In many cases, different ideals of home, unfolding across different temporalities, can compete with each other with the same physical and social spaces. For instance, the chapter by Adam Bobbette explores tensions between extractivist logics, and ones grounded in local cosmology and a less linear conception of time and presence, which contend to shape the home-making practices of those living on the side of an active volcano in Indonesia. Meanwhile the chapter by Faten Khazaei zeroes in on a particular movement of home-unmaking: looking at how police responses to domestic violence cases in Switzerland can work not only to interrupt the quick temporalities of violence, but also rhythms forms of family care and stability around which victims of domestic violence might hope to rebuild.

If imaginaries of home span across time, then this leads us to an understanding of homes as dynamic, rather than as stable entities. Home is understood as a process. This idea is already present in Carsten and Hugh-Jones (1995: 37) who state: 'Houses are far from being merely static material structures. They have animate qualities; they are endowed with spirits or souls, and are imaged in terms of the human body.' Brun and Fabos (2015: 12) position the idea of home-as-process at the centre of their categorization. They describe it as a set of everyday practices, while 'such practices involve both material and imaginative notions of home and may be improvements or even investments to temporary dwellings; they include the daily routines that people undertake ... and the social connections people make'. In a classic formulation of this idea, Douglas (1991) advances a minimal definition of the home, as the act of bringing a particular space under control. For her, a home is first and foremost a localized activity of ordering and control in the present, produced through the accumulation of meaningful objects and the enacting of familiar routines in a certain space (see also Easthope 2004: 135; O'Mahony 2013). Nikita Simpson's chapter in this volume also focuses on the dimensions of time and the process of home-making for her Indian informants as well as herself as a researcher. Reflecting particularly on how many of her female informants developed from strangers to confidants by regularly visiting Simpson's house-turned-sanctuary, she paints the process of doing fieldwork as one of developing intimacy together – or of home-making.

Botticello (2007) takes the idea further away from a fixed dwelling towards a 'site of practices where comfort, familiarity, and intimate sociality occur' (2007: 19; see also Capo 2015). This is very much the understanding of home taken up by Gagne, here, for example, as he examines the interstitial home-making practices of gay men in Beirut, situated in the small spaces beyond the family home and state control, and in the quick and intermittent rhythms of hook-ups, which nonetheless contribute to a more enduring, if fragile, sense of home. Home-as-process hence does not have to concern a fixed structure, but a set of practices and routines; it is a 'highly complex system of ordered relations with place, an order that orientates us in space, in time, and in society' (Dovey 1985: 39).

From the idea of a home in the continuous making, comes the possibility of imagining a *better* home – often as a continually receding horizon, towards which action is oriented. There is always room for improvement in home-making:

architecturally the house or hut could be bigger, it could be in a more secure neighbourhood; socially homes can be more inviting, more open to visitors and guests (Derrida 2005) or on the contrary more secure, more exclusive, as in the case of gated communities (Low 2004; Pow and Kong 2007). Alongside Gagne, Ott and Samanani, the chapter by Johannes Lenhard confronts this entanglement of home and hope. On the one hand, participating in the production of care and hope, though activities such as volunteering, allows Lenhard to make a home with his roughsleeping participants in Paris. On the other hand, the aspirations of his interlocutors for a better future throw up a range of difficult dilemmas for Lenhard, particularly in cases where people themselves may not fully know what future they desire.

Mallett (2004) connects the temporal and processual characterization of home explicitly. She positions home as always in-between the real – in everyday home-making or practices – and the ideal and imaginative. Following Jackson (Jackson 2005[1995]) she (2004: 80) claims that home relates to 'the activity performed by, with or in a person's things and places. Home is lived in the tension between the given and the chosen, then and now'. Coming from a phenomenological position, Mallett argues that 'people spend their lives in search of home, at the gap between the natural home and the particular ideal home where they would be fully fulfilled' (2004).

In the literature on migrants, refugees and mobile home-making, this double character of the home as spanning time and as being dynamic and processual has been widely explored. In their literature review of work on migration and home, Ralph and Staeheli position home for migrants explicitly in between several poles: 'Mobility and stasis, displacement and placement, as well as roots and routes go into the making of home' (2010: 3). Home is about relationships as well as location; it is connected to people as well as objects and includes both lived and ideal aspects for most migrants. In all these dimensions, they depict home as fundamentally processual, arguing that it 'emerges out of the regular reiteration of social processes and sets of relationships to both humans and non-humans' (2010: 4, 5) usually between the past, present and future. As Ralph and Staeheli conclude, 'Contemporary migrants continuously negotiate identities between "old" and "new" worlds, forging novel configurations of identification with home in both places' (2010: 7). In Wagner's contribution to this volume, mobility as a practice of home-making among Syrian refugees she experienced in Jordan figures prominently, also as a way of surviving. Her informants struggled to survive both in camps and in Jordan environments as guests, workers but also because of kind-ties while also developing ties of attachment and belonging. She shows how (temporary) home is in a setting where survival is at stake and also very much depends on relationships and dynamic re-negotiations of identities.

In her recent study of refugees in Georgia, for instance, Brun (2015) finds that returning home is important for her informants, having escaped from the Georgian war in the late 1990s. Home is to do first of all with an 'absence' of those 'social relations and practices possible to enact in the familiar home environment' (2015: 7); it is related to a feeling of nostalgia for the home of the past: 'People long for the home they lost' (2015). Talking about the longings of refugees, Brun and Fabos (2015) argue that 'understandings of home are often based on the past: people long for the home they lost', and the broader familiarity this evoked, whether that of a particular neighbourhood, or nation. Often, this longing for a past home is related to a homeland, to the 'geopolitics of nation' as Brun and Fabos (2015) describe what they call an (all-capital) 'HOME', particularly referring to the memories of people in situations of protracted displacement. In this sense, coming home or the 'myth of return' are quintessential parts of how many migrants understand home (see Christou 2002; Duyvendak 2011; Lindley 2010).

At the same time, practices of mobility themselves may come to constitute home. Nowicka (2007) in her work on UN staff members deals with the idea of how home can come about in a world of constant mobility. She understands home as an open space with 'permeable borders include[ing] elements of [its] environment' (2007: 73), a shifting, territorial 'set of relationships to both people and things' 'bind[ing] times past and present' in recurring routines and connection-making (2007: 83). As Rapport and Dawson (1998) conclude in their important early overview of the field of home and movement: 'For a world of travellers and journeymen, home comes to be found far more usually in a routine set of practices, in a repetition of habitual social interactions, in the ritual or a regularly used personal name' (27). In this volume, Melissa Wrapp's chapter on the politics of housing in Cape Town, movement is also at the core. By telling the story of one of her interlocutor's struggle to return to his family house, Wrapp, however, foregrounds questions of the power to move: who is allowed to move? Who stays put? What persists within the movement of home?

Meanwhile, Ahmed (1999) identifies home for Asian migrant women in Britain as something located largely in the future. Against a difficult and sometimes unhomely experience of the present, home is located within one's hopes, and is made in an imagined place where one has not yet arrived (c.f. E. Bloch 1995). For many refugees in particular, in fact, both a home in the sense of a house or a secure place to be is in fact first a dream: many of the contemporary refugees escaped from their supposed homes into the unknown, coming to dream up new homes (or remember idealized old homes) in the future (Jansen and Löfving 2011; Doná 2015). In a similar sense, many homeless people continuously 'struggle along' in the present longing for a better home in the future, a place to sleep and a way to have meaningful relationships as well as objects (Hecht 1998; Desjarlais 1997). Jansen's (2009) claims that, rather than seeing home as a 'remembered site of belonging', it should be seen 'prospectively as a socially constituted object of longing' (57; see also Jansen and Löfving 2011).

Across these engagements with home as an ideal, as something articulated and changing throughout time, and as brought into being through practice, we can once again trace a similar tension between unalienated and alienated characterizations of home. On the one hand, when explored in terms of familiar routines, closely held ideals, or a site of comfort or intimacy, home emerges as a domain where subjects' sense of who they are is bolstered and reproduced. Here, home is the space, the practice, or the imagined idyll where alienation might be undone. On the other hand, however, home may be a site of displacement, a place where one is made to feel out of place, an ideal that has not yet arrived, or something which is subject to continual improvement. In these conceptions, home is characterized by a *distance* between subjects' sense of selfhood, and their experience of home, however articulated. It is a domain that may be complicit in reproducing a sense of alienation, experienced as exclusion, dislocation, instability, or simply a desire for something other than what is given. In many cases, alienation and its escape may be present in the same account. For instance for the migrant women whose lives Ahmed (1999) traces, both try to make home in the everyday – even as their everyday experiences are often characterized by a sense of unhomeliness – and yet see in the future the promise of an ideal, unalienated home. In this volume, the contribution by Ott about *TeePee-Land*, a squatted encampment in the middle of Berlin, similarly has this tension between present/future and unalienated/alienated at the core. Ott focuses on the potential for constant creativity and renewal which the squat offers to its inhabitants; home here can be constantly remade according to the collective desires. At the same time, however, this creativity is not really a choice but a necessity – the sense of home would break down without it. Even when both alienation and its opposite are present, they continue to remain in tension, negotiated across space and time, through contending imaginaries, or through differently oriented practices.

Ethnography: From dwelling to home-making

In the preceding section, we traced a tension between characterizations of home as an alienated domain on the one hand, and as an unalienated domain on the other. The literature on home is vast and diverse, and this tension by no means exhaustively characterizes what scholars have said about home. And yet we find that whether explicitly or implicitly, most writing on home has something to say about the relationship between home and alienation.

In this section, then, we turn to what this tension between home as unalienated/alienated might imply for ethnographic practice and method. What we suggest is that these two conceptions of home as unalienated/alienated map onto two models for doing ethnography, one characterized by *immersion,* which might be thought of as *dwelling*, and the other by *active interventions* in the field, which may be thought of as *home-making*. In contrast to ethnographic dwelling, ethnographic home-making involves being an active participant in our interlocutors' efforts to reproduce the ever-changing social world which makes up our ethnographic field.

Ethnographers frequently speak of fieldwork as an intimate practice. If this predominant account is to be believed, these intimacies begin developing, bit by bit, starting from the moment the fieldworker steps off the boat or into the tower block, or arrives at the end of the long, dusty trail. These stories present an ethnographic meet-cute, where despite the hurdles thrown up by differences in power, positionality and perspective, through persistent presence, the ethnographer eventually gains access to intimate understandings – to the up-close 'stuff' of life in a particular place, or for a particular group, that remains inaccessible, invisible or unspeakable to the world at large. And, in turn, the model for doing ethnography so as to gain access to such intimate understandings has been one which relies on immersion. In this model, as much as possible, the role of the ethnographer is not to intervene within the field, but simply to immerse themselves within, soaking up knowledge and experience, while trying to live as closely as one can to one's interlocutors. Our argument here is that this model of ethnography as immersive dwelling, is reliant on the related idea that home is an unalienated space. As such, there is much it occludes.

To be sure, there is a sizeable body of work which has pushed ethnographers towards a more reflexive, critical practice. And yet, this work has largely left this ideal of immersive fieldwork untouched. This seems to be the case for two reasons. Firstly, the critique of positionality and power in ethnographic practice, and the model of reflexivity which has developed out of it, has largely been focused on ethnographic texts (and writing), rather than on the practice of fieldwork. Secondly, and relatedly, while this critique has led many ethnographers to abandon ideals of *objective* understandings, they have come to valorize *mess* instead. Across this shift, immersion has persisted as a favoured technique; where it was once used to access an objective perspective, it is now deployed to come-up-close to the messiness of 'real' life.

In anthropology, the set of critical interventions which prompted a turn towards reflexivity have collectively been termed the 'writing culture' or 'reflexive' turn – the former after the landmark volume of the same name (Clifford and Marcus 2010[1986]). This critique took as its starting point Geertz's 1993[1973]) call for an interpretative approach to culture, which approached culture as a collectively written, rewritten and interpreted text, rather than a static arrangement of meaning. The move made by writing culture theorists was to take ethnography itself as a text, and to scrutinize the conditions and tropes involved in its production and reading.

On the one hand, they scrutinized the literary tropes of ethnographic writing, unpacking how such work claimed a supposedly objective perspective. Among such tropes were the use of narrative frames which stuck the subjects of ethnographic knowledge in a frozen past, the use of analytical abstraction to tidy, and thus claim authority over, messy realities, the repositioning of knowledge gained through particular conversations with particular interlocutors into a generalized, third-person-plural voice, and the erasure of the (often troublesome, inevitably subjective) presence of the ethnographer themselves. Regarding this last point, in considering the presence of the ethnographer particular emphasis was put on the fact that ethnographic knowledge is *inescapably mediated* by the ethnographer's particular presence: their gender, class, pre-existing knowledge, analytical interests, personal commitments, and so on (Clifford 1983; Clifford and Marcus 2010; Denzin 1997; Fabian 1983; Geertz 1988). On the other hand, many of these same works were concerned with how ethnographic writing might engage productively with the messy surplus of life: the excess of historical interconnections, varied perspectives and shifting subjectivities that resisted neat containment within singular, authoritative texts. Broadly, these latter approaches came to be thought of as poetic approaches to ethnography.

The strategies proposed for contending with the limitations of ethnographic perspective and the messiness of life, however, have been overwhelmingly focused on the ethnographic text. This is evident in the literary-theory origins of the reflexive turn, in some of its key metaphors ('writing culture', 'poetics') and in the very model of reflexivity it sets out: In different ways, both Marcus (2002) and Salzman (2002) make this argument (see also Handelman 1994). Marcus argues that the ethnographic response to social complexity and to the inescapable problem of ethnographic positionality has been to produce 'messy baroque' texts that evoke a sense of surplus, uncontainable by the text or analytical frame itself. However, he argues that the development of these textual strategies has *not* been accompanied by the 'sorting out relations of complicity as an equally baroque imaginary for … the complexity of the fieldwork process itself'. Critical of this textual approach to self-awareness, Salzman suggests that the postmodern genre conventions they go on position the author's own subjectivity as the only source of knowledge. If distanced objectivity is no longer a viable ideal, and if all accounts are contingent on perspective, then it becomes impossible to challenge the ethnographer's subjective account of what they felt. If taken as a primarily textual practice, reflexivity solipsistically positions the ethnographer's subjective experience as the ultimate origin of all knowledge within ethnographic accounts.

Meanwhile, feminist critiques have contrasted this textual model of reflexivity to longer-established feminist approaches to epistemology. While feminist approaches share a commitment to principles of equality and collaboration, which often ground knowledge in shared experience and practice, the postmodern literary approach abstracts away 'dissolv[ing] feeling and commitment into irony' – that is into detached, suspicious reflection (Mascia-Lees et al. 1989: 14). Some works seem to embrace this suspicion. Thus, Borneman and Hammoudi (2009) document an increasing tendency for anthropologists and other ethnographers to favour deep-dives into historical and cultural archives over fieldwork itself. While motivated by a more complex set of considerations – including a desire to confront the historical roots of power and to engage with existing documentary practices – this turn to the archive has provided refuge for those distrustful of intersubjective and embodied encounters as a source of ethnographic knowledge.

Others, however, have taken pains to offset the impression of ironic distance by re-enchanting the ethnographic encounter itself, through renewing tropes of ethnographic immediacy and immersion. For example, Johannes Fabian has famously argued that ethnography produces its 'object' through the production of accounts where the entangled co-presence of the field is reified into a static, mono-vocal and abstracted account, set in another time and place from that of the writer and implied audience (1983). In later work, he concludes that this problem stems not from the act of representation itself but from 'a tension between re-presentation and presence' (1990: 755) where representation works to produce distance, and where empirical accounts privilege the abstracted distance of representation to the immediate vicissitudes of experience. Against this, he argues for a mode of ethnographic writing that works 'to revendicate the primacy of experience as something that requires presence (as sharing of time and place)' (1990).

In other words, for many reflexive ethnographers, textual reflexivity relies heavily on an immersive mode of ethnographic practice. The ethnographic text may be fraught and baroque, but its very ability to attend, however partially, to the complexity of human experience, derives from the immediacy and subjective intensity of the ethnographic experience. Paradoxically, the homes of our interlocutors may be understood as messy and multiple – rather than neatly unalienated – but when it comes to their own practices of dwelling within the field, ethnographers are nonetheless encouraged to strive (or to portray) as unalienated a perspective as possible. Thus, Marcus (2007) notes that, reflexive, messy-baroque texts continue to rely heavily on narratives of arrival and immersion that paint ethnography in terms of immediate, intense presence. Indeed, even after the reflexive turn, we have continued to see various explicit conceptualizations of ethnographic fieldwork itself as entailing deep immersion – as 'being there' (Watson 1999), as 'epistemological intimacy' (Herzfeld 2016), or as 'witnessing' that which cannot be easily put into words (Taussig 2011).

Moreover, Marcus (2002) points out that these two tendencies emerging out of the wake of the 'writing culture' critiques – of privileging textual sources and methods of critique and of valorizing the immediacy of the ethnographic encounter – are not always contraposed, but often present within the same 'messy baroque' texts. Or, as Sam Hillyard puts it:

> Ethnography is animated by this desire for intimate communion. It wishes to 'be right there', participating immediately and directly in the lived experience of others. The reflexive self-doubt that typifies non-realist ethnography is not the negation of this élan but one of its proofs, as is the assiduous regard of scientific method.
>
> (2010: 183)

To sum up: While the reflexive turn within anthropology has made reflexivity a commonplace concern for anthropologists and other ethnographers, it has done so by privileging a textual model of reflexivity. In the first instance, ethnography is imagined as the capture of texts, be they written or intersubjective. It is only in the second instance, when it comes to writing that one's relation to these texts and matters of interpretation are engaged with reflexively. Guided partly by this model, some ethnographers have moved to privilege the textual materials or modes of critique in their ethnographic investigations. Others, however, have sought to emphasize that the intersubjective experiences of traditional ethnography are immediate and rich enough to facilitate 'messy baroque' accounts and reflexive analysis. As such, they have insisted on a vision of ethnography as immersive dwelling, which allows the ethnographer access to the messy realities of life as lived. This ideal of ethnographic immersion mirrors and draws on visions of the unalienated home as the template for ethnographic dwelling.

As a consequence, the dominant model ethnographic fieldwork – when not oriented towards the archive – privileges acts of immersion over what might be thought of as acts of intervention. Positionality is something to be aware of and accounted for, and thus be woven into texts, but it is not something to actively play with. So, for instance, when considering the implications of feminist standpoint theory for ethnographic practice – the former of which argues for the fundamental situatedness of all knowledge – Judith Okley concludes that 'the researcher's presence and positionality must be *confronted*' (2013: 81, emphasis added). In this vision of fieldwork, ethnographers ought to participate as well as to observe, so as to access embodied forms of understanding, but this participation is one which always follows cues – it is participation *in*.

Hillyard (2010) argues, however, that if ethnography is inescapably mediated – that we inescapably come at ethnography with a particular *perspective* – then we ought to see these mediations as technologies of knowing. Particular positionalities and practices within the field itself serve as techniques and as ways of knowing particular things over others. Building on this, what we would like to suggest is that while *dwelling* is a familiar, well-established and resilient technique within ethnography, ethnographers could also do with adopting *home-making* as a counterpoised practice.

If techniques of dwelling emphasize immersion, receptivity and following the lead of others, techniques of home-making emphasize taking part in the choices and labour which creatively reproduce the ethnographic field. We suggest these techniques are complementary but counterpoised: an overemphasis on dwelling risks obscuring the field as a site of creative labour, contestation choice and dilemma; it often subscribes to the most powerful accounts of life in the field for fear of becoming embroiled in struggles in which one has no part; and it limits the sorts of commitments that ethnographers can come to share with their interlocutors, and so come to understand. As Salzman (2002) suggests, to fail to take part in shared process of meaning making, when one is ultimately out to write a text, is to effectively insist on one's own subjectivity as the ultimate source of all possible knowledge. Or, again, contra Fabian and others, ethnography produces its object not only in writing, but in each moment when the ethnographer approaches the field as something given, rather than taking part in the creative, laborious process of ensuring life goes on.

Meanwhile, an overemphasis on home-making would entail running roughshod over the field, imposing one's own understandings, commitments and practices onto others, often from a position of material or social advantage. Ethnography at its best gains much of its insight through deep humility, where ethnographers work to suspend familiar understandings, beliefs and values and work instead to take seriously the lives, understandings and experiences of others, in their own terms. And yet the history of the social sciences is marked less by humility and more by the use of ethnography to shore up Western-centric modes of knowledge and hierarchies of value. Divorced from the insights gained through genuinely humble ethnographic immersion, home-making as a technique risks reproducing the worst excesses of this history. Yet, despite this peril, we would like to suggest that when practices of ethnographic home-making are informed by sensitive practices of ethnographic dwelling – and vice versa – there is potential for a richer portrait to emerge.

Dwelling may be our most familiar ethnographic technique, but home-making as method has its own particular history among ethnographers. A particular strong inspiration comes from the 'material semiotic' tradition, which has picked up and extended the feminist debates on domestic labour. Here, we take a lead from figures such as Donna Haraway (1988; 1994; 2016), who reminds us not only that claims to a neutral standpoint are never more than assertions of superiority but also that knowledge can emerge through actively *building* relations; we follow Bruno Latour (2007) in understanding that to produce an account of the world is never simply to describe it, but to intervene within the world, both through technologies of knowing and through the text itself; and we draw on Webb Keane who reminds us that all relationships, whether social or material and including those produced through ethnography, are stores of potential that enable all parties to act on the world in specific, interdependent ways (2005; 2016).

Collectively, when it comes to ethnography, the material semiotic tradition reminds us that producing accounts is more than just a matter of arranging words on the page. Rather, accounts are articulated through arranging elements of the material world in a particular way. These arrangements 'enrol' others, who bolster or challenge these accounts. The clue is in the name – 'material semiotics'

– which indicates that the making of meaning is not simply a textual practice, but a practice of arranging the physical and social world in a particular way. Such accounting is a continual process, but when ethnographers enter onto the scene and seek to understand the field, they do so in ways which inescapably implicate them in the production, maintenance or challenging of particular accounts.

So, for example, to decide that a particular high-rise building in Glasgow is initially modern, durable and comfortable (homely), and then later to decide it is decrepit and not fit for inhabitation (unhomely), are not simple, factual claims. Rather, both these versions of reality are 'assembled', by announcing them in newspapers or activist meetings, getting city councillors and town planners to behave *as if* they were true, and by highlighting particular material arrangements. Strong steel pillars and big open living rooms help assemble an account of durability and comfort, and help get this account accepted; small cracks in an interior wall, the presence of asbestos and some tenants moving out assemble an account of decay, even though the steel pillars, open living rooms and other residents living happily are all still there. In both cases, researchers, journalists and other storytellers are key players in giving each account reality (Jacobs et al. 2007).

From this perspective, the home – or indeed any other element of the social world – gains its reality from being enacted in diverse material ways. Home is the place where we sleep, the place we keep and use furnishings, the place where we eat, drink and interact with close kin. Perhaps it is also a place where we express ourselves, painting walls and building up wardrobes. Perhaps, again, we define our ideals of home in terms of images in magazines, cherished childhood stories or conversations with friends. Perhaps it is the familiar walk, arriving in and winding through our neighbourhood, with its bent trees and colourful playgrounds, rather than the house itself, which plays the most decisive role in making us feel 'at home'. Material or social, imagined or instantiated in practice, every form of home is enacted within the world in a particular way. And so, any different arrangement of these elements inevitably enacts a different sort of home.

When accounts are brought into the physical world in this way, the warning that there are no neutral, non-mediated standpoints from which to understand the world takes on greater weight and importance. Read in this way, reflexivity cannot be simply understood as an exercise for when it comes time to write. Rather, to participate in the world is to be involved in the reproduction of particular accounts – particular arrangements of reality. And to participate in the world by insisting on not participating, as much as possible, is at the very least to become a stubborn physical limit to the accounts of others. Many ethnographers who have been present during a family meal and have attempted to refuse food will know this very well; people insist we eat, not merely because it is customary, but because if they are unable to feed us, then other familiar truths begin to fall apart: perhaps this refusal suggests they are not good hosts, or caring companions. Perhaps it suggests that food lacks the ability to bring people together or produce kinship, even though everyone says so. So we eat. But do we learn to cook for others, and to insist in kind that they eat? If not, are we suggesting that ties of intimacy can be forged in one direction, but not in the other? No matter how we act, we are taking part in the making or unmaking of worlds. As Borneman and Hammoudi (2009) argue, ethnography is inescapably a practice of ethical risk, to which the only response is ethical commitment. And if we accept this, then ethnography may need to entail not only immersive dwelling, but decisive action as well.

Just as there is an intellectual tradition which grounds the technique of ethnographic home-making, so too are there strong examples of this technique in practice. Take, for example Paloma Gay y Blasco's accounts (sole- and co-authored) of her life and friendship with Liria de la Cruz Hernández. Even in the initial stages of their relationship, as ethnographer and informant, entanglements emerged quickly. Lira, a Spanish Gitano (gypsy), details in her own words how welcoming Paloma into her home was related to her curiosity around the fact that 'Payos [non-Gitanos] live more independently in their lives' and her ongoing frustrations around living in the shadows of constant gossip and judgement while dealing with a difficult marriage (Gay y Blasco and De La Cruz Hernández 2012: 4). Over time, Paloma learns of the consequences Lira has faced in housing her, in terms of the intense Gitano culture of moral scrutiny; Lira has not only taken her in, but in doing so has re-positioned herself as a disruptive figure and has instigated a range of rumours and questions that she must constantly manage. Paloma reciprocates by helping Lira fulfil her curiosity around Paya life – helping her lie to her husband and leave the neighbourhood, to share her own experiences of middle-class Madrid.

When Lira leaves her Gitano husband for Younes, a young Moroccan immigrant, these experiences of autonomy and exploration help inform her decision, and she turns to Paloma for support. After Lira is found and returned to her husband, her family reach out to Paloma to convince her to stay: 'They knew how close Liria and I were, and were desperate for me to take sides' (ibid). Torn between conflicting commitments to her interlocutors and to her close friend, ultimately Paloma acts to help Lira escape her family, seek a divorce and gain custody over her daughter, in defiance of the Gitano customs that she had spent so long wanting to understand, and writing about – and in defiance of other friends and interlocutors. Paloma's presence in the field was involved in the active unmaking of one home, but was also the catalyst for the construction of another.

While leaving room for the voices of others, or even co-writing accounts, are ideals emerging from the tradition of reflexivity-as-writing, Gay y Blasco's ethnography is instead an account of co-action, where her presence in the field triggered a series of shifts in perspective and contestations in which she was forced to choose to whom her commitments lay, and to act accordingly. In her accounts, these entanglements not only precede the act of writing, whether solely or jointly, but also cannot be negotiated through writing alone (Gay y Blasco 2017).

Gay y Blasco's reflections chime with Audra Simpson's work on 'ethnographic refusal' among the Mohawk of Kahnawake (*Kahnawakero:non*) (2007; 2014). While Ortner (1995) argues that to refuse to write about negative, potentially unflattering depictions of informants is to produce 'thin' and ultimately dehumanizing accounts, Simpson inverts this characterization. She argues that written accounts often have political consequences for the individuals and groups depicted within them. Supposedly rich, tell-all texts may lead to new forms of stigma, exclusion and governmental control – new forms of dehumanization – which can dismantle and thin out the possibilities for life within field sites themselves. This is no coincidence, she suggests. Colonial anthropologists certainly understood that their accounts would have concrete consequences for how lives were lived and governed. Contemporary anthropologists who claim only to be motivated by providing rich accounts not only forget this history and its consequences, but also overlook that the contemporary accounts our interlocutors produce continue to be inescapably entangled in efforts to prolong or bring into existence particular visions of the world. The questions we ask, the processes we do or don't participate in, the conversations or forms of change we do or don't initiate, and indeed the texts we write, all have implications for what happens to the worlds spoken by our interlocutors. As ethnographers both our presence and our texts make, transform or undo particular forms of home in material ways.

What might home-making as a technique of ethnography involve in practical terms, then? Firstly, it would involve carving out moments of reflection during fieldwork, during which emerging forms of implication and commitment might be traced and scrutinized. Such reflection should strive to move beyond those modes of understanding and judgement which are most familiar to the ethnographer. However, even when striving to be sensitive to, and to think with, forms of judgement found within the field, there is always scope to think about positionality and commitment. Secondly, it would involve making conscious choices between these commitments, while remaining aware that one cannot be everywhere or understand everything at once. Third, these processes of reflection and choice may lead to the explicit chasing of new commitments, with those who may be inaccessible, marginal or otherwise less visible from one's position within the field, rather than simply continuing to 'go with the flow' of engaging with the most readily available interlocutors. It is necessary not only to recognize any field site as criss-crossed by different perspectives, commitments and power relations, but to decide actively how to respond to this plurality; we must choose who we will become entangled with, and how.

Fourth, this might involve a more conscious and intentional use of ancillary technologies, such as daily schedules, purposeful 'networking' and virtual forms of connection, in order to foster or manage particular commitments. Different constellations of commitments will lead to different understandings of the field, and it would be a mistake to privilege only those relationships which are most readily available. Techniques such as explicitly managing one's time, in order to divide it between multiple, differently positioned interlocutors, working deliberately to cultivate elusive relationships, or even intentionally cutting ties from overly confining relationships offer the potential of revealing new perspectives on one's field site.

Fifth, there may be moments where one might choose to make deliberate interventions within the field. Recognizing that one's very presence is always already a disruption, requiring novel responses from one's interlocutors, ethnographers may opt to deploy this presence in ways which invite *particular* responses. Whether in inviting people around for a home-cooked meal, or leading in the formation of a campaign group, there are interventions which may prove ethnographically productive. The language of 'intervention' ought to highlight the colonial roots, and present-day structures of power and inequality in which academic research and ethnographic methods remain entangled. And yet recognizing that one's presence in the field itself is an intervention, we might use insights gleaned from techniques of ethnographic *dwelling*, to engage in practices of ethnographic *home-making* which serve as more empowering, caring or responsive interventions, than that posed by our more passive presence.

Sixth, deploying home-making as a technique would involve understanding that all commitments have costs, some of which may be unacceptable. Recently, attention has been cast on the ways in which immersive models of fieldwork can put ethnographers at risk (Clark and Grant 2015; Hanson and Richards 2017; Pollard 2009; Stacey 1988). When faced with danger, abuse or difficulty, fieldworkers may find themselves reluctant to cut ties, ask for help, or confront others, if they are convinced that doing so would be a failure to fully take part and immerse oneself as an ethnographer. This reluctance may be compounded by the prospect of limited institutional support in instances where one's colleagues also subscribe to a view of ethnography primarily as an immersive practice.

Seventh, again recognizing that field sites are full of different perspectives, which provide different accounts of the world, we ought to be attentive to the various forms of labour done to reproduce these varied perspectives, and the costs associated with maintaining them. In other words, we need to recognize that the homes of our interlocutors – those spaces, imaginaries and practices which ground their perspective, their sense of belonging and their feeling of subjecthood – are always themselves products of particular forms of labour. And, recognizing this, our task cannot simply be to dwell in such homes. We must also ask how we ought to relate to these varied forms of labour. Doing so is likely to direct our ethnographic attention in new directions – whether towards particular humans and non-humans whose life-sustaining presence goes unacknowledged, or towards the global forms of exchange which mediate access to particular domestic goods, or ideal visions of home.

Eighth, recognizing the inescapable entanglement between the labour of reproducing or remaking particular worlds, and the production of ethnographic knowledge, we need to recognize ethnographic knowledge itself as a collaborative enterprise – as something also sustained through distributed labours – rather than the product or sole possession of the lone fieldworker. In turn, this ought to push us towards other ways of conducting ethnography – for instance, working in teams, or through reciprocal collaborations with those in the field. Likewise, this should prompt a broader reconsideration of the 'ends' of ethnographic knowledge, beyond the production of academic texts and towards approaches which better honour and support the world-sustaining labours through which we come to know.

Finally, and perhaps most significantly, drawing on practices of ethnographic *home-making* would shift ethnographic reflexivity from a *consideration* of positionality, to a *practice* of co-implication. Co-implicated, we would be forced to grapple not only with the presence of ourselves in our interlocutor's homes, but with their presence in ours. Taking the relations, commitments and obligations which emerge out of ethnography seriously may involve inviting interlocutors into our own homes, within the field, within the academy and within the texts we produce. For some scholars, this may mean producing pieces of writing together, for others it may mean making our own status, knowledge and time available to our interlocutors to turn towards causes that are important to them. For all of us, it would pose the challenge not to see interlocutors as mere 'informants' but as collaborators and companions.

Again, there are limits to how productive techniques of ethnographic home-making will be, as well as limits on how ethical they may prove. The challenge, however, is not to simply consider our taken-for-granted techniques of *dwelling* as *necessarily* more productive or more ethical. By intertwining techniques of dwelling and home-making, we hope for a richer, more reflexive and more engaged ethnographic practice than either method would produce on its own.

1

Studying gay sex in Beirut:
The lascivious suture of home/field

Mathew Gagné

In the summer of 2013, I met Nadeem – who became a key interlocutor and dear friend – over Manhunt.net, an online cruising service. Having just returned after a long period of studying in Europe and North America and again living with his family to the north of Beirut, he was keen to use the website, and other apps like Grindr and Scruff, to meet new men and develop a queer social life. A few months later, during a brief visit to Beirut in December, I asked Nadeem what he thought was the greatest impact of the apps among men in Beirut. 'They're having more sex', he quickly responded. While unquantifiable, his claim drew my attention to a quality of digitally mediated gay sex in Beirut: the appearance of gay sex as more accessible and abundant in queer male life. I began to think about sex as a social terrain within which ineffable feelings are shared, negotiated, communicated, lived, disavowed and frustrated in an intersubjective field of experience among queer men. Sex supported social life as a complex circulation of emotions and connection that created the conditions of possibility for queer male social worlds in Beirut.

My doctoral research – conducted intermittently between June 2013 and May 2017 with the primary period from July 2014–July 2015 – explored the question of how queer men in Beirut used hookup and social media apps to create their intimate lives. My entry into the field was both one of physical arrival and digital presence: simultaneously being a profile in a series of hookup apps while physically in Beirut.

Upon arrival, all I had was a set of apps that gave me access to a seemingly endless number of users. I was quickly dispersed within networks of men, technologies, and spaces in and around Beirut. I was immersed in the chaos of many conversations that gradually became substantive connections and important ethnographic relationships. Gradually, random encounters with strangers in the early months of my fieldwork accumulated and morphed into a more structured and familiar socio-sexual life with men who became so many things to me.

In the beginning, Beirut may have been strange to me in ways that home ought not to be, but over time I created the relationships that made it more intimate. My fieldwork was about more than arriving and then finding a place to dwell within Beirut's queer male socio-sexual world in order to observe its practices. Rather, I became entangled within people's socio-sexual networks, and part of the very production of the ethnographic field I was studying among the intimate life-worlds of these men. Even the casual encounters and random chats online I had coalesced into something more intimate when these men became interconnected within the wider socio-sexual networks we all inhabited.

In ethnography, the intimacies and connections that grant access and insight into everyday life develop slowly as ethnographers get to know people, which largely happens in small moments that make up the ordinary aspects of life. They accumulate over time, creating social relations that tie the ethnographer and their interlocutors to shared spaces and experiences.

Sex enabled me to think about the field and home not as distinct places, but as joint sites of negotiated feeling and sensation among others that formed over time. In the time I spent in Beirut, I was a part of the lives and homes of others. I made Beirut home through a patchwork of encounters that were shared among me and my interlocutors in ways that grounded us to a city as host to our experiences, relationships and negotiated intimacies. Home was always in the process of being (re)made through my relationships with others that provided affective and personal grounding. Sex created bonds of respect, knowledge and emotion that transcended the mere social connections often instrumentalized in ethnography, giving my fieldsite the feeling and quality of being home.

The connection between sex and the labor of home-making meant having to position myself as a participant in the production of my fieldsite. I had to acknowledge the many ways I became entangled in people's affective and intimate lives by becoming part of each other's experiences, tales and decision-making. I asked a set of ethical questions about how to have sex while also being a researcher.[1] I couldn't only take into consideration my positionality in the field but had to approach the field as a series of practices of co-implications that were all part of a vaguely named thing called sex that was made of many different kinds of relationships, moments and affects.

In anthropology's canon, sex in the field has been relegated to an anxious place. It risks making relationships awkward, leading to possible dejection, and fans fears of exploitation based on asymmetric power relations (Irwin 2006; Kulick 1995). Further trouble emerges from the potential for sex to challenge the conditions of difference embedded within anthropological knowledge production, by posing the risk of enveloping the subjectivity of the anthropologist into the 'otherness' of interlocutors (Kulick 1995; Newton 1993). Yet, proponents of sex in fieldwork insist upon the importance of acknowledging sex and sexuality as part of ongoing negotiation of social relations within the field (Irwin 2006; Kasper and Landolt 2015; Spronk 2015). Their perspective refuses an understanding of researcher positionality as static or controlled for one that places the researcher in a social milieu of constant negotiation of different social relations. The ethical question becomes not one of acting but *reacting* to the shifting intersubjective conditions that are present within the different interactions with interlocutors. These encounters become ongoing emotional relationships that create new opportunities for commonality and intersubjective learning. The field is a space of knowledge and familiarity structured through intimate ethnographic encounters.

Yet, sex was a form of embodied learning among interlocutors and me. There is an emerging literature that insists upon taking erotic interactions as a site from which to theorize meaning-making and embodied realities of social structures (Spronk 2015; Valentine 2007; Wekker 2006). Techniques of learning in the field privilege the deployment of bodily senses in situ to experience the action of the context (Irwin 2006; Wacquant 2004;), but less often sensations, or 'sensual immersion' as 'bodily and emotional immersion' (Irwin 2006: 157). This involves extending embodiment beyond a moment and using a full range of sensations and feelings to learn through the constant negotiation of one's position in the field towards others. Being attuned to these sensations requires flexibility and reflexivity of the ethnographer vis-à-vis others as he is negotiating a place within a social world. In my project, sex served as a site of body-sensorial knowledge about the pressures and conditions the structures and norms of Beirut that queer men dealt with constantly. Sex allowed me to immerse myself in the production of social worlds within a socio-sexual network of men. In fact, the challenge of ethnography is often one of managing complex feelings that come from being part of the life-worlds of others, while simultaneously being accountable to them.

Gay sex and the home in Beirut

In Beirut, queerness was largely banned from the heteronormative space of the family home. Home, as a site for the reproduction of heteronormative intimacies and kin relations, exerted power over their sexualities by marginalizing and limiting queer intimacies. Creating the kinds of sex lives men wanted often meant having to go outside of the home, towards the queer spaces and social networks that had formed over the past three decades. Rarely were queer intimacies anchored to the stability of home as a private place.

Queer men in Beirut created a sense of queer home through social labour that formed and solidified sexual and intimate ties outside the norms and social reproduction of the heteronormative domestic sphere. Men felt a sense of home among queer friends and lovers and against power hierarchies and relations that tried to quell and marginalize them. Participating within the socio-sexual worlds men created outside the domestic sphere led me to learn much about the limits and potentialities of queer male life in Beirut.

Gay sex inhabited a precarious place between a history that had seen the expansion of queer social spaces, politics and visibility as well as the (often violent) power of state, legal and socially conservative forces that sought to quell it, sometimes leading to arrest and imprisonment, social marginalization and abandonment, loss of economic stability, and physical and verbal abuse. Reconstruction of the city after the civil war in 1990 created new queer spaces and commercial establishments. At the same time, the internet enabled individuals to connect in queer-themed chat rooms, gradually forming social networks, and, later, activist groups and non-governmental organizations, thus precipitating new forms of political activism. In the past decade, a multitude of organizations have emerged, mounting contestation to state, legal and socially conservative forces on the basis of claims to queer visibility and rights, particularly against article 534 of the Lebanese penal code that criminalizes sex deemed against nature, often taken to mean homosexuality.

Despite these complex forces, queer men created a robust socio-sexual sphere outside traditional notions of the home that emphasized a version of gay sex that was about the private, individual pursuit of desire's fulfilment. A user by the name of 'Always Horny', who insisted upon the sexual nature of the apps as I tried to resist his attempts to engage me in sexy talk, lambasted me for trying to be 'creative' in my approach to the apps for something more than sex. When I asked whether he would like an encounter that is more than sex, he wrote: 'I am happy in my life [and] sex is one of my happy times.' Men valued sex for its simple pleasures and ability to fulfil their individual desires. Gay sex, in everyday life, meant creating the pleasures and intimacies that defined a feeling of enjoying life. Take, for instance, a profile called 'top^2 mesh tob' (meaning in Arabic: [top, not tob] which is him mocking those men with poor English skills who may spell top with a *b* given that Arabic does not have a *p* sound). His image was of a bare, toned torso with the headline: 'Just enjoy this fucking life.' Despite the aggressive tone of his statement, in the context of the apps, he was alluding to the ordinary pleasures of sex in life. His free space read: 'Not gonna talk about myself only locos do so. To cut it short, I want a short, smooth, muscled bottom to play with.' The apps fostered a socio-sexual sphere where men could achieve intimate pleasures within an expanded social field that created a sense of home outside the home.

My own sex life

Understanding the emotions of sex, and how sex created meaningful and material social worlds meant availing myself of all kinds of intimate possibilities with men in the field. Home-making meant finding affective and social connection in many possibilities that flourished through emotional and sexual production with men in the field.

I met Jalal in September 2014 over Grindr while I was out with Nadir, a friend and steadfast interlocutor, as well as Milad, Nadir's infrequent lover and friend. Jalal's gathering with friends had ended but he wasn't ready to go home. So, he took to the apps to find someone to occupy him. We had spoken a few months earlier over Grindr, but our conversation history didn't extend beyond a few hours. Here we were again, this time with tangible plans to meet. I left my friends at the gay bar in Ashrafieh, a large neighbourhood in Beirut, where they were indulging in some Wednesday night karaoke, and met Jalal – who refused to come into a Beiruti gay bar – in a nearby parking lot. We greeted each other from opposite sides of the driver's door. He was tall, broad and a bit nerdy with an endearing smile. After a few words serving as a pause to assess and confirm offline attraction, I climbed into his black SUV and we headed for a drink and later to my place. Thus began our short romantic affair.

We saw each other regularly, but hardly ever planned it. Rather, Jalal would spontaneously contact me to meet in those moments when he found himself with nothing to do for a few hours or for an evening between his social and familial obligations. While he was an avid traveller with no qualms about his sexuality outside of Beirut, he kept his sex life separate from the density of his social and familial life in Beirut. He saw the apps as a social venue to reach into for pleasure and sex when he wanted it. To him, the apps created a sphere in which he could find sexual fulfillment with a sense of freedom from the forces that otherwise limited his sex life.

Jalal was attentive, optimistic and romantic, qualities I admired in him. We went on excursions to Lebanon's mountain sites, dinners and walks. It remained casual: we both already had barriers between us. Yet it was awkward. I recall one night, we were completing the services questionnaire after eating at *Zaatar wa Zeit*, a popular chain restaurant serving fusion Lebanese food. When it came to the question about who we were with, we jostled over the categories of 'date' or 'friend', him choosing the latter while I felt inclined to choose the former. A few days later, while strolling along the seaside promenade, we had a cryptic conversation to express what was clearly a mutual affection yet agreed to keep our relationship casual. I was in the midst of my fieldwork and Jalal was looking to disentangle himself from the complexities of Beirut for better employment abroad. Neither of us was ready to emotionally open up nor to commit. Tensions between our mutual affections and unwillingness to let them flourish would eventually separate us.

Jalal and I were the object of each other's affections, but he was also an interlocutor. He didn't seem to mind my status as a researcher simultaneously learning from him and our intimate relation: in fact, he sat for an interview, and spoke about gay sex and love in Beirut through the apps (I even got his consent to write our tale specifically for this volume). We created sexual intimacy alongside a research relationship. Yet, my research into the sexual lives of others did, as he would confirm, make him feel a limit to our intimacy.

In early November 2014, Jalal travelled to the United Arab Emirates to explore employment possibilities and ended up staying for three weeks in pursuit of a job opportunity. I saw him next in Istanbul, a trip we had planned before he spontaneously left. Over dinner in Nevizade Sokak, a narrow path bustling with restaurants and bars just off Istiklal Caddesi in Taksim, he told me of his job offer, and asked if he should take it. I insisted he accept it. He left Beirut again two days after the end of our trip. Our erstwhile affection was stymied by the economics of life in Beirut.

Weeks later, he returned to prepare himself for permanent relocation over the holidays. One night, we drove to the northern city of Byblos to see their famed annual Christmas display. Stuck in traffic, we began to disinter those feelings we both quelled. He told me of his frustration over the times when he began to think that something more intimate and committed was possible between us, but he felt unsure I could provide what he wanted. He accused me of not showing him the intimacy and desire he needed to feel secure. Acknowledging my part, I raised the problem of his own distancing from me: his early insistence on keeping it casual and his desire to leave Beirut. He dropped me off without resolution. I saw him once more: two months later he returned for a weekend visit. He called me late one February night from the airport, wanting to see me before he drove north to his family home.

My own experiences with Jalal resonated with those of Kaseem, who, a year before, ended a long-term relationship because his partner left for an employment opportunity in Europe. He told me the tale while sitting wistfully near the waters of St. George Bay in central Beirut. To him, love in Beirut was weighed down by economic structures that encouraged young men to leave. He was feeling hopeless about finding love again – although he did eventually but only because he, too, left Beirut a few years later. In that moment, we shared an intimate world where we both experienced the emotional departure of a lover drawn away from the country under stymied economic opportunities. Both Kaseem and I have tied a piece of our personal history, a narrative of love come and gone, to Beirut's economic structures.

With Jalal, not only was the inescapability of desire obvious, but more so was the inevitable labour of having to actively account for that desire, reflect upon it, and deal with the necessary awkwardness of Jalal and I having to remain open towards each other, our limits, and the conditions of Beirut that were closing in on our relationship. The relationship required that I accept my own feelings and desires in the field, rather than dispelling them, or struggling to keep them away as the good ethnographer. Our entanglement was part of Beirut, whose limits would disentangle us.

Apart from the intersubjective nature of home-making, what I learnt from being with Jalal was the feeling that queer male intimacies were hardly anchored to a time or place, but insecurely lived between pressures of heteronormative social life. We lived out intimacy sporadically, when the time permitted. Intimacies unfolded within the interstitial geographies and temporalities between routine daily life. It was never anchored to a certain place, or to a wider set of social relationships. It happened between these things, requiring us to work at creating it through conversation and negotiation because there were few social relations to which we could anchor it.

Creating shared worlds of experience and affect

Home in the field was about my relationships to other people and places as they became more familiar and intimate over time. I shared with my interlocutors a range of intimate experiences through which we reflected upon and negotiated the many ways that Beirut shaped queer life. Take the following scene as an illustration of a moment when diverse socio-sexual experiences glue together some friendships between myself and two interlocutors through shared frustrations over the apps.

Michael – a dear interlocutor and friend – wanted love, yet, like many, became hopeless from the sense of its difficulty in Beirut under heavy cultural forces impinging on queer intimacy, and the common desire for non-committal sex. Having been raised in the United States, he moved back to Lebanon – his natal home – only a few years before. He often imagined his intimate life elsewhere, in a place better suited to his desires and sensibilities. On the night of his twenty-sixth birthday, nearly two years after I met him, Michael told me that he had always wanted to be married – with talk of children – by the age of thirty. He spent the day in bed, feeling despondent that his wish seemed more unlikely with each passing year. Despite a few passing crushes, he had never had a serious relationship. He attributed the difficulties in his intimate life to both a wider set of familial norms that stymied queer intimacies, as well as the ways that men primarily used the apps to find sex over other possibilities like dating and love.

Nearly a year later around his twenty-seventh birthday, and still on the apps, Michael was having a bad night. He had gone out to some clubs with one of his best friends but was feeling lonely. He wasn't the type to have random hook-ups. He was, rather, aroused by a version of sex that followed from a bit of conversation and interpersonal bonding. He rushed home, and, at 3 a.m., completed an overhaul of his Grindr and Scruff profiles to see if he could make something different happen. It wasn't his first attempt. A few weeks before, he had replaced his longtime bare torso profile picture with his face as an experiment. The next day, he arrived at Sinan's place, where we often whiled away the evenings with junk food, conversation, and YouTube videos, and declared: 'Well, the experiment failed. I am officially ugly.' He received messages from only two men, neither of whom he was attracted to. The technology had played to intense, oscillating registers of pleasure and validation often undercut by feelings of insecurity, and frustration. 'We are all ugly on Grindr', Sinan chimed in. 'I have been asked "what's wrong with your face" a few times,' he said, seemingly unaffected by the casual insult. He was aware of his handsome face and that such a comment was the effect of the social distance over the apps that enabled men to vocalize their meaner sides. I added that a random user on Grindr had, after I casually greeted him and sent some face pictures, called me a 'very ugly man', I commiserated, thereby connecting our individual experiences into a shared emotional moment. Michael put his torso picture back, and his words became about his personality and what he wanted as opposed to some quips about gender and drag. I suggested that he use an image of his upper chest and the left side of his face to show only enough face and chest to leave room for imagination. In the weeks that followed, Michael received more messages, not always of the kinds he wanted, but that increased opportunities for sex.

In that moment, we inhabited the same affective world of desire and frustration, where we showed care and empathy towards the experiences of one another. The social mechanics and technological operations that facilitated these connections were one layer of a mutual understanding that gave way to a shared affect of rejection and measurement of self-worth and physical attraction. Beirut as a home became part of the experience of these moments when interlocutors and I were connected through inhabiting a social space that was larger than us, within which we found a place in it together. We jointly navigated the more grisly and hurtful aspects of gay sex in Beirut, reckoning with the dilemmas that we all experienced using the apps.

Sharing socio-sexual experiences that gave meaning to the boundaries of home meant that I, as the ethnographer, became part of the unfolding and decision-making in men's sex lives. I was implicated in the experiences that defined home through sex and intimacy. Yasser, whom I met through a mutual friend, invited me to stay with him in the north of Lebanon for a few days. On the second day, we were driving to Beirut to meet friends for an excursion to Zahle, a city in the Bekaa Valley. Five minutes from his house, a one-time sex partner invited him for sex. Yasser was fortunate to live alone, and Rayan wanted to bring along another guy, Mahmoud, for a threesome. Yasser, telling me they had good sex the first time, was aroused by the proposition and contemplated postponing our plans and dropping me off at a café for a few hours. But he said no to Rayan. Rayan insisted that it happen. All the conditions he needed were nearly in place, except for the place to have sex. Rayan worked to ensure their plans remained: 'We could come in the evening; it wouldn't take long.' Instead, Yasser invited them over for Thursday, but Rayan had to work that day. They were free and horny then and now. Eventually, Rayan stopped trying to convince Yasser.

Three days later, as Yasser was driving me back to Beirut, Rayan again contacted him for a threesome. Yasser did not immediately say no. Again, he thought about turning home and leaving me to take the bus. This time Yasser asked questions about the third guy, Mahmoud. 'Hmm', Yasser hummed to me, 'he is an Ayoub [a family name] and they are known to be hot and aggressive wild men.' Rayan sent Mahmoud's picture – fully clothed in an awkward pose with his arms crossed and body leaning back. We agreed it was an unattractive image. Yasser asked for Mahmoud's body picture. Rayan didn't have one. Yasser requested Mahmoud's phone number to ask him directly. Rayan responded: 'He doesn't send body pictures to anyone, but don't worry, you will like him. He is hot, and versatile [referring to his sexual position as interested in both penetrating and being penetrated].' It wasn't enough to sway Yasser. Rayan, after Yasser said he couldn't meet, became upset and dramatic. He berated Yasser for engaging in the negotiation, equivocating, and then saying no. Yasser brushed it off, and said that he was busy, but that they could come over this weekend. Their engagement ended here because my engagement ended there: I never asked Yasser if the proposed threesome ever came to pass. But, for those few days, I was imbricated in his sex life. As part of his tale, I was both a limit and a potentiality in his intimate life. I acted as an obstacle to the novelty, yet uncertainty, of the sex that clearly enticed him. Yet, our friendship was a plain of potentiality for an intimacy that could be creatively widened into an affective anchor for making a sense of home together.

The stories of others

In general, these apps created a space of familiarity among strangers who were connected through a history of chatting and interacting with each other's profiles over and over, seeing one another out in the city, on the street and in the queer bars. Through the apps, a dense network of men emerged who may have been strangers to some degree but became familiar through their profiles in the apps. The apps fostered a history and memory among users that turned the apps into a medium through which users saw strangers over and over, or where strangers became familiar through frequently seeing the information in their profiles. Men came to know so much more about one another even if they remained strangers.

Take, for instance, an afternoon spent sipping coffee on a patio with three interlocutors, all of them friends. Across the street we saw a young man whom we all recognized from his profile. He particularly stood out since his profile had long been an image of his bare torso, with the text that he is looking for friends and something serious. Yet, he was always the one to start a conversation asking about our dick pics or sexual desires (a common contradiction too big to cover here). We had all seen him before at the few gay clubs and parties around town. In that moment, we shared a common history with him, the fodder of which create ties that defined home. One among us told the story of a date he had with him, how much all he could do was talk about sex, and gossip about others in the scene. As we shared our overlapping experiences with the young man across the street, the brief moment of storytelling among us revealed the dense network of queer men that we all inhabited.

In a small city, storytelling crossed many social networks, connecting men within circulations of information. Storytelling gave meaning and structure to random and individual intimate encounters and moments in a social venue where one shared his affects and reactions among others, gaining validation and affirmation, or not, for them. It was a way of narrating and collectivizing experiences we shared, helping make our shared world intelligible and populate with familiar characters. I shared my desires and lusts and stories with interlocutors as much as they did with me. I refused to treat their experiences and emotions as mere objects to be collected while I painted myself as the privileged researcher without any. It created a more reciprocal basis for collecting data, based on friendly bonds of trust, all while knowing why I was there, and that I was out to collect this very information. I asked for their stories, their lingering and powerful emotions, and ethically I had to reciprocate. In collectively producing narratives of their lives, we built up a sense of a world in which our individual lives coalesced into a wider history of meaning and connection. In other words, we were jointly creating a shared affective and experiential home.

Sex and ethnographic positionality

My place among the home-making processes of my interlocutors was constantly negotiated from a series of standpoints I inhabited in the field. This involved a different set of ethical questions: how to be a good friend, lover, researcher and participant in Beirut's gay sex culture?

In sex, emotions and insecurities can be fragile, requiring sensitivity to how my words and actions affected others. While I could not always prevent or undo sour feelings, I could at least act as ethically as possible by trying to minimize harm and actively repair injuries. This took a practice of honesty and openness about my feelings for others. I had to be aware of my own needs and desires, limits and expectations. I found it difficult to engage with those who just wanted quick, nameless sex. I had to be aware of this limitation, so that I could act responsibly to what others were looking for knowing the limits of what I was prepared to offer. A key ethical question of sex was whether I had been ignorant or neglectful of the expectation others had of me, and my role in creating the expectations I could not meet. I also had to be aware of the kinds of power I had with men as a white, cis-gendered, normatively embodied gay man affiliated with a prestigious university in a country with a history of foreign intervention.[3]

This relationality is based on having to recognize my fundamental vulnerability in the field while making it the ethical task for myself to bear the emotions I incited in others rather than making them primarily the responsibility of my interlocutors. As a researcher, this involved not simply adopting a fixed, pre-given ethical stance, but attuning myself to the lives of others by understanding how to react to something that had been done towards me. In fact, these ethical questions fuelled home-making processes because they attuned me to the intersubjective emotions that also entangled us. They made me aware of how I was affecting others and being affected by them, making each other part of our emotional lives.

Take, for instance, Nabil, whom I met one afternoon for a stroll and sex after speaking to him for a few weeks over Grindr then WhatsApp. I hoped to continue being intimate with him, but, as he left my house, his body language and eye contact told me he was less interested in more than a one-time fling.

The next day, he messaged telling me I had too many rules in sex, referring to my refusal to do a few things during sex. 'I should let go more' he texted me, suggesting that I abandon my limits and surrender to the pleasures of sex, specifically his desire to contort my body in the ways that he wanted it. Perhaps he felt that his desire and pleasure were stymied and unfulfiled by my rules. Or it meant to construct an environment of mutual pleasure where the satisfaction of his pleasure was meant to be the source of my pleasure. In which case, giving into his pleasures was actually about expanding my pleasures beyond my own limits, and not about abandoning them. Perhaps I simply didn't live up to his expectations of sex with me. In this case, it wasn't intimacy and closeness that required strong ethical consideration, but the negation of mutual pleasure that became the grounds for his sense of injury. The moment made me question my relationship to sex and pleasure, challenging the very models I had concerning sex and intimacy, the scripts and expectations to which I held. He had exposed some of my vulnerabilities, and perhaps I had also exposed his. I had never been told this before but had to react to what he was telling me and wonder about what I had done wrong towards him to incite this response.

A tension arose that was about divergent pleasures: something between us didn't add up to mutual pleasure. At stake in the sexual encounter was not the potential for intimacy but the promise – and failure – of shared pleasure. Given the fleeting nature of our encounter, I didn't necessarily owe him emotional and sexual reparations of the sort he was critiquing me for. Yet, the sense of injury I inflicted upon him – seemingly strong enough that he felt compelled to text me the next day just to call me out – was due to my violation of the terms of pleasure within a wider sexual culture among queer men in Beirut. In a context where the constraints upon gay sex forced men to pursue new horizons of pleasure and connection in those times and spaces they could claim for sex, perhaps my misstep was to reintroduce a feeling of constraint into a moment meant to overcome it.

On Being Welcomed Home

January 2016: I entered Bardo, a popular restaurant-cum-weekend gay dance club, and found Amin greeting me with a smile at the end of the corridor connecting the street to the door that doubles as a catwalk for men to assume a strut as they enter. 'Welcome home,' he said, giving me a big hug. I had just returned to Beirut from Toronto between fieldwork periods. His affection was a warm welcome back to the city where I had spent much of the past two and a half years. Yet, what did he mean by 'home'? Was he simply hearkening to Beirut as a familiar space, intimating the irony that I had recently spent more time in Beirut, a relatively new and foreign city to me, than Toronto, the city where I was based?

For a moment, his words disquieted me: I interpreted his use of 'home' as an epistemological category that suggested I had transgressed national and cultural differences between me and my Lebanese interlocutors, thereby obfuscating my subjectivity as a white North American scholar, an anxiety-inducing transgression for an anthropologist diligently working to keep a reflexive positionality. Yet, Amin's gracious words suggested something much more poetic: that I had found a home in his home within the home of many others. He was welcoming me not only back to Beirut, but back into his life: the spaces he frequented, the people he associated with, and the stories he told. I was back to being directly involved in the unfolding intimate lives of my Beiruti friends and interlocutors. It also meant that amidst the vulnerabilities of queer male intimacy in Beirut, and the fragile and shifting processes of home-making that was fraught with dilemmas, there was place for feelings of home among the lives of others.

The poetic sense of home highlights the various positions I, like all ethnographers, assumed during fieldwork as I built relationships with men. In my socio-sexual relations, I was often many things: ethnographer, white, North American, app user, gay man, sexy, ugly, lover, friend, stranger and so on, which required that I constantly work at negotiating these positions in relation to the various positions others assumed, which shift in moments. Sex as a practice of home-making meant negotiating a dense terrain of positions with others, allowing a foreigner anthropologist to cultivate a sense of home within differences of space, cultures, people (family, friends, lovers) through producing an affective place within networks of queer men based on a spectrum of difference and similarity.

Notes

1   This research was approved by the University of Toronto Research Ethics Board (REB) with minimal concern. I made clear in my REB application that sex would be part of my fieldwork, as well as its illegality. The REB agreed that my research did not increase illegal behaviours since it did not ask men to engage in illegal activities they were not already engaging in. The REB asked me to address risks associated with identification of research participants given the illegality of gay sex in Lebanon. In response, I developed a robust method of data security to ensure that personal details of my interlocutors were stored securely on an external hard drive and not on my phone.
2   Top refers to his preferred sexual role as the one who penetrates.
3   Ethically, I had to protect the visibility of interlocutors in space as an out gay man: I managed my utterances and body language in social situations where being associated with me could 'out' an interlocutor. I concealed from authorities and people outside of this world my focus on gay sex because of the illegality of gay sex. I had to be careful about my engagements with security authorities, lest they search my phone (a common and illegal practice in Lebanon) and entrap interlocutors through their contact information.

2

Curtains, cars, and privacy: Experiences of dwelling and home-making in Azerbaijan

Sascha Roth

'For Azerbaijanis the home is like a fortress', Reşat told me. 'We highly appreciate our privacy and do not want others to observe us in our daily life. That's why the first thing we do is building a wall around our property even before we start building the house.' During my fieldwork in Azerbaijan's capital Baku, I soon noticed an important characteristic of the city's built environment: walls, which were widespread, not only in private residential neighbourhoods. In public space, the state as landlord of the national home extensively uses walls in order to hide the poor and unfavourable areas alongside major roads that stand in contrast to the aspired vision of national progress, prosperity, and a modern, independent state. Hence such undesired urban spaces are concealed from the eyes of visitors and local inhabitants likewise (but also from the very eyes of the country's president, Ilham Aliyev). For me, this form of 'cultural intimacy' (Herzfeld 2016) shows many parallels with how people in Azerbaijan represent, talk about and act around homes including their physical and symbolic barriers such as walls, doors and especially windows.

Reşat's statement on Azerbaijanis' concerns about privacy was supported by the impressions that my wife and I gained during the first months after moving to Baku in Autumn 2013 with our two-year-old son for my yearlong fieldwork. Since the end of the Soviet Union, many parts of the city have experienced a construction boom of private family homes. Hence, within twenty-five years the vast and previously unbuilt space of the urban periphery in which we rented a small apartment in a *həyət evi*[1] has become a densely built low-rise housing neighbourhood. The streets and small alleys were flanked by high limestone walls and closed metal gates, shielding the property from people's curious gaze. For an anthropologist interested in the changing housing strategies and home-making efforts of locals amidst the large-scale transformation from Soviet socialism towards market capitalism, this was not the most encouraging observation. Indeed, even at the end of my fieldwork there were still many neighbours whose houses, courtyards and family life remained a well-kept secret to me. However, occasionally, the family privacy became porous in the same ways as walls which do not provide sufficient protection to the soundscapes of social life in the courtyards. Reşat's remark on the local importance of walls was further confirmed by observations that I could gather on my initial excursions through our neighbourhood. Not only houses but also the few vacant and unbuilt lots were protected by walls or other improvised alternatives. In one case, for instance, there was a twenty-metre-long and three-metre-high patchwork of rusty metal sheets in different sizes, colours and stages of corrosion. Another plot was enclosed with scrap parts of train wagons in yellow, greyish and rusty colours – a surprising contrast to the rather monotone impression of unplastered limestone walls in the area.

The multiple understandings of 'home' as outlined in this volume's introductory chapter are often imagined as a delineated intimate space that provides refuge and protection, that is, privacy from 'the other' – whether this 'other' refers to neighbours, the public or other spatial concepts such as homeland or nation. The popular proverb 'an Englishman's home is his castle' emblematically stands for the widely held perception that Reşat made implicit reference to in his statement.

Rural architecture in Azerbaijan (and the Caucasus in general) has traditionally been characterized by walled property. Consequently, pre-socialist neighbourhoods in Baku are dominated by the typical courtyard houses (*həyət evləri*) and walled plots as well as those being built informally by rural migrants in the post–World War II era. During socialist times, this inward-oriented domestic architecture was counteracted by the state's approach towards spatial planning, mass housing and micro-districts. Focus was laid on open space and collective life for dwellers within the inner yards amidst mass housing blocks (that often turned out to become a kind of semi-private space for dwellers themselves). After socialism, private dwelling construction seemed to make inflationary use of walls, as if to compensate for decades of prescribed fencing standards (also made partly necessary by the constant shortage of construction materials).

Based on my own home encounters in the field, my ethnography will illuminate ways of negotiating family privacy vis-à-vis the public, and the meaning and possibilities of negotiating a more individualistic notion of privacy.

Because privacy is considered such a crucial characteristic of the home, I will then describe the importance of material thresholds from public into the private home and their symbolic qualities. Most important here are curtains which further serve as a trope to unravel different expressions of privacy and its enactment in everyday practice. Finally, I will provide some ethnography that allows us to grasp another central capacity of cars beyond their function of providing us mobility – their capacity to being transformed into a private and intimate space that conventional homes rarely provide for. In many ways, local understandings of home, home-making and privacy differ significantly from what I and my family knew from our own home context.[2] Hence, our sense for privacy felt challenged in significant ways: At times, the courtyard was highly frequented, either by our hosts or another tenant neighbour family, or clients to our landlady's informal tailor and beauty business. The co-presence of others right before our front door often made my personal attempts for securing a sense of privacy impossible, notwithstanding the visual barrier of thin curtains which proved unsuccessful in preventing noise from the outside into our home. Furthermore, our small living room was separated from our landlords' shop by only a thin wall. Sometimes until midnight we were unintentionally following his conversations with customers or the local TV programme he was watching.

Experiencing privacy: Gender and the 'Other' home

In spring 2014, my friend Elbəy (age twenty-nine) invited me and my family to jointly spend a weekend at the dacha in his home village. There, around three years ago, Elbəy's father had bought around thirty hectares of land and planned to start a cattle-breeding business and the commercial cultivation of vegetables. Elbəy was responsible for planning and coordinating these plans. He had recently built the dacha which he visited regularly for enjoying the 'good energy' of the place but also to supervise the ongoing works during the summer months. Since I first got to know Elbəy at a friend's place in Baku some months ago, he sought my company whenever possible and soon became one of my closest friends in the field. He frequently picked me up at home with his white Hyundai Santa Fe and we spent most of the time just cruising through the city, picking up friends and making conversation. Hence, I soon got introduced to an extended social network – not only in Baku but also in his home village.

Two things which at first were really surprising to me are worth mentioning here: Firstly, every time he came to pick me up, he vehemently refused to enter our landlord's courtyard that led to our apartment, let alone to spend a short visit at our place. Instead, he stayed in his car sending a message via phone to announce his arrival. Vice versa, we went to his downtown apartment several times, sometimes with other friends too, but I have never met his wife or two children there. What was the issue? Over time it seemed to me that people in general deliberately avoided visiting each other's property or home for informal or spontaneous visits – relatives or very close, long-term friends excluded. Even neighbours that had questions or concerns hardly ever entered the yard; instead they would yell the name of the addressee from the outside. Such behaviour seemed much related to people's respect towards the homes and private space of others, mostly due to the presence of other family members. I can hardly explain otherwise that Elbəy was so skilfully manoeuvring our informal visits to his home around the co-presence of his wife and children. Thus, meeting together with our families required a formal invitation. Eventually, we received exactly such an invitation to the villa of Elbəy's parents not far from Baku. The invitation to Elbəy's dacha was the second time we met each other's families.

Secondly, for me as an anthropologist having my family with me also meant managing my time between work and family life, between professional and private responsibilities. And usually, fieldwork merges all these levels as many different things can be considered part of fieldwork or at least as part of making one's home in the field. Building friendships, being invited to weddings or other people's homes (whether with or without my family) is important in both ways. Hence, negotiating between these dimensions and the various expectations from different directions sometimes created challenging situations and required an increased awareness for the emotional well-being of my family. For instance, I had difficulties turning down Elbəy's rather spontaneous intentions to meet, if I wanted or was expected to stay at home with my wife and son. If I declined, I was immediately facing questions about why I could not join, what I was expected to do instead, etc. And spending time at home with the family was certainly not considered by Elbəy nor most of my other acquaintances to have priority over the male company of friends. The process of home-making in the field involved much joint efforts by my wife and me to make all three of us feel *at home* in our rented apartment.

But much of this home-making involved very different gendered expectations. It took me quite some time not to perceive it contradictory that people around me constantly expressed the unique importance of the family or the home but seemed to feel little obliged to physically spend time together. Hence, the home was usually represented by my male company as a gendered space attached to women rather than men. Male responsibilities towards home and family were attached to ideals of masculinity and rather connected to providing for and representing the home: going to work (which necessarily means not spending too much time at home), engaging in all kinds of 'biznes' for earning money – all things which largely depend on people's social network, a reason to spend time fostering and maintaining it (or increasing it by spending time with a foreign anthropologist as a potential future capital). In contrast, my German socialization raised my awareness that spending time with the family is most important for making a good and caring husband.

*   *   *

On a Friday we left Baku with two cars in the late morning and planned to arrive at the dacha by noon. I was driving our car and followed Elbəy's lead. After two hours we were approaching his home village. Similar to many Baku neighbourhoods, walls constituted a dominant feature along the roads. We passed the village towards the open fields and, after some minutes, arrived at the dacha. We unpacked the cars and Elbəy showed us our sleeping room on the second floor to put our luggage. While we were enjoying the landscape and nice weather, the children were playing in a parked tractor – a Soviet original in blue colour whose cabin looked very homey, due to a comfortable seat upholstery with flower motives and red velvet curtains with ornaments on the rear and side windows.

After one hour, Elbəy told us to get into his car for visiting his relatives at his uncle's home for lunch. When we arrived, Elbəy's cousin opened the oversized and ornamented metal gate to let us enter the spacious yard in front of the house. The open yard had a corrugated metal roof about six meters above floor level and about ten-by-twenty-five meters in size, whose fringes were embellished with elaborately ornamented zinc sheets. This kind of construction is a typical feature of rural homes which serve to host hundreds of guests for weddings and other lifecycle feasts of the family. We entered the house and got introduced to everyone before we were served tea as lunch was being prepared. Elbəy's uncle was absent and his cousin has disappeared as well; only female relatives were present. After lunch and more tea, Elbəy's brother Samir arrived together with his cousin and told Elbəy and me to join them. Meanwhile, my wife and our female hosts tried to engage in conversations by using a curious mix of different languages. When I was about to leave with the other men, she asked what we were up to but I could tell her neither where to nor why we were leaving. I literally got 'kidnapped' by our male company. At that time, neither my wife nor I could anticipate that I would be absent for more than eight hours.

When we returned around midnight, I had already felt bad for hours because of my long absence; my wife did not even know where we were or when we planned to return home. This was a bad conscience that none of my local companions seemed to share. As I learned from her later, she in turn got introduced to numerous female relatives who visited the house and was drowned in black tea. And when she inquired about where the men had gone and what we were doing, the women simply replied that she should not be concerned with it; we just had things to do and would return sooner or later. I could have called my wife but it felt weird to me as none of my companions was doing so. The impact of local gender norms, roles and male pride was overwhelming and made communicating with my wife impossible without violating these norms. I decided to go native in that regard as I was trying hard to keep my status among our group and I did not want to risk any intervention to the flow of our activities. While my wife and son were more or less 'trapped' in our hosts' house with quasi-strangers, I felt as if I'd been introduced to every uncle, cousin, relative and friend in the village who was available. And after dark we were driving around in the flood plains of the Kura and Aras rivers in a pickup truck with my hosts being excited and engaging in hunting animals. Elbəy was driving the car, his uncle on the front seat was armed with a loaded shotgun carefully watching out for rabbits or jackals while his cousin on the backseat next to me was handling the spotlight which was connected to the car's battery. I, the anthropologist, was trying to pretend a similar level of excitement for this hunting rally sitting amidst the noise and smell of gunshots.

On my return, my wife braced herself not to start a scene in front of our hosts while I felt sorry and tried to appease her: I would explain myself later in a more discrete setting. Right then, Elbəy suggested that we should not return to his dacha tonight, as it was very late already. Instead, my wife and son should stay here overnight while I would stay with Elbəy in the house of his other uncle just opposite. That was too much for my wife! We had come here with nothing but a few diapers for our son. She insisted to return bringing forward various legitimate reasons. Instead, every reason was replied to with a counter-reason for why returning was not convenient. It was a strange and delicate situation for everyone and I did my best to support my wife's interest, though I found myself in a serious conflict. In the end, although my wife had not yet swallowed her anger, we gave ourselves up to our hosts. So, my wife and son were sharing one king-sized bed with Elbəy's wife and children while I was staying in the other uncle's house.

*   *   *

'In Azerbaijan there is no privacy!', I was told by Vusala, one of my students in a seminar on qualitative research methods. Regarding mine and my wife's experiences described earlier, I guess one can easily sympathize with this statement. The fact of having been separated from my wife during the night and hardly seeing her during the whole weekend deprived us of what we thought to be *our* familial privacy. On the other hand, it shows that privacy has many nuances with rather ambiguous notions. At our stay in Elbəy's home village, for instance, men and women enjoyed an enormous level of privacy, though in rather collective and spatially separated ways.

Vusala's statement about privacy could also be understood in individualistic terms, that is, as respect for an individual's need of privacy, which, arguably, might be the dominant spontaneous association among many Western anthropologists. I, personally, appreciate the times I can dedicate to myself, although such moments have become rare with now two children. And that fact, over time, also shifted my understanding and expectations of privacy away from emphasizing its individual notion towards its familial notion. However, it has never occurred to me during fieldwork that someone complained about a lack of individual privacy. On the contrary, when I was probing my interlocutors about the value they attach to it, I received many comments similar to the one made by my friend Nizami, who lived in a shared flat with many other men: 'Your whole lifetime, you share sleeping rooms with others: as a child at home, in the dormitory when you study … that's normal. Being alone is just considered weird and boring. Man is a social animal.'

The kind of privacy that Vusala referred to was the collective privacy enjoyed within the home that was mentioned by Reşat at the beginning of this chapter when he explained the meaning of walls as protection from the curiosity of other people. But how could Vusala claim that there is no privacy in Azerbaijan when people's own emphasis as well as the architecture and materiality of homes and neighbourhoods (e.g. walls and thick multilayered curtains) point in the opposite direction? Following her initial remark, she added that 'people in Azerbaijan constantly talk about their relatives and neighbours. Here, *everyone* is into gossiping – not only elder women'. Indeed, among my friends and acquaintances it was common practice to gossip about and compare yourself to others, which seemed to constitute an everyday topic in conversations. Especially weddings offered plenty of fodder for conversations, comparison and criticism with regard to the number of guests, the location, its prestige and quality of food, live music, etc. Hence, as talking about and comparing with others plays such a prominent role, people in turn place high value on protecting close family members from becoming subject to criticism in public; home architecture can be interpreted as representing these efforts in material and symbolical terms. But the more something is considered to be endangered, the more likely do people attach special meaning to it. Thus, the home ideally enables families to enjoy privacy, protection and control from the outside world. Furthermore, it is a space that ensures a kind of mutual loyalty, trust and integrity among its dwellers. This is well captured in a telling proverb a local linguist shared with me: '*evin sözünü çöldə deməzlər!*' (the word of the house must not be told in the desert.) Hence, the boundaries and thresholds of the home (e.g. walls, doors, windows or curtains) that separate private from public space obtain a crucial role and have long been discussed by anthropologists in other settings (e.g. Cieraad 2006; Douglas 1966; Van Gennep 1960). Such thresholds of the home are discussed in the next section.

No Home without Curtains: Of Home Boundaries and Thresholds

The Baku neighbourhood we were living in represented an extensive mixture of dwellers' social standing and economic situations. For instance, I perceived our landlords' home as being of average quality within the neighbourhood (though much better than the homes common in other parts of the city). Within twenty years they had significantly extended their residential space whenever money was available; now they were renting out partly to foreigners. However, up the road there were also luxurious villas of the nouveaux riches – Baku's economic and political elite that has been attracted to this part of the city within the last decade. Often, these homes appeared like fortresses because of high walls around the houses, huge gates for huge cars, and window grills even on the houses' top floors. Showing off was obviously much more appreciated than modesty. Walls and gates reflected the wealth of the owner and provided a contrast to their solely functional counterparts in average houses.

These examples show well that thresholds of the home do not only provide physical or visual protection and privacy for the family. They also serve the public display of status and wealth, whether real or aspired to, of its dwellers. Their quality and visual appearance are immediately visible to outsiders. Additionally and independently of the economic background, gates and doors also were used to announce important lifecycle events to the public. Red ribbons were put on yard gates and doors of the home to signify the marriage of a (usually male) household member and the arrival of the bride (*gəlin*, literally meaning 'incomer') to the house. Similarly, a black ribbon served to announce bereavement.

Interestingly, I observed the very same dynamics in local mass housing estates from Soviet times. Within the buildings' dull monotony, it is the apartment doors which represent a personal touch and socioeconomic distinctions among the apartment dwellers. From simple steel doors with peepholes to the more elaborate ones, layered with imitations of expensive wood, often embellished with iron doorknockers, each door has its unique appearance and also raises certain expectations about the dwellers' economic standing. This is quite common across the Caucasus and comparative accounts from Armenia do equally attach special meaning to the door as the home's 'safeguard' and 'calling card', which 'often represents the home as a whole, especially under the conditions of modern house planning on a mass scale' (Abrahamian 2007: 272–3).

In the remaining part of this section, I want to share some impressions on another threshold, the curtain (*pərdə*). In Azerbaijan and in the Caucasus in general, it is impossible to imagine a home without curtains; they are traditionally considered to be part of the bride's dowry and usually consist of up to three layers of different materials, transparency and thickness. Among other factors, curtains are an important indicator for whether an apartment is inhabited or not. When I was looking for a place to rent and therefore visiting the available and newly renovated apartment of our eventual landlords, it did not yet have curtains. It was among the first things that my landlady assured me they would do by the time we moved in (although I did not raise the issue at all). Later, my wife and I were used to opening the curtains regularly during the daytime in order to get more sunlight (as we both like to have plants in our apartment, their need of it was an additional reason). At first, our landlady was very surprised by such behaviour and asked about the reasons for it. Eventually, she seemed to realize that as foreigners we had a different approach to curtains.

Curtains are arguably the most vivid but also ambivalent symbol for privacy. In Azerbaijan the curtain figuratively stands for the private and secret aspects in any social interaction. Hence, the curtain attains the Western meaning of a person's or group's intentional façade or appearance. It describes the representation of the home, the family or oneself at its best towards others that people constantly attempt to create and maintain in everyday life (see Goffman 1959). In Azerbaijan, this is reflected well by the expression *pərdə saxlamaq*, which can be translated as 'maintaining the curtain'. To me, this phrase bundles and represents all the aspects of home as a private sphere that I describe in this chapter, including the importance of walls and thresholds: constant and active efforts to maintain collective privacy in front of others. At the same time, this, in turn, also implies expectations towards respecting others' privacy and secrets. In its ideal conception, 'maintaining the curtain' is a joint effort by all parties involved to prevent any direct confrontation and endangerment of the façade, collective privacy or 'curtain' respectively. Such curtain politics of everyday life can be applied to myriads of social settings and processes and I have given many implicit examples in my ethnography so far.

The following is a rather trivial but descriptive example. I was invited to the wedding of a friend's son. Weddings are huge feasts with several hundred guests and have become quite an industry. Dishes and all kinds of food (and liquor for male guests) are served throughout the evening. Although many men smoke, young unmarried men usually do not smoke in front of their parents and relatives. In order to *maintain the curtain*, they frequently leave the hall in small groups and smoke in an appropriate, more private place. At the specific wedding I was attending, some of the groom's cousins and friends asked me to join them for smoking. We left the celebration but instead of just having our smokes outside, they preferred to sit in the car for an even higher degree of privacy. We got in and took a twenty-minute ride through the lavishly illuminated city centre before we returned to the wedding.

The car, here, enabled us to enjoy a gender- and age-specific kind of privacy that allowed for a temporal retreat from normative social expectations. In the final section I will further reflect on men's home-making activities around cars and how they shaped my own relation to our car at the time of my fieldwork.

Caring for cars, or home-making the other way

The son of our landlord had a white Lada which he was treating with meticulous care. Several times a week, and sometimes on a daily basis, he would clean his car in our courtyard. Generally, I perceived such practice as part of car-owners' daily routine. His obsession surprised me, however, especially because of the time but also because of the huge amount of water it required. Baku has an arid climate and water is officially considered a scarce resource. This is why the provision of water in many districts is limited to certain hours a day (hence most people were filling their private water tanks to secure a 24/7 supply). Those who could afford it were making use of the countless car wash places that have recently become widespread across the city. Many people with a sufficiently spacious garage at a large road would open such a business, which was often blessed with a constant flow of customers. Within half an hour one or several men were cleaning the car inside and outside.

The common statement I received on my questions about this frequent and also time-consuming ritual was simple: 'It is dirty!' The perception of a car being dirty or clean obviously diverged greatly between me and the locals. I have frequently wondered about the state of cleanliness that some men were aiming at when they were washing what appeared to me to be an already clean car. But admittedly Baku, known as the 'City of Winds' and located in a semi-desert region, is characterized by dust and sand. On some days, when leaving the window open for some time (unfortunately we did not have air-conditioning, which is considered an indispensable feature of the home among locals), the floor and window sills would be covered with a thin layer of dust. Under such conditions cleaning felt as if tilting at windmills (which I assume was another reason for the necessity of air-conditioning and keeping windows closed).

As a foreigner I was touched by the intimate and caring relationship of men and their cars and the diligence with which they approached the cleaning process. Among overambitious car-owners the cleaning culminated in an almost meditative ritual: they would for instance rub the tires' surface with glycerine to give them a dark black and shiny gloss just as the leather shoes of the driver. Alternatively, people were using a mixture of pomegranate juice and water to do the job. I more than once found myself comparing the male obsession with a clean car and the housewife's ideal of keeping the home clean. Both the home and the car had to be kept clean as both were gendered sites to receive visitors. And owners wanted to make sure to present their private space in its best condition.

Over time, these widespread habits among many local men also had an impact on my own relation with our car. In contrast to other locals, the dusty conditions in Baku did not raise my motivation to invest a comparable amount of time for cleaning a what I perceived to be primarily a functional item. Why should I clean my car weekly, let alone daily, when just a couple of days later, it would be covered in dust again? I had little interest in wasting my time and being caught in the treadmill of car aesthetics! Hence, for a long time I limited the cleaning to situations where it seemed a requirement, such as when we were invited to weddings. For locals it was obligatory to arrive at a wedding with a freshly cleaned car. Firstly, to avoid gossip by others and, secondly, out of respect to the hosts. At such occasions I took the service of a car wash. But usually I did not care much about whether my car, which I parked on the street, was of immaculate appearance. That changed at once when the son of our landlords approached me asking whether I would not want to clean my car which was pretty dirty in his view. He obviously felt slightly embarrassed to approach me with his rather rhetorical question pointing at something that was usually considered common sense. With regard to the *everyday curtain politics* the situation can be well understood. Eventually, I felt obliged to follow his hint. From then on, I engaged in a similar, regular cleaning ritual whenever I sensed the emergence of a slight pressure towards myself and a whiff of shame. So, I cleaned my car occasionally out on the street which at times became slightly unpleasant as neighbours and shop-owners were often standing in front of their house: were they observing me? What did they think of me as a foreigner and the quality of my cleaning skills?

During my fieldwork, a car turned out to be an advantage not only in terms of mobility. It also supported those aspects of my home-making in the field that went beyond the physical space of home for building up a social life. Of course, for friends and interlocutors without a car, I was also an important resource for their mobility and it therefore enabled me to participate in their everyday life much more than would have been possible without.

Cars, especially in the post-socialist context, have long been important substitutes or temporary extensions of the home for males that have grasped the attention of scholars. In the Soviet Union, the early 1970s marked a turning point when the mass production of cars took off. As by far most car-owners were men, Soviet society's automobilization resulted in a gendering of time and space: For men, 'the interiors of cars … served as refuges from the crowded conditions of apartment dwelling' (Siegelbaum 2008: 7). Furthermore,

> courtyards, alleys, roadsides, and fields, previously gender-neutral spaces, were appropriated for the predominantly masculine activities of car work and car talk. The interiors of parked cars served as alternative living rooms for men seeking privacy or a place to withdraw after a row with their wives.
>
> (Siegelbaum 2008: 248)

Probably anywhere, cars provide an alternative space for enjoying privacy – for individuals, for couples, for peers, etc. But in former socialist contexts cars obtained special meaning in regard to privacy, not only because people had to wait for years or even decades before being allocated a private car. Socialist housing policy, despite all its merits, hardly managed to provide sufficient living space for its citizens and contributed to cars obtaining the role of gendered and mobile living rooms for men. My ethnography has aimed at underlining such dimensions of gendered privacy and processes of dwelling and home-making with regard to houses, homes and cars. One characteristic was the spatial separation of men and women according to the varying duties, expectations and moralities of dwelling and home-making. Our efforts as anthropologists towards home-making in the field necessarily engage with the manifold differences and potential tensions in diverging notions of home. Enabling a sense of privacy, for instance, might count as a universal expectation towards the home. But as I have shown, understandings of how appropriate modes of privacy shall be constructed and maintained are diverse and inevitably become part of the anthropologist's home-making.

Notes

1 *Həyət* means 'courtyard'. Hence, the term *həyət evi* (literally 'courtyard house') is generally applied to one or several dwellings around a joint courtyard, often inhabited by an extended family group.

2 When speaking about the concept of home, it is noteworthy to say that in Azeri, unlike in English, the term for 'home' is the same as for 'house' (*ev*). As in most other Turkic languages, it is the root of the verb 'to marry' (*evlənmək*) which literally means 'to become enhoused', though from a rather male perspective. 'To marry' from a female perspective is *ərə getmək*, which literally translates as 'going to the husband'. A more gender-neutral translation of the former could equally mean 'home-making'. This points to the house/home as being primarily a social and gendered concept. Accordingly, home-making here is much about social and gendered processes. It is social because, as such, home implies the reproduction of the family, the kin group and the formation of a new household. Hence, when I am married, I am *evli*, that is, 'with house/home'. It is a gendered concept because responsibilities towards the home's ideal production, use and maintenance are defined and legitimated in 'traditional' and symbolic terms. Obtaining the physical structure – a house or an apartment – is regarded as a prerequisite for marriage and the responsibility of the bridegroom's family. Making the house a home is expected to be the bride's family duty. This finds expression in the bride's dowry (*cehiz*), which includes almost everything that belongs to a home's inside, for example, furniture, domestic appliances, chandeliers, porcelain, carpets and curtains.

3

A lonely home: Balancing intimacy and estrangement in the field

Nikita Simpson

In the days before I left for fieldwork, as my classmates peeled off one by one bound for exotic destinations – Iquitos, Bhubaneshwar, Surin – I thought a lot about loneliness. I'm not used to being alone. I grew up in the Sydney suburbs, in a house of multiplying siblings, lost friends and a steady stream of relatives from Delhi and Bangkok. Mornings involved finding a new cousin in the bathroom while brushing my teeth. Privacy was rare and none of my things were sacred. Maybe this is why my good friend and fellow anthropologist left a package as he slipped away from our final meeting. I tore away the crisp brown paper to reveal a copy of Olivia Laing's *The Lonely City: Adventures in the Art of Being Alone* (Laing 2016). I flipped open the front cover – 'If you're lonely, this one's for you.' Even her words looked lonely, swimming on the grainy page. He had inscribed the following page:

> *You are about to go away. I wish you all the strength in the world to fight through this, my love. I trust that you bring the energy, the curiosity and the love you need. Come back safe and don't suffer too much from the loneliness – it can be a good thing.*

The lonely plight of the anthropologist is well documented, even assumed. Our first ethnographic encounters as bright-eyed undergraduates are with Malinowski, left 'alone on a tropical beach close to a native village while the launch or dinghy sails out of sight' (Narayan 2012: 15). With Lila Abu-Lughod, as her father leaves her in a Bedouin tent somewhere in the Egyptian desert (Abu-Lughod 1986). Leaving behind your loved ones, for a period of wild adventure, yet ultimate loneliness, is a salient trope in ethnographic literature.

Yet reading back on this inscription, after almost two years in the field, I realize that the kind of loneliness I experienced was particular. It wasn't the loneliness of loss – it was never that sharp. Neither was it the loneliness of solitude that I felt. *Middlemarch* was there for the evenings, and I always had my *Suitable Boy*, dog-eared and familiar. I feel like a fraud when friends and family commend me for my bravery at 'doing it alone'. For in that village at the foothills of the Himalayas, surrounded by welcoming strangers, I don't think I was allowed to eat even one meal by myself.

The kind of loneliness I experienced was peculiar to the experience of going to a new place, where I was entirely strange, and hoping, desperately, that I would be able to build a home there. This home had to encompass sufficiently intimate relationships such that I would have something to say about that place when I left again. But my home also had to remain sufficiently estranged, or alienated, from the rest of the community such that I could observe, clearly, the happenings around me. At the heart of this task, and essential to participant observation, is an oscillation between intimacy and estrangement. You're strange when you arrive. Then intimacy grows over the process of home-building. But you become almost too intimate as you get to know your informants' inconsistencies and contradictions. Then you have to become strange again as you depart. In this chapter, I hope to give but one example of what an anthropologist might experience in balancing intimacy and estrangement while building a home. I point to the kind of loneliness that grew from this tension in my own home, and how it played an important role in the practice of participant observation.

Divya's story

The home I built was nestled high in the foothills of the Dhauladhar Range, and looked down on the sweeping Kangra Valley of Himachal Pradesh in India. I shared it with a vibrant housemate, Simi, a designer from Manipur who had lived in the village for more than five years; and Ram, a mountaineer whose knowledge of the range was unparalleled. My partner Tom came and went over the course of my stay, the source of many raised eyebrows and whispers. The four of us were tightly wrapped up in the daily comings and goings of the house, and of the hamlet it was set in. We rented the house from a retired army man who (like many village entrepreneurs) seemed to construct and rent out a new pillarbox every summer. We took the upper storey that had been hurriedly built. The entry to the bathroom was in the middle of the kitchen. The sitting room was sealed up, without even one window overlooking the magnificent valley below. It was cheaply made from chipping asbestos. But the glorious verandah made amends. It wrapped around the whole front of the house, and was lined on either side by the tops of almond trees. Sparrows flitted along the already-rusting railings, Red Starts craned to listen to our conversations, Hornbills came majestic in the monsoon, a hungry Kite circled and dipped above. On a Sunday, when the village children came at sunset, we would play bird sounds from our speakers, and they would flock in, curious, responding to our tinny calls. Like a tree house, it felt removed, slightly, from the prying eyes of the village below.

We had employed a young woman from a village across the river, Divya, to work in our house – helping us with the cooking and cleaning.[1] Slowly, Divya became one of my cherished friends and intimate interlocutors as she came, day after day, into my home. My relationship with her exemplifies the tension between intimacy and estrangement that both of us had to balance. One day last April, Divya[2] had come early, as usual, to wash the dishes and sweep the floors. She came up the stairs slowly. Her *tuni* (scarf) was tied practically around her body, and her pants were scrunched up to reveal her feet stained green by the *lipai* (dung) paint that she used to refresh the *culha* (mud stove) that morning. Her step seemed tired, but as she looked up she took in myself and Tom sitting on the verandah in the usual setup – with our cane table and two chairs, looking out towards the plains, computers hooked up to the charging point, a freshly brewed pot of tea on the table, with a cup waiting for her too – she cracked a smile. 'Hello Di', she sang, 'Hey Bro', she put out her hand to high-five Tom's. She instantly seemed more at ease. 'Why do you drink that kind of tea?' she asked, stopping to pick up the pot and peer at it strangely. 'You don't boil it?' I shrugged and told her to taste it. I poured her a cup, adding a dash of fresh buffalo milk. The milk curdled slightly as the hot tea was poured into the cup. She stared at the swirling colours, and slowly sipped it. She made a face, 'Sugar?!' I smiled and she followed me into the kitchen to get it. She set the tea down and rolled up her sleeves as I went outside to continue with my work.

After some time, Divya swept the last of the dust and dirt out the door with a big low movement of the palm broom, and set it aside at the edge of the verandah. She re-pinned her hair, and came to settle down next to me on the spare cane stool. 'Di', she asked, 'will you teach me some things about the computer?' Divya explained that she had worked very hard in school, she had enjoyed being there with her friends, she had revelled in the full days. But then when she had finished she was just *aise* (like so) 'sitting' at home, filling her days with the same cycle of chores her brothers refused to do. In our home, she was thrilled by the strangeness of the way we sat together as boyfriend and girlfriend, the way we tapped away all day, even the way we brewed our tea. For Divya, the stuff of our home had an uncanny quality. It was simultaneously achingly present in her daily life and her surroundings – through the memes on her Facebook feed, the dark cars with Punjab plates that raced up the road beyond her house. But it was also just as achingly absent in the time-loop of domesticity. She wanted to bridge this gap, to touch the world that lay just beyond her reach.

When she asked for computer lessons, I believe she was trying to bridge the gap between her world and ours. We agreed to begin with typing. She would come and settle down beside me, pour herself some strange tea, dollop in three generous spoons of sugar and wait until I had finished what I was doing. I would pass over my Mac, with a fresh word document blinking back at her, and she would begin to type. We began with some questions and answers. She was slow, hesitant to pick up the spacing, how to move back and forth with the cursor, how to add a capital letter. She looked frequently back at me for affirmation before gingerly continuing. For me, it was an exercise in patience; I had to suck in my breath and clench my jaw to stop myself just jumping in and doing it for her.

Evidently, her computer class at school, that was meant to be a weekly occurrence, had been a failure. A bright young teacher had lobbied the education board to set up a 'Smart Classroom', and been successful in acquiring four computers, and a projector. The school was very proud, painting a big sign above the gate saying 'School Smart Classroom and Computer Room'. But after some months it became clear that this young teacher only wanted to show this off as leverage to get a transfer to a better school in town. He left promptly, leaving the computers and projector to the merciless mould of the monsoon.

Divya and I progressed to writing short paragraphs. She would bring a small notebook to carefully write down the English words that she was learning and their Hindi equivalents. She was determined and committed. I would leave her to work on her own during these times for half an hour, an hour at a time while I got to work preparing lunch. Sometimes when I was out doing an interview, or away in that other world, she would let herself in and use one of the old laptops, tracing the keys out onto a sheet of lined paper in her exercise book, trying to establish the pathways between the high *W* and the low *B*, the lines across from *P* to *R* and back again from *E* to *Y*. Though in these moments, I was nagged by an unsettling sense that our intimacy was fleeting. Divya was teaching me so much about what it was to be a young woman in this place, but how long would, or could, our friendship last?

Becoming intimate

Divya was just one of many bouncing kids, shy girls, tired housewives, toothless old women who passed by our house. It was mostly girls and women who came, despite often being confined to their own homes by responsibility. I believe my place was sufficiently close to their own homes to permit them to come, but sufficiently far to remain thrilling. I had come to this village in North India to work with women and girls. Witches, widows, wayward girls, victims of violence, single women, mad women, depressed women, possessed women. I wanted to hear the stories of them all. As I crafted my proposal, I thought I would be lucky if I were to collect the stories of just two or three. I thought it might take me until I left to be close enough to reveal even a little bit of intimacy. As it panned out, I realized that building a home was proving an important strategy for eliciting stories. The women came to me. I didn't have to prod and probe. I believe they came precisely because I was a stranger. In the beginning, they were curious about this strange half-Punjabi, half-Australian girl who had come to their village with broken Hindi and a dubious boyfriend. It seemed as they began by sticking their heads through the door, sniffing out the new smells of the house, that they were simply inquisitive. But the initial scouting led into a steady stream of visits. I learnt quickly from Simi and Ram that this visiting, dropping in, was a very important tenant of sociality in the village. And that it warranted an effusive and precise form of hospitality. I followed suit by dutifully offering sweet tea served in porcelain cups on a tray, an array of biscuits and a comfortable seat to anyone who dropped by – whether they were explicitly invited or not.

Why did they keep coming back? Apart from neighbourly curiosity, it felt as though there were certain freedoms, possibilities, that existed for these visitors in my home. One reason they came was to play. We had games and puzzles, pencils, pens and endless reams of paper, but most importantly we let them use the computers. The children would rush back from school, lugging their giant backpacks up the hill, panting and laughing as they bumbled in the door, braids askew. Our place was removed from the responsibilities of their own homes, and such removal made it a kind of sanctuary. In our place, they knew they could put off washing the clothes, beating the rugs or making evening *roti* – even just for a little while. In our place, they could be experimental, sometimes do things that were otherwise forbidden, deviant. The girls would strip off their scarves and undo their braids. Simi told me that one of the boys even felt comfortable enough to try on her dresses, wigs and lipstick. Intimacy with these kids grew rapidly;

they were the first to cross boundaries, to ask me difficult questions, rifle through my things and instruct me if I was doing something culturally inappropriate (Allerton 2016). For instance, one evening the kids came over to our kitchen to make a cake for one of their birthdays. As they entered my kitchen they saw I had hung my underwear over the curtain rails, trying to dry them out of sight of my landlord and his son. They looked at each other, and burst out laughing, then pointed and slapped each other's hands in fits of embarrassed laughter. 'You can't do that!' one of them exclaimed slowly, kindly, clutching her stomach. 'What if Uncle comes in here?' My cultural faux pas made me childlike in the eyes of the children who visited my home, and allowed me to seem somewhat equal to them.

A second reason they came was to unburden themselves. Visitors of all ages dropped in of their own accord; at morning tea to tell me of their illicit romances, at afternoon tea to whisper about their troubles with neighbours, and at evening tea to complain of their alcoholic husbands. Children zipped up and down the stairs, screeching of troublesome siblings and fighting parents. Even some men dropped by after a few drinks to accuse their wives of this or that. Some of these encounters were quiet, concealed. I brought a sobbing girl on her way home from school into the privacy of my bedroom to comfort her about her ill father. Others were performatively public. One woman would grab me by the waist and slap my hand as she told me about her flirtatious banter with her employer at the hotel where she worked. It seemed, because they were unable to trace my context, they didn't quite know my people, that I represented a window of opportunity for them to open up, share, confide. These were often half-stories, partial truths, inchoate and tender. These encounters became the stuff of my fieldwork, the data I recorded carefully and filed away. But these intimate windows could close as suddenly as they had opened, as Divya's case illustrates.

Divya presents one such case of 'unburdening'. Sometime just after the spring wheat harvest and before they planted the monsoon corn, Divya began to stop halfway through her typing; she would look around to see if I was busily doing my own work. I would avoid catching her eye, so I could see what her next move was. She would swiftly switch to the Safari browser and sign into her Facebook account. I was surprised by how adept she was in all of this flicking screens and closing windows, compared to her wary movements on Word. I wasn't sure if I should stop her from doing this. I wasn't here to discipline her, but I wasn't sure I was comfortable with allowing her to scroll through selfies of her cousins, or videos of Folk Dance posted on community pages. But I soon realized that the reason why she really wanted to go on Facebook was to speak with her fiancé.

I began to probe by teasing her. I touched her shoulder and gave a knowing smile – 'Who's that?' She looked away shyly. She told me in a coy outpouring how much she liked him, how much she was dying to get married, how much she wanted to leave her chaotic home to go and live in his newly built concrete house, with its three tiled bathrooms, marble kitchen bench and freshly painted peachy walls. It was clear that thinking about this boy – part romantic fantasy, part exhausted dream of rest – filled many of her idle moments.

But by the time the corn stalks had grown high with the deluge of monsoon, her voice had begun to crack a little as she spoke about her pending marriage. She would sigh and put her hand to her head, 'I have so much *tension*,[3] Di.' Day by day, I would hear a little more of the story. Her troubles seemed to multiply. The guilt of being born a girl to a family still fixated on nurturing boys and sending girls away. Her father's meagre wage doing labour work at a hotel construction site, 200 rupees a day, machinery slicing his fingers. The realization that her first fiancé wasn't right and the shame of such a blemish to her future marriage prospects. The long and precarious second engagement she had to endure while she waited for her cousins to marry first.

As she revealed these troubles, they thickened the air between us. I watched a new kind of intimacy grow between her and me, between her and this place. Coming to my home became a different kind of sanctuary, less the place where she could pretend to be carefree and relish in the strange elements at the cusp of her life, where she could experiment with being part of this life, one typed word at a time. It became more a place of unburdening. '*Itne sare soch, Di*' – I have so many thoughts – she would explain how the thoughts and worries whirred around her mind. I started to find dishes left soaking under the sink, and dead flies caught between the bottles of masala. Instead of coming out to peer over my shoulder at the computer screen to wait her turn for her lesson, I would have to come into the kitchen to find her sitting on the cane stool inside, staring blankly at her mobile phone. 'When are you leaving Di?' she asked one day when I walked in on her stopped halfway through washing the breakfast dishes. 'What will I do when you go?' I reassured her it would be another year before I even thought about leaving, and even then we would make sure she was able to continue her lessons with someone else.

One evening she came tramping up the stairs, as the last pinks and oranges scattered into blues and purples across the valley. She had missed her morning duties. She explained that she had a new job. 'Di, I'm going to work with my sister for a new couple … me and my sister … it'll be the whole day. We earn more money.' Tom and I looked at each other. Divya suddenly looked smaller, younger, I was aware of how thin her wrists were, how I towered over her by a good two feet. In this moment, I was surprised to notice a rush of that peculiar sense of loneliness.

Becoming strange

Thinking through the case of Divya we can see the lilting tide of intimacy and estrangement – the way she entered my strange home, our friendship grew, she sought sanctuary, we became close, she recoiled, retreated from my home, and we grew distant, strangers again. To understand this tension, we can look more closely at what is entailed in intimacy itself.

Through this steady '*ana, jana*' – coming and going – between the four of us, our two acquired shepherding dogs, the birds and succession of callers, I realized we had built a sanctuary. The people who visited us were our real friends. Our neighbour, Sonam, would drop in with sour *amla* for me to suck when I had a bad stomach. I would quietly advance her small amounts of cash when her daughters needed new school uniforms. The home I had built was underpinned by intimate, reciprocal relationships. But this home wasn't just a sanctuary for me. It seemed too to be a sanctuary for at least some of those who passed through it. The home we built was founded on something shared. To borrow from Lauren Berlant – 'intimacy also involves an aspiration for a narrative about something shared, a story about both oneself and others that will turn out in a particular way' (Berlant 1998). However, our home seemed to be a sanctuary precisely *because* I was strange, removed from their usual networks of kinship and care, removed from their usual norms of respect and responsibility. Girls were able to tell me things they couldn't tell their mothers, women were able to tell me things they couldn't tell their sisters, wives were able to tell me things they couldn't tell their husbands.

But this is clearly not the whole story. Why did Divya leave? As Berlant warns, 'this view of "a life": that unfolds intact within the intimate sphere represses, of course, another fact about it: the unavoidable troubles, the distractions and disruptions that make things turn out in unpredicted scenarios' (Berlant 1998: 281). Intimacy clearly entails brevity, that some things are left unsaid, unexplained, ignored. What was I, and my interlocutors, ignoring or leaving unsaid in pursuit of intimacy? And what would be the unintended consequences of such ambivalence? I believe that there are three tacit and shared fantasies that underpinned the home I created, sustained by both my interlocutors and myself. Unveiling these tacit fantasies show the limits of my home, and the points where it chaffed with the norms of the village it was nestled in – as had been the case with Divya.

The first was the shared fantasy of time. During my first few months of fieldwork, I was careful to immerse myself completely in the temporal rhythms of the place I was in. I didn't leave the village for many months, and tried to mirror the routine of the family I lived with. I woke in the morning to take the cow to graze, I helped the landlord's daughter to make morning tea, then *roti* for breakfast, and washed up with her after the meal. I left early to cut grass and returned late after wedding festivities. Living like this proved, as the months went by, tiring and I began to build my own time into my day, working, reading or writing fieldnotes. I increasingly formed my own temporal rhythms that were separate to the time I spent with my interlocutors. Hence my home, that was initially always open, at any time, for a friend to wander in, became closed for big chunks of the day, where I would turn away visitors. The initial, rapid intimacy that grew with my informants was underpinned by a hope that these friendships would last a longer duration, even forever. Some of the relationships that grew in my home have lasted the test of time, some have even grown stronger, but others have fizzled away, or rapidly been cut short. But maintaining the home I built, and the relationships that it encompassed, entailed a kind of time-tricking. In order to build this home, both the strangeness of the past and the strangeness of the future had to be truncated. The desire for something shared entailed living in a constant present (Day, Papataxiarchis and Stewart 1999). Ultimately, the destinies of my interlocutors and myself diverged, the limits of my home became apparent, and we again became estranged. The home I built lasted for but a moment in time.

The second was the shared fantasy of equality. In order to build intimate relationships, of play or unburdening, my interlocutors and myself had to imagine ourselves to be somehow equal. This does not mean that we assumed that we were the same, but that we inhabited the same lifeworld. We had to ignore the obvious inequalities between us. For instance, I was in a vastly different position to Divya on almost all counts – class, caste, religion. Such difference ushered in inevitable hierarchies within my home. She was being paid to work in my house. She had few other job prospects, and was pressured to work for me by her family. This house was owned by a family who had quadruple her own family's income precisely because they were able to rent out this place to foreigners like me. What is especially problematic about this fantasy on my part, is that it allowed me to impose a form of tacit social control. The intimacy that grew in my home was on my terms, animated by my rules of conduct and care. The people welcomed, or desires expressed, in my home were often those considered odd or inappropriate elsewhere in the community. However, such spaces should not be romanticized, for while unusual norms may be tolerated, there still exists (as in any setting) judgement regarding degrees of normalcy and deviancy expressed through peer pressure and policing (Johnsen, Cloke and May 2005). Inevitably, the invitation to enter my home was not extended equally to all people, and the experience of my home was not uniformly positive. Therefore, the fantasy of equality was fragile and the openness of my home limited.

The third was the shared fantasy of privacy. As I have mentioned, the home I built felt slightly removed from the village it sat in, both physically because of its position on a second floor hidden in the treetops; and normatively because of the range of possible identities and behaviours permitted. This removal from the community, or estrangement, made possible a sense of privacy. My interlocutors felt like they could share what they wished in this space confidentially, without the usual consequences. However, such occlusion of my home was not only tenuous and temporary, but also dangerous for my informants. I had forgotten the influence of the village itself on my home and those who entered it. My house sat in the middle of a bustling hamlet, bordered on either side by well-used roads. Everyone could see what was happening on our verandah, just as we could see what they were up to. It, and the women who went in and out of it, were as easily surveilled as we could provide them sanctuary. Ultimately, it was this last fantasy – and particularly the actions of Vaani, a precocious sixteen-year-old visitor – that set the limits of my home.

Vaani's story

Vaani had been gone for four hours by the time they called us. We had just stacked the dinner dishes in the sink when we heard Priyanka, our landlady's dutiful and ever-working daughter, shouting for us on the steps. Usually they were all asleep by this time, their lights off and doors bolted against the February chill. But today something stirred in the *tika* (hamlet).[4] We met Priyanka on the balcony – 'Is Vaani here?' she asked quickly, eyes darting behind us. We hadn't seen Vaani since a few days before, when she had come for a movie night with the other girls. She regularly dropped in to see us, after school, or in the early evening – she would flash her coquettish smiles and come to look at herself in the mirror that was hung on our almirah. Vaani was one of the '*frank* girls' at school – popular but risky. She wore thick black eyeliner on her top lids, and never brought her *tuni* out with her. Sometimes she even wore jeans and plimsoles. She also used our home as a sanctuary against her turbulent family. Priyanka sighed – she knew Vaani wasn't here before she even asked – and headed back downstairs to tell her father.

We woke in the morning to shrill shrieking. At this point in my time in the village, I could identify the shriek as that of Neha, Vaani's mother, as she fought with her mother-in-law in their front courtyard. Such shrieking blended into the usual morning sounds of Barfi – the goat bleating below my bedroom window, the bells of Calli, the cow and her calf being taken to graze. Their house was slightly up the hill from ours, such that from my window as I peered out I could see it like a raised stage. The village was set along the tiered farms at the foot of the Dhauladhar. Cracking old mud houses were set in courtyards paved with slate. Usually, these courtyards were buzzing with activity; wheat or rajma was laid to dry, children played impromptu cricket games and women hung daily washing. But today the courtyard served as a theatre. Through the crack in the curtains, behind layers of apricot and walnut trees, I could see a number of people milling around two women who were clearly pitched against each other.

The younger woman, Neha, pulled at her thinning hair and appeared to double over as the elder, her mother-in-law, waved a long stick just above her bowed head. Neha's fraying kurta hung loosely on her slight frame, it seemed skewed to one side, baring her shoulder like a boiled hen's egg. Her mother-in-law sneered; Neha's hysteria only made her insults cut with an even more cruel precision. She brought the stick down against the slates, missing Neha's feet by centimetres. I could just see Vaani's face behind the door frame, her eyes wide. It was as if the publicity of the scene was specifically for the benefit of the neighbours. I asked what was going on and they told me that this fight went on all night last night. Then again they started this morning. They told me that Vaani went missing last night. Vaani had gone with two girls from the upper village to a DJ party in the nearby military cantonment, but she hadn't asked her parents' permission before going. Her father and uncle went to find her; they searched every wedding that was going on in the neighbouring villages, but returned empty-handed. It was not until well after midnight that Vaani had returned home in an unmarked car with two other girls, driven by an unknown boy. The fight had begun when Neha picked up a long stick used to swat the cow and began lashing out, as if possessed, at her mother-in-law and husband for not finding her daughter. Then her mother-in-law had grabbed it and started to hit Neha, screaming that Vaani's behaviour only mimicked her mother's. She waved the stick around above her head and each time it came down a little closer to Neha.

*   *   *

That evening, Ram, Simi and I were huddled in my room around the strip heater, when we heard a knock at the door. 'Nikitaaaaaa', Sonam's high-pitched nasal voice made us cringe as she poked her head around the door. 'Do you have a broom? I need it to do the floor in the morning.' Sonam's voice always proceeded her; she was Divya's aunt and at that time also helping with the cleaning while Divya was away. A thick-set lady with a sweet face that was beautiful when she was younger, before her daughters came one, two, three, four, five, and the hope of having a boy faded into lines webbing her eyes. Sonam knew precisely where the broom was, upstairs in the cleaning cupboard where she had put it back earlier that morning. I had expected her to drop by soon after the story about Vaani broke. Sonam was another woman who often came to our home and loved to share the whispers of the village. Whenever you met Sonam, you were sure to hear of some elder woman who had found a pile of ash in her kitchen pantry – a spell laid by a jealous sister; some young girl run away with her college boyfriend – only to return with flowering bruises.

Sonam excused herself humbly for disturbing us. She drank in her surroundings; she had never been into my room before. It was itself a treat for her because Tom and I shared it scandalously before we were married. Satisfied, she crouched down in front of us, and promptly forgot the guise of the broom. It was clear that things had changed since the morning, and the tide had shifted against Vaani – within the space of the day she moved from being a victim to a dangerous influence. First, Sonam told us about what exactly had happened. The incident was clearly an opportunity to let the flood gates open against Vaani and her mother. Her visit to us was a means of distancing herself from their shameful ways, setting herself and her own daughters safely in the shallows of critique. Sonam paused, allowing us to fill the gaping period with our dangerous speculation. 'There is no knowledge of where she was or what she was doing', she accentuated. Sonam's tone changed, and she leant forward slightly on her haunches. The reason she was telling us was purely, she said, to warn us. And here she paused to allow the sense of danger to fill the space between us. Vaani's behaviour was unacceptable. And the village consensus was that it had happened because she had been able to come to our home. She warned us not to allow Vaani, or any of the other children, to come to our place, else we might be blamed for facilitating their errant behaviour.

After the incident with Vaani, most mothers stopped sending their kids out to run from kitchen to kitchen. Women became more suspicious of one another, especially those coming back late in the evening. Even we kept to ourselves more. Just as Divya had used our house as a place of escape from her mundane chores, Vaani had used our house as a place of escape from her family and as an alibi to slip away unnoticed. Indeed, Sonam's warning was also a threat. Pursuing this kind of open home was not just dangerous for me, but also for my interlocutors.

A peculiar loneliness

My intention in this piece was to chart just one example of an anthropologist attempting to build a home in the field, and the oscillation between intimacy and estrangement that underpins this task. Building a home required, for me, a kind of blind optimism – both desire and belief that I could and would build intimate relationships with my informants that were private and equal and would last the test of time. My informants only entered into my home, and such intimate relations, because I was, in the first instance, a stranger. But as my home grew and its occupants weathered the inevitable events of village life, our intimacy and its animating desires matured, revealing how our life worlds could not always match. Our destinies diverged, our equality slipped and our sense of privacy was shattered. The moral boundaries of the village came crashing down on my home. I was reminded of just how temporary, just how fragile that home really was. It had appeared, for but a moment in all of our lives, when some unlikely stars aligned. This process of moving from strangeness to intimacy and back again to strangeness has allowed me to recognize the contingencies of my own assumptions. As Shah puts it,

> [Fieldwork] requires us to dive deep into the sea of other people's lives and find a way to swim with them. It requires commitment, endurance, constant improvisation, humility, sociality, and the ability to give oneself up to and for others. It also entails the ability to retrieve oneself and be prepared to rethink, from this position, everything one thinks one knows. And then it needs one to swim back to the shore and be prepared that this shore is almost always going to be different from the shore where one began. (Shah 2017: 7)

I understand now that the loneliness that is the plight of the anthropologist is not a condition of solitude or separation. Loneliness is the realization that any intimacy built in the field is temporary and fragile, and contains within it its opposite, strangeness. To borrow again from Berlant, – 'I didn't think it would turn out this way' is the secret epitaph of intimacy (Berlant 1998: 281) and indeed the secret epitaph of any ethnographic monograph.

Notes

1 Many women and girls had work in the village in the homes of foreigners or people from Delhi or Chandigarh who also kept a house in the hills.
2 All names are pseudonyms and characters are composites.
3 'Tension' is an emic term that encompasses everything from everyday stress to severe mental illness.
4 A group of houses, like a hamlet.

Ethnography of police 'domestic abuse' interventions: Ethico-methodological reflections

Faten Khazaei

The assumptions of home as an intimate, private and secure place – in sum an unalienated space – have long been taken for granted, not only in anthropology but also in the broader social sciences. Studies of domestic violence, however, have served to directly question the supposition of home as mainly an unalienable space and to put troubling experiences of exploitation and insecurity centre stage (Maynard and Hanmer 1987). Accounts of domestic violence disrupt the imagination of home as a secure space, demonstrating how home can become a site of violence and terror. For women, home may be the most insecure place within their lives, a place where they are most at risk of being subject to physical, sexual and psychological violence (Maynard and Hanmer 1987). In contrast, men are mostly victims of violence in public spaces (Maynard and Hanmer 1987). The gendered nature of domestic violence, intersecting with the gendered nature of household spaces, provides a challenge to normative understandings of a private/public divide. Accounts from scholars and others focusing on domestic violence have revealed the widespread nature[1] of domestic violence and have transformed an up-until-then private matter into a public social problem demanding public intervention.

Later accounts from black feminists (Richie 2000) as well as classical studies of social control (Donzelot 1997) demonstrated that the homes of poor and disadvantaged groups have always been the site of public intervention/intrusion, where poor/black domesticity was problematized/criminalized as a space of social risk in terms of future delinquency. These studies deconstructed the idea of home as a private secure space to a site of ongoing state intervention and intersecting power relations.

Departing from this deconstruction or denaturalization of home as a secure private sphere, in this chapter I draw on my own sociological research into institutional responses to domestic violence in Switzerland. I will reflect on my own ethnographic experiences of accompanying a police emergency unit intervening in such cases. The emotions and affects evoked by such events can bring into focus a specific process of home (un)making, in which I was caught, and which presented a challenge to me as an ethnographer and an analyst. My ethnography revealed the deeply contested nature of domestic space, and the lived tensions which exist between characterizations of home as an unalienated/ alienated space. Attending to these tensions in my fieldwork meant resisting and deconstructing a romanticized vision of ethnographic immersion that limits the space for pain, conflict and feelings of unease as modes of knowledge production. In this chapter I explore the possibility of an intimate ethnography of violence. I suggest that emotional commitments in ethnography are not only matters to attend to reflexively but also resources which open up the field as a space of encounter between affects (Mazzocchetti and Piccoli 2016).

Accompanying the police: Ethical considerations

Accounts of violence in intimate spheres cannot be separated from forces of structural violence including those related to the state or to poverty (Hearn 2012). As part of my broader research project, which focused broadly on how various institutional actors intervened in, and provided support to, cases of domestic violence, I set out to conduct an ethnography of police interventions. Remaining aware of the police's role as a major force of control and discipline, this fieldwork required careful ethical consideration around which I was willing to be implicated or involved in, as an ethnographer. When considering these dilemmas in my research design, I believed that cases of police domestic violence constituted a special case, where police intervened at the request of the victim – or at least in her benefit, in cases when they are alerted by a third party.

Domestic violence can be considered as a process of home-unmaking whose harm can be minimized by the police intervention, that may, in contrast, be considered as an attempt of home-remaking. Such interventions offer the possibility to bring peace – at least temporarily – in the middle of a violent crisis. Critiques of racial profiling and the criminalization of racialized and marginalized groups and spaces relate differently, and less directly, to domestic violence interventions, which are not initiated by police officers' identification of cases or suspects. As police intervene at the request of those involved or implicated, these interventions are different from the stop-and-search practices which, for example, are a primary focus for critiques of racial profiling.

These considerations around the central objectives of domestic violence interventions, and the focus on supporting victims, were crucial in my choice to conduct ethnography on police interventions, but also in my processes of ethical decision-making throughout my fieldwork.

In terms of obtaining consent, ethical issues can emerge out of the tension between transparency – the necessity to disclose the research and its objectives – and any 'instrumental' relations between the researcher and participants, motivated by the necessity of collecting and producing useful data (Pollner and Emerson 2001). Scholars have highlighted the ethical issues not only around conducting ethnography covertly but also around the cultural ideals, demands and ethical limitations emerging from an often-impossible ideal of 'full disclosure' or transparency (Lofland 2009). It has been shown that obtaining consent can sometimes be linked to coercion, and so every decision should be evaluated in light of its outcome for participants and for the research. Consequently, the need for social researchers to prioritize the avoidance of harm has been emphasized, as a frame for evaluating questions of transparency (Iphofen 2009).

In the case of my research within the police corps, as a 'formal organization', further ethical considerations emerged around the formal requirement to adhere to police security regulations. These security issues related to emergency interventions, and included the mandatory wearing of bullet-proof jackets by interns and observers and the need to obey the instructions of the chief of the patrol. These were conditions that I had to accept to be able to conduct in situ observations of these interventions. The legal obligations of police officers to protect any 'civil element' within their company made it impossible for me not to don the blue intern bullet-proof jacket. The acceptance of police regulations also entailed not speaking freely with the subjects of domestic abuse cases.

For my study, following the model proposed by Iphofen (2011), I prepared a checklist detailing the pros and cons of not disclosing my identity to the subjects of domestic violence cases in police interventions. The outcome of this process of ethical decision-making was two pros and six cons for disclosing my role. While according to many norms of research ethics full disclosure and establishing oral or written consent are ethically preferable, the assessment of my checklist showed that not introducing myself and my research to victims and perpetrators to seek consent during emergency police interventions presented less risk of harm than the opposite.

First, there was a risk that my presence as a researcher could generate uneasiness that could impact on the statements given by victims and perpetrators. This was an unacceptable risk considering the seriousness of the situations and the possibility that future cases could be harmed as a result. A second consideration was my intention to cause minimum disruption to the work of the police officers, so that they could follow their security protocol. The third concern, related to the fact that even *if* I could have introduced myself and requested the consent of the protagonists, I could not have been sure whether their consent was given freely. As I was accompanying the police officers, they could have felt compelled to accept my presence and may not have dared to resist the will of the police officers whom I accompanied. After all, police officers must have already agreed to my presence as they had brought me with them. Fourth, as I abided by the first two principles of anonymity and confidentiality, whereby real names and addresses were never disclosed, the risk of future identification and potential harm was negligible. Fifth, the focus of my research was on how police officers conducted their interventions and asked their questions. Consequently, other protagonists, including domestic violence victims themselves, were secondary sources of information for my research. I did not concentrate on the identifying details of the incidents or on personal information and backgrounds of the people involved. Sixth, there was no other way of obtaining these kinds of data using other sources of information. For instance, conducting interviews with police officers would have provided access to their discourses on their practices but not on what actually happened during the interventions. The report on an intervention comprised a one-page document that was succinctly presented but only focused on the final procedure that the police officers had decided to apply during that intervention, omitting the entire process of decision-making that was entailed. Thus, the process, which was of primary interest, could not be studied using other methods and without being physically present.

Taking account of the theoretical and ethical debates around conducting ethnography covertly, I followed the principle of minimizing harm, and opted not to systematically present myself as a researcher to the people in whose homes we intervened, with the police corps. The most important factor in this decision was my intimate conviction that accompanying a police emergency unit which intervened at the demand of victims of domestic violence, or to their benefit, and which aimed to stop an ongoing violent scene, was an acceptable goal. This was a goal I could accept to be part of even covertly, without having the time to introduce my work and ask permission, even if their intervention meant intruding on people's intimate sphere of home in which I was not personally invited.[2]

In the following section, I will narrate a police intervention during which I did not have the opportunity to introduce my work and ask for consent from those whose home I entered. An intervention during which I experienced a specific process of home-unmaking, in which I played, even if passively and unwillingly, a part. This intervention was a critical moment of fieldwork when 'those personal and emotional experiences … significantly affect the researcher's understanding of the setting in general or of critical activities within it' (Emerson 1981: 370). Critically, it was a moment where my own emotional experience attuned me to the lived realities that emerge at the intersection between intimate and state-structural violence. Emotions enable a different sort of knowledge around how 'violence occurs within violences' (Hearn 2012: 157) and how intimate violence unfolds in relation with broader structural social relations. This emotional attunement was not possible without sharing and seeing what constituted the most intolerable violence in the eyes of a woman who had experienced domestic violence and who had asked the police to intervene to help her about it.

An account of the encounter

It was a mild evening in May 2016, and I had already been carrying out fieldwork with the police emergency squad in a French-speaking city in Switzerland for one month. I was spending the evening and night in the front office of the police station, chatting with the commander, when I heard on the radio that a teenage girl had called the police to inform them that her parents were having a fight. The chief of the section assumed that this case was domestic violence and knowing my specific research suggested that I accompany the patrol in the intervention. He told me, 'You may go now, but they will be on their way in less than fifteen seconds.' 'OK, thanks', I responded. I grabbed the intern flak jacket from the corner of the room and ran to the parking lot.

It was precisely 9:10 p.m. when the patrol came to the parking lot to fetch me. I got in the car quickly behind a young police officer, the driver. A more experienced officer who was in charge of the patrol sat on his right side. As I was thinking to myself 'imagine if someone got killed because I delayed them', the officer driving announced, 'we will go into emergency mode' and asked me to let them know as soon as I had fastened my seatbelt so that 'we hit the gas' he said. Before having fastened my seatbelt, I told them I was ready, not wanting to cause any additional delay for an emergency intervention. At the chief's prompt, the driver pressed down hard on the gas pedal and sped across the city. Meanwhile, I struggled to stay in place, holding tightly to the handle above my head.

The chief of the patrol told us the case concerned a Cameroonian family. He had received information from headquarters that police had once intervened at that address in 2015 for another domestic violence incident, where the victim had been punched in the face. He asked me if I had already participated in domestic violence interventions and I responded affirmatively. He then observed, 'So you know that we need to first secure the place before and then you can enter. Because interventions at the people's home are dangerous for us, in their apartment, an environment they know well but not us.' He told me of an intervention back in 2005 which ended in a police officer shooting a man in his home, because he attacked him with a knife, which he had hid before the police arrived.

When we arrived at the location, a large building containing several apartments per floor in a working-class neighbourhood, we struggled to enter. No one answered the police officer's ringing. Finally, we saw a neighbour in one of the balconies and the officers asked her to open the entrance door for us. While waiting nervously the chief of the patrol turned and told us, 'I hope he is not smashing her up!' Finally, the door opened, we found the mailbox and the floor number of the apartment we wanted. Once in front of the door, the younger police officer knocked hard on the door announcing the presence of the police. The door opened and a young teenage girl appeared at the door, guiding one of the police officers to her mother who was waiting in a bedroom. I followed. It was a children's bedroom with two bunk beds in one corner. The beds were dishevelled and there were a considerable number of clothes resting on the lower bunk and scattered over a little dressing table on the other corner. A woman in her late forties was standing in the middle of it with an expressionless face. She nevertheless looked exhausted. The police officer went to her; I said hello and stepped aside to let him face the woman. I stayed in the bedroom with the young police officer, the woman and her daughter, while the chief of the patrol went to the living room where the husband was waiting.

The police officer asked the woman, 'I need to know what happened.' 'I am tired', she answered and explained briefly that she had slapped her husband and pushed him when he had punched her repeatedly in the face. She said she had two loose teeth and there was blood in her mouth. She then had asked her children to call the police. Meanwhile, her daughter was standing behind her; she was now seated on the chair in front of a dressing table. She was trying to comfort her mother by caressing her hair when she suddenly let out a gasp,

'Oh', as several of her mother's narrow braids remained in her hand. She joined in her mother's explanation and added that the father had dragged her mother by her hair on the floor. The woman explained that her children were holding her while her husband was trying to drag her by her hair and that was how several braids were torn from her scalp. 'Did he beat the children?', the police officer enquired. 'No', the woman answered. The police officer turned to the girl and asked, 'You confirm?', 'Yes', she said.

We learned further that the violent scene had started with a quarrel over a phone call between the husband and his lover back in Cameroon, when he had mentioned the wife's name. The woman went to ask why her name was being mentioned in that conversation. The man finished his call and began to quarrel with his wife, before leaving. Shortly, however, he returned even angrier and announced that he did not want to stay in the home with them anymore, then started to beat her.

The police officer decided that this was indeed a case of domestic violence and that he needed to take statements right there in the apartment. He told his colleague to take the woman's statement and asked the woman if he could send the children to the playground outside the building so that they would not witness the intervention. She accepted and the officer called all the children and told them to go and play in the yard and come back in half an hour. The couple had three teenage daughters and one son who were in the apartment with us but waiting in another bedroom. I remember thinking to myself while taking notes, 'why only half an hour? That will never be enough!' Waiting for the police officer to return I watched the woman who despite her exhaustion kept her composure and remained emotionless, as if she was accustomed to going through police interventions. I was feeling out of place, desperate and useless. I suggested to the woman who was standing again to sit down and relax and asked her if she needed water. I wrote in my notes how terrible it felt that it was all I could do to help.

The young police officer came back with a whole bunch of forms, while chewing gum and trying to organize his papers. He did not seem to find what he wanted. He asked her, 'Are you afraid?'

- Yes, for my children.
- Do you want to press charges?
- Yes, I am tired. I do not want to see him anymore.
- Is it frequent?
- Every day! And he does not pay the rent nor the bills.

The chief of the patrol came in and asked his colleague to take pictures of the woman's mouth and the right side of her scalp where her hair was torn out. The woman explained that her husband wanted her to accept his lovers, whom he frequently visited in Cameroon. After a few moments of searching among his forms, the police officer chewing gum announced to my shock that he would also register the woman as a suspect because she had admitted to slapping her husband. But the woman remained calm while the police officer was rummaging through his forms. He asked:

- Do you work?
- No, I am a housewife.
- Do you have any other income?
- No.
- Do you have any debt?
- No.

The police officers clarified that 'these questions are because you are also held to be a suspect' and handed her a form to sign. The woman complained faintly saying she was angry with her husband and only slapped him once, that it was the first time, but then remarked, 'I know the procedure' and signed the documents resignedly. I remember taking notes of their conversation but writing in parenthesis about my frustration over the fact that they considered her a suspect, wondering what it meant. Did it mean that they were expecting her to receive the blows passively without reacting, and that if she behaved otherwise, she would be treated the same as the perpetrator and have her case registered under that category in the police database? The police officer handed over another form to sign for a centre who would help people who used violent behaviour. He repeated his question again about the woman's profession and how much money she earned and announced to her that she could have an attorney, but the case would be sent to the prosecutor for later decision.

After asking for information on the history of the couple, we learned that they were together for fifteen years but got married recently, within the last three years. The woman said the first five years went well but since 2011 things had changed,

- What changed?
- Always the same problem, his lovers. We got separated in 2011.
- Divorced or only separated?
- No, only separated, then he promised that he would change.

In 2011 she had pressed charges against him for domestic violence, but ultimately withdrew them, declaring in court that she would stay with him because he was her children's father. The police officer then asked about what the children had told him, that there had been three prior episodes of physical violence, and the woman admitted that she had not informed the police in the two previous cases.

After a few moments, the older police officer returned from the living room and asked the woman to pack a bag for the husband because, in following the law, they would expel him from the domicile for fourteen days. And as he was drunk, it would be easier if she prepared his luggage with what he would need for two weeks. 'It is for your sake, so that he will leave as soon as possible, we have time otherwise.'

It was at precisely this moment that the children came back, arriving as I had feared for the worst part of the intervention. The man started to shout from the living room, angry that the police wanted to expel him from his home: 'You are at *my* home, this is *my* home, I pay its rent and you raise your voice to me here?' We saw him enter the corridor which was visible from the bedroom we were in. He started to open the cupboards of a small storage space at the end of the corridor, throwing things on the floor. He shouted that if he had to leave, this would be for ever, that he would not come back again, and he would take all of his possessions with him. At his reaction, police officers came back to the woman asking her to prepare the luggage quickly, so that they could take him out sooner. But they did not send him out while waiting for her to pack and he continued to shout and throw out clothes and other stuff on the floor. The children were gawking, and some went back to the other bedroom in front of the one we were in. The police officers went to the man in the storage space. The woman and I did not see them, only hear them threatening him, 'Do you want to end up in the police headquarters or what?' but he continued to shout. The police officers reminded him that it was the law and he did not have the right to come back for fourteen days. He replied, 'I won't come back at all!' Then we heard some noises, something like a fight between the police officers and the man. They finally asked him to turn his back so that they could put handcuffs on him, because he was not cooperating. At the sight of this the woman's composure finally broke. Tears began to run down her cheeks, letting her expressionless and resigned mask fall and she turned to the police officers and asked brokenly, 'Where are my children?' I was in the corner watching and filling my field notebook, trying to suppress my own anguish and guilt when I heard her. I looked at her, I saw her crying and so did I. But everyone was too busy to notice us.

The police officer answered the woman's question from the corridor saying the children were in the other room. She started to prepare a sack of clothes, while the police officers were telling her to call back on the emergency number should there be any problem. They informed her that they will keep the husband at the police station for the night, because he was not respectful and cooperative. But they insisted that they were not the judge, and the rest would be decided by the prosecutor later.

Feeling the woman's deep concern for her children, I left the room and went to the other room where the children were waiting, to try to reassure them. I explained that to calm the situation down, the police officers judged it was better for their father to leave for the night. Then, I came back to say goodbye to the woman, 'Take care of yourself', I told her. We said goodbye and left her apartment at 10:45 p.m. Not far from the apartment, in the car, we received a call from the woman, asking for the police to return the residency permits that they had mistakenly taken with them. They promised that they would bring them back later. And we drove back through the city towards the police station.

Domestic violence interventions often start with the intrusion into people's homes in the middle of a crisis, in an emergency situation, which leaves people's lives and homes open to scrutiny, without granting the time to manage how things are presented. I had persuaded myself that the police interventions, even in those circumstances, was an attempt at a home (re)making, bringing peace and calm to people who asked for their intervention.

The experience of this incident, however, reminded me powerfully how much ethnographic fieldwork itself is a politico-relational space traversed by visible and invisible power relations. Home reflects broader socio-structural relations in – it is traversed by relations that precede the home, and which are transformed and reproduced both within and beyond the home. Although I was aware of literature which revealed the domestic spheres of racialized families as sites of state control (Richie 2000), this experience brought my ethnographic attention beyond those forms of violence which were perceptible and visible at first sight, to other forms of violence more imperceptible and insidious. This experience revealed how emotion could be a way of seeing, when feeling in a real-life situation can bring deeper understandings, of the lived experiences of violence, beyond what can be easily captured on the page, in the research accounts of others. The different forms of violence I witnessed made me think about my own role and part in the infliction of additional forms of violence on this woman and my ethical commitment in considering, analyzing and reporting it.

Hearing the victim also named as a suspect served as a sort of symbolic violence, destabilizing my hopeful and supportive image of police interventions. Then there was the mortifying ritual of a police intervention asking her over and over about her professional and financial situation, forcing her to repeat several times that she had no income, that she had no job. There was also the behaviour of the young police officer, chewing gum and rummaging carelessly through his forms and repeating the same questions without really listening carefully to her to avoid making her repeat her uneasy answers. Then the way statement-taking of the husband was handled, and the decision to announce his expulsion before first taking him out of the house to avoid surprises. And finally, there was the way the officers let the situation get out of hand, to the point where they were forced to handcuff him and drag him out, before the eyes of his children, after miscalculating the time needed for the intervention. This scene finally broke the numb resignation and composure of the woman, who, worried about her children and seeing her husband handcuffed and dragged out, burst into tears.

If the ethnographic experience is to enable us to understand everyday life, then attending to the emotional currents of particular situations inevitably forms a part of this. Such attention can result in a sensitive ethnography (Laplantine 2015) when the ethnographer lives and feels in her body and mind what the interlocutors go through. This experience can shed light on 'the very construction of what counts as violence' (Hearn 2012: 163) and who defines it. In my case it provoked irreversible changes of perception and positioning leading to new understandings of violence as a continuum. To clarify this, it is helpful to review four viewpoints within the encounter about what constitutes violence, for different actors in different ways.

As a researcher on domestic violence, I was there to look at a concrete case of a specific type of violence – domestic violence inflicted by a man on his wife, within the intimate spheres of the couple's life, and of the home. For the police officers, domestic violence was instead a category of public action, framed by law, and governed by conventions they needed to follow, forms to fill out, questions to ask and people to hear, arrest or leave alone. Home was an insecure, dangerous place for police intervention, where the familiarity of home to residents presented a strategic threat, which was met with an attentive and controlling presence, and a willingness to use force. For the perpetrator violence came from being expelled from his own home, while for the woman who had asked the help of police, it was ultimately the act of her children's witnessing their father being dragged out in handcuffs – a second symbolic act of violence in the wake of domestic violence – that broke her self-control and resignation.

In addition, she faced symbolic degradation in being registered as a suspect of violence, because she had pushed and slapped her husband who had beaten her, and in being repeatedly and dismissively questioned about her livelihood.

How could this confrontation with the various forms of violence inherent in a real-life police domestic violence intervention be explored? This was a multilevel violent experience that I shared with this woman and her family. The strong emotions I felt being there, but also when later transcribing my notes, and even when coming back to my notes months later, were bodily and emotional experiences revealing the embodied experience underlying what one reads about the interrelation between intimate partner violence and broader structural violences within which it takes place. Questioning myself when I was there, about where I was, what I was doing and what I was part of, recalibrated my understanding of which violence mattered and to whom. This encounter demanded that attention be paid to unspoken violences that were not at first sight visible, that were silenced or absent if one focused only on a physical act of domestic violence. Attentiveness to these emotions helped to decipher the woman's concerns from her reactions, and helped to analytically frame police domestic violence interventions as also possible practices of home-unmaking (and not only home-*re*making). As Hearn writes, there is a need for 'a change of perspective from seeing violence as always "caused" by something else, to one in which the practice of violence is itself a form of social inequality, an unequal and unequalizing social structural division and relation *of its own*. Violence is a social distribution of *who does what to whom*' (2012: 164; emphasis in original), within which a wide range of actors – including those who seek to intervene, support or indeed, observe – are inevitably implicated.

Conclusion

Ethnographers' emotions are often considered as biases to be expunged through reflexive writing, or as irrelevant sensationalizing (or miserabilism), and not recognized as an integral part of the investigation. But silencing or ignoring them does not make them disappear. So, without embracing sensationalism there is interest in the consideration of the ways in which emotions might attune ethnographers to lived realities. As Mazzocchetti and Piccoli (2016) observe, being blind and deaf to one's own emotion, the researcher can sometimes become blind and deaf to her interlocutors too. If the emotions can reveal what words and institutional frameworks silence, it is not only helpful but the responsibility of an ethnographer towards her interlocutors, to take seriously what they experience. All the more so in my work, where I intrude into my interlocutors' homes, accompanying police officers – embodying powerful forms of social control – even if with the intent of helping the victim and arresting a perpetrator. Emotions are born from confrontations with fear, injustice, vulnerability and helplessness, shame and distress, all of which shape lived forms of inequality and ought to inform the gaze of researchers. Emotional attunement to the experiences of those excluded reveals not only new dimensions of power but also how power flows through and animates particular bodies, making the ethical dilemmas which surround research a distinctly embodied matter that resists being neatly resolved in advance of the encounter, no matter how carefully one plans or prepares.

Foregrounding emotions does not mean reducing ethnographic methodology to matters of emotional empathy. Rather taking emotions seriously opens up a range of potentialities in both scholarly understanding and the forging of ethical commitments. Emotional encounters are not only methodological tools but also data themselves. Following Mazzocchetti and Piccoli (2016), I have attempted to interrogate the potentialities and the ethical challenges around including one's own emotions within ethnographic data, without falling into the trap of pure subjectivism. I attempted to show how the researcher can experience her own emotions and lived situations around her in a given ethnographic encounter, when the encounters involve situations of suffering, trauma or violence which affect subjects profoundly. Such emotional attunement expands understanding beyond the silences of everyday life and of power, allowing for a critical interrogation of powerful emotional affects. One can then get closer to things impossible to say when the researcher and the interlocutors are taken in the same lived moment, through a common experience and when 'being with' transforms to 'feeling with' (2016: 2).

Notes

1   Based on a 2013 analysis of data over 80 countries, the World Health Organization concluded that worldwide, 1 in 3 of women who have been in a relationship have experienced physical and/or sexual violence by their intimate partner (www.who. int/news-room/fact-sheets/detail/violence-against-women).

2   At the time of my fieldwork in Switzerland, the Federal Act on Research involving
    Human Beings required the ethical assessment of research projects by cantonal
    ethical committees mainly in the case of biomedical research (Perrin et al. 2018).
    Following this requirement, my project was evaluated by the General Prosecutor of
    the Swiss canton under study as well as my supervisor at the University of Neuchâtel.
    During these negotiations, confidentiality and anonymity were guaranteed and were
    respected in my data management as well as in my final account of the research.
    These negotiations led to a differentiated strategy of obtaining consent. On the one
    hand explicit consent was sought from all those professionals involved in domestic
    violence interventions or support, who were the primary subject of my research.
    On the other hand, when dealing with those who interacted with these services and
    interventions, whether as beneficiaries or otherwise, I followed a principle of seeking
    consent whenever I could be confident this would not lead to a harmful situation.
    In practice, this meant I obtained consent in some police domestic violence
    interventions but not all.

5

Digging holes, posting signs, loading guns: Constructing home near the Grand Canyon

Susannah Crockford

A census-designated place

Going up to the land meant a two-hour drive first up narrow winding switchbacks and through the city of Flagstaff and then a long lonely route on a single-lane highway through ponderosa pine forest, watching warily for elk and deer, especially around sunset. The ponderosas thinned travelling north, replaced with pinyons and cedar dotted among bare scrub and yellowing brush. The turnoff was an unmarked dirt track, after which there were several turns on other dirt tracks that gave a dizzying sense of turning around on oneself in a circle even though that was not the case. At first going out there, I would often drive past the turning into Rand's acre and reach the end of the dirt track and have to turn around. There was nothing visible from the track that indicated where his land was. Looking carefully revealed a little wooden sign with the number of the lot and the name of the street written on it in black marker and a bamboo cane marking the corner post of the acre, a little flag, and a sign saying 'beware of the dog'. Rand had brought the sign up from his old house in Tucson. He said he was home once he put that sign up.

Rand had to make his own signs because most of the street names were not marked by the municipal authority in the area, Coconino County. A few of the main routes, such as the track that connected to the highway, had a green sign with white writing on a tall pole, designating that the county deemed it significant enough of a road to officially mark. The other tracks had names labelled on county maps, Google maps, and US Geological Survey data but on the ground there was no way to tell one path of rutted red dirt from the next. When Rand first came to live on his acre, he posted signs to show that he was there and he was occupying the land. The sign at the front of the acre with the name of the street and the number of the lot, taken from the county map; the sign declaring the warning about the dog; and a number of small yellow signs put up on trees, downed logs or small metal poles that said 'posted' and 'no trespassing'. These signs are required under Arizona law to mark private property that has no other ostensible indications of habitation such as structures or fencing; entering an area so marked without the owner's consent is therefore trespassing, a criminal offence. For Rand, the sign about the dog added extra potency; he had three large black dogs and he always put that same sign up wherever he lived. It was a connection to his past, to the relations he considered most important (those with his dogs), as well as a practical tool for claiming occupancy of the land and warning potential trespassers. For him, that sign made his empty wooded acre on which he had pitched his tent, home.

Rand's first step in creating a home on ostensibly empty land was symbolic, much as flags laid claim to the land under the Doctrine of Discovery[1] when European occupation began in the fifteenth and sixteenth centuries. Laws further signified which land belonged to whom. Rand's legal claim to the land was materialized through his ownership deed. In a society founded on the expropriation of land as private property for a specific cultural group, the piece of paper that symbolizes the ownership of the land was the first step towards making a home. This reminds us of the fact that there is no such thing as empty land. American land had been taken by force from its previous occupants – the indigenous peoples of the continent – and parceled out for the use of white homesteaders for several hundred years, a move legitimized through the legal system put in place by the colonial state. Rand's attempt to transform a piece of land with no prior structures or connection to amenities (beyond a dirt road) into his home was situated at a confluence of these physical, legal, historical and social processes.

The differentiation of inside from outside was vital to the creation of privacy and to evoking a sense of ontological security, both of which form core components of American cultural definitions of home (Easthope 2004: 134). Ontological security is a sense of being safe in one's abode. This feeling of safety is inescapably subjective. A home that may feel safe to one occupant may feel threatening and constricting to another. Indeed, this became the situation on Rand's land; his ontological security came at the expense of my own. My presence as an ethnographer and as the only woman complicated the process of home-making, opening up some possibilities and closing off others for all those, including myself, who dwelt on Rand's land. I was in Valle from September 2013 to April 2014, from May to September 2015, and from July 2016 to January 2017, as part of my ethnographic fieldwork on spirituality in Northern Arizona. That I was the only woman regularly living on the land brought in a web of gender relations that had implications for both how home was made and how my fieldwork proceeded.

The land (as Rand and his friends called it) was in a 'census-designated place' called Valle. The only infrastructure in Valle was at the intersection of two highways that led on to the Grand Canyon National Park, the entrance of which was about thirty miles to the north. At the intersection there was a petrol station, a motel, a Flintstones-themed campground, a rock shop, a small private airport with adjacent air museum, a hardware store and a storage unit yard. The local economy was focused on servicing visitors to the Grand Canyon National Park, and many residents of Valle worked either in the park or in the businesses clustered around the intersection. The population as of the 2010 US Census was 832.

The plateau to the south of the Canyon itself was rocky, with clay dirt, a short growing season of only three months and inhospitable weather conditions: baking hot in the summer, blankets of snow in the winter and winds that could reach up to 75 mph. It was easy to miss the occupation of the land leading up to the Canyon from the highway; it seemed as if there were only services put there for the convenience of tourists. Those that did live there were at risk from varying levels of precarity: lack of connection to infrastructure such as electricity, gas, trash collection, water; physical isolation, being at least forty miles from the nearest urban centre; economic marginalization as many of the residents were on lower incomes[2]; many of the buildings were not built to municipal codes, and were therefore not insurable, in a place with significant risk from forest fires as well as structural fires. Valle was, to those who did not live there, a weird place. A police officer from the County Sheriff's department told me that the majority of calls the department received from Valle were for domestic violence and UFO sightings.

Yet this weird, marginal place offered a way of living preferentially counterposed to mainstream on-grid society. The people I knew in Valle, by and large, wanted to be out of the way, beyond the view of the state, outside of the busyness of urban environments. There were two main cultural frames referred to by my interlocutors in Valle to explain this preference. The first was survivalism: a millenarian practice aimed at provisioning all of the material needs of life for oneself without reliance on wider social structures, particularly the federal government. The second was frontierism: a romanticized view of the history of homesteading and pioneers in the western US, who were idealized as living in self-sufficient independence from the state, identified primarily as the federal government. Rand's occupancy was part of this history, and he invoked this history in his espousal of survivalism and frontierism as justifications for living there. At various times, Rand called his settlement a homestead, a commune and a fort. It was a place he built himself with his friends that provided both shelter and safety. It was his home.

Building a home

The acre of land that Rand called home was legally purchased through a rent-to-own agreement. When he first received the paperwork, Rand proudly showed me the deed with his name on it. This piece of paper meant that he was a landowner. Previously he had always rented apartments, something he found hard to maintain financially and thus never felt secure doing. The agreement he made required no credit check and had monthly payments he could afford, even if the result was paying over six times what the land was actually worth. Rent-to-own was an industry that catered to the poor; its strictures were one mechanism through which the poor paid more for less, contributing to socioeconomic inequality. Rand was just happy he owned something; the status of being a landowner was more important to him than the particularities of the contract.

When I first met Rand he was spinning fire. Fire spinning was a spiritual practice in Sedona that I was participating in as part of my research into new age spirituality (Crockford 2017: 135–67). This circus art, popular at Day of the Dead festivities in Arizona, came to signify much of Rand's character to me: impressive and aggressive, but unpredictable and mutable. Imperiously tall and broad shouldered with wild long blond hair, there was something about him that seemed to not quite belong where the other humans lived. He seemed to belong more in the forest, accompanied as ever by his three large black dogs. The next time I met him he was camping in the Coconino National Forest, living between homes and between jobs. When he was able to put down his $200 deposit on the land, he simply packed up his things and moved them to his land, pitching his tent there instead.

The tent was hard to keep clean; when he opened the door the mud came in from the ground outside. Each day he would sweep it out several times. Rats got into his food supplies, which he kept in a backpack. He found an outsized metal cage and placed it there for his dogs so they would not run off when he was not there. After he found his things disturbed by an intruder one day, he moved his sleeping tent inside the dog cage for security, locking it with a padlock. He dug a pit for an open fire, which oriented the camp as it grew. The tent and the cage created initial boundaries, albeit highly porous, between the inside and the outside. The fire pit centred the land and the signpost at the roadside demarcated the front. In the absence of any other markers differentiating Rand's acre of land from its neighbouring plots, these features provided orientation as well as inside/ outside boundaries – the basic requirements for a 'minimum home' (Douglas 1991: 290).

Rand's house, which began as simply a tent, and the other structures – RVs, trailers, cabins, vehicles, tents, teepees, in one case a series of converted grain silos – that people lived in around him, did not fit the normative American image of what a house should look like. Yet it was not only the single-family house that typified the ideal American home; it was also ownership, rather than renting, of accommodation. For Rand, even though the structure was rudimentary, he had a piece of land that was his to develop as he saw fit. That one fact made it preferable to the apartments he had rented previously, even though those apartments did not suffer from the same problems of dirt, rats and lack of amenities.

To resolve the problems of the tent, Rand bought a dilapidated thirty-two-foot trailer from a neighbour for $300, and put his tent inside it. However, the trailer turned out to be infested with mice and rotted wood. Rand spent weeks trying to refurbish it, before giving up as the winter approached and the risk of freezing at night when it snowed became possible. Instead he purchased a barn of Mennonite construction, also on rent-to-own, and refitted it with insulation, a wood stove, carpet and drywall to make a basic cabin. Once there was more than just a tent on the land, Rand's friends started to move in with him. His best friend, Matias, was the first to arrive, sleeping in his car at first, and later moving into the trailer. Matias was slightly taller, darker and thinner than Rand, and there was always a noticeable pecking order between the two. Rand liked to be in charge and would overtly and subtly put Matias in a subordinate place. Often this would create conflict but Matias's gentler nature was such that he generally accepted it. Indeed, once he told me that he liked being 'number two' because that was less pressure. Together they built most of the edifices on the land. Putting up structures, signs and fences were gradual processes of creating physical barriers against the elements, demarcating the inside space from the outside, and creating privacy. This demarcation of private spaces further contributed to the sense of social hierarchy, which also had significant gendered aspects.

The American cultural norms that connected women with domestic tasks and men with manual labour inflected the activities we took responsibility for on the land. Construction work, vehicle maintenance, fetching water for the tank, installation and maintenance of solar panels for electricity and a wood stove for heat and gardens for food were Rand and Matias's responsibility. Once I lived on the land full-time, my tasks became washing up, washing the clothes and tidying up. Living off-grid meant no conveniences like running hot water, central heating or air-conditioning, electricity wired in to structures available via a switch, a washing machine for clothes or roadside rubbish collection. Everything required more human labour and that labour emerged along gendered lines, following familiar patterns.

For washing dishes, the sink from the trailer was set up outside on workbench legs, using cold water poured from a three-gallon jug, which then drained directly onto the ground. I was the only one who washed up; the others simply left the dirty dishes to pile up if I was not there. Trash was a constant challenge, blown in by the wind or dropped carelessly by the inhabitants. I was the only one who took the time to pick it up. Washing clothes was done at a laundromat in Williams or Flagstaff, a procedure that took all day and required a hundred-plus mile round trip, or in a hand-cranked washing machine. This was also my responsibility; it was tough physically and also took a long time. A neighbour came round and saw me turning the handle as the green plastic tub sat on the back of a truck and said I looked like a 'squaw', an ethnic and sexual slur for a Native American woman. I did not wash up, wash clothes by hand or pick up trash because I particularly wanted to, nor because I was somehow better at it or more suited to it physically. I did it because the men did not and otherwise it did not get done. There was an unspoken assumption that as the woman, I would take care of tasks related to cleaning because it was an aspect of life that in American culture was associated strongly with both domesticity and femininity. This created an awkward emotional response for me. On the one hand, I did not mind pulling my weight around the land and I certainly was more able and experienced in washing dishes than I was in wiring solar panels or gardening. On the other, I felt like I had been manoeuvred into doing what they regarded as women's work and that I was participating in gendered forms of labour in a way that I would not have so meekly consented to back in my old life. I felt uncomfortable, but at the same time unable to express that discomfort.

Why these forms of labour were left to me was never fully articulated while I was in the field. As already hinted at, it was an unconscious assumption of Rand's that he would take care of the power, the water, the vehicles and any construction.

It was not something we discussed. I took the position of watching and assisting in Rand and Matias's construction projects and noting down the continual jockeying for status and dominance that went on between the two. My initial understanding of ethnography was that of immersion, rather than intervention, so it never occurred to me to try to build my own structures. Even giving my opinion on what structures they should build felt inappropriate because I knew that I would soon leave and I would not have to live with the result. Moreover that felt like overstepping the bounds of my role as an ethnographer, trying to change the field to suit my liking instead of observing what was there as if I was not. Instead I followed the men, assisting them with what they were doing in order to learn about them and their way of life. At the same time, Rand would ask me to do domestic tasks, such as the washing up that he did not want to do. I did them at first to provide a contribution to the group that I was seeking entry into, and then as time went on, it became an accepted part of my responsibilities. It helped assuage the anxiety I felt over wanting to offer some form of labour in exchange for being accepted into the group. It seemed that, as a woman, the primary way I could gain acceptance in this group of men was by doing what they considered women's work.

Despite continuous attempts to demarcate the inside from the outside through putting up fences, building structures, tidying up and posting signs, there remained a pervasive sense that 'outside' predominated the land. Most activity except sleeping occurred in exterior spaces, and the borders of structures were continually permeated by dirt, wind and wild animals. There were no locks that could not easily be forced and no perimeter fence to keep people and animals out. Looting was endemic in Valle; any place left abandoned or unattended would be progressively ransacked by neighbours. Rand had looted his wood stove from abandoned land nearby, as well as many other resources including tools, fencing and a generator. Rand called it 'recycling' because the materials would rot if left and he was putting them to use again.

These rudimentary boundaries meant that a sense of safety had to be augmented through the display and willingness to use weapons. Creating a home required controlling its boundary; turning the wild, unpredictable, threatening open space into domesticated, tamed, dominated space.

This was expected of all occupants, regardless of gender. When two neighbours whom Rand identified to me as 'tweakers' (a slang term for methamphetamine users) came over unexpectedly when he was not there, my suspicion was that they were there to try to steal something. When I called him to tell him what had happened, Rand asked me to carry the .22 calibre rifle openly as a warning in case they came back. I spent the remainder of the afternoon, perched in a tree, holding the rifle, pensively watching.

In other Arizonan homes I lived in prior to moving on to the land, this control of boundaries was taken for granted. Houses were built with solid walls, behind fenced-in yards, sometimes with extra security systems, and the awareness that infractions would be dealt with by the criminal justice system. However, for Rand and many of the other residents in Valle I spoke to, this meant owning and openly carrying firearms. If it was suspected that a resident did not have a gun, they would be perceived as weak and their property more susceptible to incursion. Home-making involved more than symbolic ownership of property through deeds and signs or the creation of physical structures and boundaries; it required visible human occupancy and even aggressive displays of dominance.

Making a home

Many would be daunted by an acre of open land with no water source or connection to power grids, but for Rand and Matias it offered a solution to a number of their problems. Owning property was a solution to homelessness for Rand, a state which he slipped into periodically following his first criminal conviction at the age of twenty. He received a sentence of three years' probation for this conviction. One of the requirements of his probation was to live within a specific municipal jurisdiction where he was unable to find accommodation because the money he earned as a restaurant cook went almost entirely to paying off the fines and fees associated with his probation. One of the consequences of his conviction, which lasted after his probation finished, was that he was placed on a publicly available registry and required to provide his address to the local police. If he was homeless, he had to provide the location where he was sleeping and update the police every week. If he did not follow these requirements, he could be sent back to jail.

Building a home off-grid also reflected his childhood home, which was off-grid, in the forest and in a state of structural incompletion. He recounted vivid stories of being sent out as a young child to fix the generator by his mother otherwise the family would be without power, and of having to jump up the stairs to get to his bedroom because there was a large hole at the top that was left unrepaired. His parents divorced when he was a toddler. From an early age, he and his younger brother were required by their mother to take on tasks, such as fixing generators and building fires, that were understood as masculine in rural Arizona. The other side of this was that tasks taken as feminine, such as washing the dishes, were often neglected, since his mother worked three jobs (as a teacher, a bartender, and a waitress) to support the family. Instead, she taught them to hide the piles of dirty dishes in the oven if guests came over. It is this gender dynamic that Rand reproduced on the land, seeing in me a more reliable version of his mother.

Rand called his land in Valle his 'sanctuary'; it was a place where he and his dogs could always go back to and be safe. When he spoke of the relief this brought him, he evoked a sense of home as a refuge or haven. This sense of home rests on a distinction between the public and the private, as well as the inside and the outside. For Rand, it also rested on a sense of privacy from the state and legitimacy of dwelling. A tent on public land placed him under more state surveillance and risk of incarceration than a tent on a piece of land he owned. Ownership of property allowed Rand to exclude some of the extensive state surveillance under which he was placed. He was able to achieve the 'minimalist definition' of home as abode, a place where one can stay (Mallett 2004: 81).

Matias did not suffer from the same extent of precarity that Rand did, so for him home-making on the land in Valle was differently inflected. Matias came from a more stable family, with more support available while growing up. In buying the land, Matias wanted a place that he owned and could build up as a self-sufficient homestead. He believed that a 'homesteading renaissance' was imminent because the poor were not allowed to thrive in America. Rand similarly believed that the state in America wanted to suppress the people, and self-sufficiency was the only route to freedom. They both evoked the cultural themes of survivalism and frontierism in their explanations for why they wanted to live in Valle. However, for Rand the land was a necessity to survive and ideology was secondary, whereas for Matias his motivation seemed to be primarily ideological. This difference undergirded the asymmetrical effort and interest evinced by Rand and Matias. Rand was far more driven in this process of home-making, by necessity, whereas Matias seemed more like he was trying out an interesting idea he had.

Despite the differences in family support, their economic positions were similar. Most of Matias's and Rand's paid employment had been in food service throughout their adult lives; neither of them had completed a college degree or formal vocational training. The land offered a promise of supporting themselves without serving food. They aimed to provision themselves from their own gardens and selling wood cut from the nearby national forest land for cash;

neither of these aims were fulfiled. The gardens did not produce enough food, and they did not sell more than one cord of wood during the time I knew them. Their productivity was hindered by their inability to agree on what to do on any given day and their habitual consumption of beer. The way they survived during the time I knew them was by working at a ski resort on the nearby San Francisco Peaks, where they worked in the café in the lodge, again, in food service. They also greatly benefited from the income that I provided once I moved to the land full time, a circumstance I return to below.

Rand and Matias were the owners of the property, but a number of their friends and relatives stayed there on an ad hoc basis. The most frequent of these was their friend Charlie, who was on probation for an array of charges involving burglary, distribution of controlled substances and firearms offences. When Matias got his RV, Rand said Charlie could stay in the back of the trailer, and Charlie was happy with that as his only other place to stay was his parents' home in Flagstaff. Charlie said he would help Rand and Matias dig lots of holes around the property. At the time many holes were needed; for the toilet, for the fence, for a pond and to expand the gardens. Charlie said he had been digging holes since he was a child. Rand said he also dug holes for fun when he was a child, when he thought he could dig through to China. Then they had had to continue digging holes for construction work, to help out family members on their properties and for community service, which both men had been required to do in the past. Charlie told me that all he was equipped to do was sell drugs and dig holes: 'That's all I learnt to do in life, and selling drugs is just digging a hole. Either way you end up in a hole.' I asked whether he meant digging holes either figuratively or literally, and he said 'yes'. I asked Charlie if he intended to get a job or just sell drugs while living in Valle, and he said he would see how things go. Charlie never maintained a long-term presence on the land, as he always had an alternative in his parents' house. He flitted between the two in order to avoid wearing out his welcome at either.

While the land lacked many comforts and conveniences, both Rand and Charlie described the conditions as 'better than jail'. Rand had been in jail a number of times over the past seven years, as had Charlie, whose longest period of incarceration was a year. Both had been detained in county jail, which they said was not as bad as the state penitentiary system, something they called 'big boy jail'. Even so, their stories of incarceration described a daily struggle involving violence with other inmates, lack of adequate food and medical treatment, and boredom. Jail was always counterpoised with home in their stories. Home was the place they called on the phone, wrote letters to and longed to return to, not the place they lived in during that time. Jail was the antithesis of home. It was juxtaposed to a '"normal" domestic house' in a similar way to how Janet Carsten described workhouses, as an 'aberration from normal life brought about by poverty and the inability to sustain oneself' (2018: 110). The land in Valle acquired its feeling of ontological security partly in contrast to jail and the experiences of physical and psychological insecurity that incarceration entailed. The land was under their control; they decided the boundaries and who could cross them. It was a minimal home, but it was significant because at least it provided ontological security. It was a place to feel safe for a small group of men who in their everyday lives, for varying reasons and to different extents, did not feel safe.

Matias had never been incarcerated and did not have the same attachment to the land as Rand. He would often stay with family elsewhere rather than stay on the land. The discomfort of sleeping in his car or in the back of the trailer never seemed worth it to him. Two years after they initially put down the deposit on the acre of land, Matias had a serious motorcycle collision that almost cost him his foot. He went to live with his father full time and he did not return to live with Rand. A similar fate befell Charlie. After crashing a pickup truck he stole while drinking heavily, he broke his pelvis and returned to live with his parents full time. He also did not return to live with Rand. Both subsequently married and made new homes with their wives, and then had children. The availability of alternative residences meant they were less invested in the land than Rand was, who had no other place to go except jail. Rand also established through manifold everyday dominance manoeuvres, both overt and subtle, that he was in charge of the land. Moreover, after their accidents, the privations of the land made living there untenable rather than simply difficult. For Charlie and Matias, the land was less of a haven than a temporary refuge, from which they both moved on.

It was also only a temporary residence for me, something that remained a continuing source of tension. My initial contact was giving Rand lifts in my car so he could get around and helping him with projects on the land, such as building gardens, during the first summer that Rand was in his tent. By the autumn, I was spending more time up there than anywhere else, and once he had the trailer, Rand suggested I move there full time to help him refurbish it. I agreed because it seemed like an interesting new field site for my research and it would be cheaper to live there than to continue renting a room in Sedona that I rarely stayed in. My initial research project focused on new age spirituality, for which the small town of Sedona was renowned. Many interlocutors in Sedona aspired to living off-grid communally as the ideal 'spiritual' form of habitation.

Living with Rand and Matias gave me the opportunity to explore what this looked like in practice. I was also intrigued by the two of them. They had both grown up in rural Arizona, and offered access to a form of life attached to that landscape that the newer transplants from the coastal metropolises that I knew in Sedona were aware of only superficially.

There was also something about living off-grid with all its related privations that seemed more like 'real fieldwork' to me, closer to the ideal of living among isolated tribes in the Trobriand Islands or the Amazon that I associated with classic anthropology. This meant leaving behind the middle-class domestic comforts of Sedona, as if an ethnographer must prove their mettle with hardship. Soon I was spending all my time on the land. Rand wanted me at the land every day especially when he went other places to work or visit, so that I could look after his dogs and there was someone there to protect it from potential intruders. His requests for me to stay there began to interfere with my ability to do fieldwork elsewhere in Valle. This was a source of frustration for me but at the same time I gradually began to feel more like it was my home. When I sat up in the tree with a rifle after the suspicious visit from the neighbours, I had the unsettling realization that I was prepared to shoot someone to keep them away from what I now called my home.

In much second-wave feminist scholarship, home was a space in which women were valued for creating and maintaining domesticity but that at the same time kept them socially isolated and economically dependent (Mallett 2004: 75). Rand rejected the idea that my research constituted real work, and felt strongly that I should stay on the land, taking responsibility for domestic work, the dogs and security. Gendered feminine labour was an important part of creating a sense of unalienated home for Rand, but he was also unable to see how this form of dwelling might not have sufficed to produce a sense of home for me.

The tension arose from the fact that unlike the second-wave feminist stereotype of the homebound housewife, I was not economically dependent on the wage Rand earned outside of the home. On the contrary the money that Rand and Matias earned from their piecemeal employment was never enough to cover the land payment, food bills and improvements to the land such as solar panels, a pickup truck and a barn. The substantial financial provision was supplied by me.[3] Douglas (1991: 295) argued that a central characteristic of home was that it was the location of planning for and provisioning of basic human needs. On a financial level, a home was not run on a market model but as a Maussian gift economy. The generalized reciprocity of home created what Douglas called the 'problem of the commons'; some provided more than they took, others took more than they provided and resources were used quicker than they were replenished. This was indeed what occurred on the land, where I found myself in a curious double bind of being responsible for both the domestic work of home-making and the economic work of money-making. It is arguable whether they would have proceeded much past a tent and a rat-infested trailer if I had not moved there. Yet for all my economic support of the land, I was the one who was left to clean, care for the animals and occupy the land (in terms of physical presence there and also as an armed defender) while the men went away into the public sphere of waged labour and social interactions.

My position as an ethnographer at home in the field was ambiguous because while my interlocutors drew me into their projects to benefit their daily needs, I drew them into my project to study them and turn the fleshy realness of their lives into the dry page-bound analysis of 'ethnography'. Immersion was my work, yet the longer I lived there the more the boundaries of work, home and life in general blurred. It became less like a field site and more like a home. This entailed a growing sense of comfort in a situation that was at the same time profoundly uncomfortable for me. It is unlikely that this immersion would have been successful if I had not accepted, at least partially, the gendered asymmetry of my relationship with Rand. He was my gatekeeper in that social context, something I was made acutely aware of when we interacted with our neighbours. After a fire in the neighbourhood for which everyone had come out to dig trenches and clear brush to stop it spreading and becoming a wildfire that endangered more homes, a small group gathered around Rand. None of the men greeted me, they said hello to Rand and he introduced the three of us and they shook hands with him and Matias. They looked straight past me, as if I were invisible. The one woman present, Bonnie, took me aside and introduced herself and asked who I was and shook my hand. She told me her name, and then followed that up with a self-description as 'Grant's woman'. Then a man wearing a cowboy hat with a pistol openly holstered on his belt, who I assumed must be Grant, whistled and cried, 'Woman! Get!' Bonnie dutifully followed him into their pickup truck without a murmur of complaint. That interaction confirmed to me what I had previously suspected: I was unable to interact with others in this place as a single woman; only with Rand there was I acceptable to others in the neighbourhood. I needed him to do my fieldwork; he needed me to help make his home.

Gaining access to a patriarchal cultural context placed me in a subordinate position, where I had less ability to decide, speak or be heard than I was used to. My presence in the field was contingent on my ability to fit in, which meant reinforcing patriarchal arrangements. Even though I wanted to complain when

I was called a squaw or I saw another woman addressed to as one might a dog, I did not. I was even praised for my silence at such junctures by Rand; he told me it made me less difficult. My complicity was not so much ethically acceptable as it was ethnographically productive. Doing my job meant not speaking out, something I commented on to my supervisor when I returned from the field who told me that it was neither possible nor wise to try to change the gendered power relations of our field sites. That was not the job of an ethnographer; doing my job meant fitting in and that meant staying in the socially acceptable spaces for women. It meant that no matter how much it felt like my home while I was there, it was never going to be my home for long.

Notes

1 The Doctrine of Discovery is the legal fiat that gave Europeans property rights over North America without the knowledge or consent of its indigenous peoples. The Doctrine is still part of international law today; see Miller 2011.
2 According to US Census data, 57.4 per cent of the population in Valle lived below the poverty level.
3 A cynical interpretation would suggest that this is the reason Rand asked me to live there with them full time.

6

Becoming a planner: Participation and anticipation in producing home

Martin Fuller

My emotional response to a scholarly confrontation is usually tempered. I am accustomed to critiques of written texts and oral presentations, but the response to my talk at a housing association meeting cut a little deeper. I was trying to gain access to a *Baugruppe* in Berlin, a community of people who are planning the construction of their future homes: an 80-unit residential and studio building in the central district of Kreuzberg. A *Baugruppe* is a group of individuals who are working together to complete a construction project, in this case a building with residential apartments, live/work units and two commercial spaces. Instead of individuals buying an apartment from a real estate agent in a newly finished building, a *Baugruppe* is formed to work together to commission architects and make decisions about their future homes together. The *Baugruppe* is a legal entity and only members can vote in the decisions. Every member of this particular group was a potential future dweller of the building they were planning. It was participatory in nature, but not every member of the *Baugruppe* was forced to participate in planning meetings, even though all had the right to attend and vote on decisions.

I was to pitch my research project at the 33rd monthly meeting of the group, with the aim of attending future monthly meetings, taking notes, arranging interviews and hanging out at various events coordinated by the group.

Standing at the front of a small room with 29 of the roughly 100 adult members of the group in attendance, I spent 5 minutes pitching the research in a way I believed least likely to generate controversy and most likely to secure access to this fieldwork.

The pitch was simple:

I am here to learn more about your ideas of home while you are planning this building and to watch as the different apartments you will occupy transform from the constructed object of a house into your 'homes', places you feel attached to, identify with, sculpt into meaningful spaces. I'd like to speak with you before you move in and follow up with conversations as you move in and a year later, after the building is inhabited. Of course no one is obligated to speak to me, but if you have time and interest, I'd be happy to meet up for perhaps an hour to have a conversation.

After fielding some easy questions by people seated in front of me, Herr Belking was the first to stand up. Belking was a leader in the unpaid management board, responsible for coordinating communication and decisions between the members and the team of paid project coordinators and architects. His tone was confrontational and sceptical: 'This is nonsense. What is interesting about this [building] project is the shared space, the working together. This is about creating a new proposal for city development, not about some old-fashioned idea of privacy. Why are you as a sociologist interested in my private life? I'm not going to talk about this with you.'

I became visibly nervous because my research depended upon this access. The grant had been sent for final approval, forms had been signed and a position secured at the university. Meanwhile, promised access to other field sites had fallen through at the last minute. Standing in front of the group, it seemed my academic career depended on this moment. To make matters worse, my German language skills deteriorate when nerves kick in, despite the decade I've lived and researched in Berlin.

I cobbled together a partially coherent response, arguing in imperfect German that the personal *was* political. Seeing confused faces, I tried another approach: 'This distinction between private and public is something I am interested in, but I'm not necessarily assuming it is the same for everyone.' This seemed sufficient.

After my response, I sat down, relieved to be out of the hot seat, and I nervously waited for the vote to be held. Should this sociologist be allowed to investigate the production of our future homes? This was a sensitive issue and Herr Belking had suggested to everyone that I might have misunderstood the whole project. The vote was held and the group approved my presence, granting me access.

This important moment in the early phase of my fieldwork showed me that I was struggling with an important task: learning how to think like this *Baugruppe*. I had envisioned a research project about dwelling, but misunderstood the significance of planning.

Over the preceding 32 meetings, members of the group had learned to work together and develop orientations towards planning that were connected to but distinct from dwelling. I imagined the primary difficulty in research on home would be of the classical variety: persuading people to let me into their private spaces and to talk about their experiences and ideas of home. But I had failed to understand that I was not merely researching homes in a building, but the social entity of their *Baugruppe*. I had to find my own place here, sitting in the meetings, learning the logic and familiarizing myself with planning. Entering the field, the emergence of this duality of planners-today and dwellers-tomorrow was a key finding that unfolded over time as I learned what it meant to think like the *Baugruppe*.

This chapter walks through a five-step process of becoming a planner and thinking like the *Baugruppe* while reflecting on the challenges this presents for research on home. These five steps allow a reconstruction of the underlying activities involved in producing a home, generating what I hope is a playful framework in which curiosities can be unpacked and my own work of researching home can be rendered more explicit. The five steps are: becoming a member, surviving the email communication, learning the lingo, becoming active and embracing shared values. After completing these steps, one has learned not only to think of home as a dweller, but as a planner.

Step one: Become a member

To become an active participant in planning this future residence, one first needed to become a member of the group. This *Baugruppe* would meet once a month to make decisions, ranging from the kinds of plants on the property, to approving quarter-million-euro budget increases. Usually 30 to 40 members attended any given meeting. Meetings began at 7 p.m. and were at least 3 hours in duration, sometimes exceeding 4; only once in 27 meetings did we go home before 10 p.m. Here they actively planned for a future of inhabiting this building together, deciding on issues ranging from approving construction firm offers, to whether or not another sealant is necessary for the flat roof, to the necessity of paying for snow removal service, to the formulation of a legal contract that guides how the building is to be used. This planning – conventionally the task of architects and other 'professionals', rather than future residents – would permanently impact their lives as dwellers. At meetings, I quickly learned the high stakes that members perceived in planning for the best possible future.

The building and this *Baugruppe* are unique insofar as both private owners and a collective ownership model co-exist under one roof. About 25% of the apartments and studios are owned by a non-profit housing collective (German: *Genossenschaft*), about 75% by private owners. Private owners paid a little more for their apartments or studios than the collective, effectively subsidizing a kind of social-democratic model within the *Baugruppe*.

Most members learned about the project through word of mouth or a mailing list of different housing collectives or alternative housing solutions in Berlin. No formal marketing was undertaken by the group or architects. A placard on the construction site provided a website address, but by this point most units were occupied. My initial access to the group came through a friend of a friend of a friend, who was one of the architects commissioned by the *Baugruppe*.

Of course knowing about the project was one thing, paying was another. The financial means to pay for a stake in the collective or to buy an apartment were also necessary. Therefore most of the members of the *Baugruppe* were economically middle to upper-middle class, with a surprising proportion of people holding higher education degrees: for instance, 14 of the 68 persons registered as private owners have a PhD. Word of mouth circulated through networks of friends, people with knowledge of the architectural firms involved or through the mailing lists.

But becoming a member was not the same as becoming a planner. Members could also be passive. Many members signed the contract, paid the money and waited for the apartments and studios to be finished. They didn't engage in the following steps involved in becoming a planner. Being a member was a necessary but insufficient condition for becoming a planner.

Step two: Survive the emails

Email was an important medium for exchanging information within the group. Often emails would come from the two coordinators who were employed by the *Baugruppe* to manage the entire project. These emails often required immediate attention: meetings were announced, information on important decisions was circulated or forms were distributed that required signatures from members, notaries and banks. Other emails were sent among the members about something comparatively minor, such as a proposal for plants on the shared rooftop. Still others were borderline aggressive: an email about the accessibility of a shared toilet in the basement erupted into conflict, the ceramic façade of the building was argued to be essential to the identity of the building or, conversely, as an aesthetic indulgence adding unnecessary costs to the ever-increasing budget.

Whether three lines or three pages, technical or emotional, these emails required active attention.

Members developed strategies to deal with this: do I read all the emails, ignore them all or skim them for relative importance in order not to become bogged down by details?

Frau Sachs was a schoolteacher near retirement age who was deeply involved in planning the shared common space of the building, a topic important for how she envisioned the future of the building and her ideas of home. At a monthly meeting she told me she wanted to meet in person again soon to discuss my research and her involvement with the project, but nevertheless it took months to arrange an interview. Follow-up emails were met with silence and eventually two months later we exchanged phone numbers at a *Baugruppe* meeting. She told me, 'I hardly check my email because I get so many now [from the *Baugruppe*] and it just stresses me out.'

Our interview took place a few weeks after *Baugruppe* discussions on the communally shared space on the rooftop; a meeting I had to miss due to travel. 'How was the extra meeting last week?' I ask. Frau Sachs had missed the meeting. 'Oh no! What? Oh I really have to finally look through all those emails.' The emails were a source of anxiety for her. Her ideal future home was not one of email exchange, but of face-to-face contact. True, the emails concerned matters relevant for the future dwelling in the building, but they also created tension today, both in Frau Sachs's daily life and in her monthly interactions at the meetings. Emails could allow for tensions to build and linger through an interface, while resolutions would usually be delayed until the face-to-face meeting. For the next year, she ceased attending meetings, due in part to the onslaught of emails.

Frau Sachs had an email address and she used to check it semi-regularly. But aside from the technical requirement of checking an online mailbox, to become a planner one also needed to foster a capacity to deal with conflicts expressed in textual exchanges. Still others simply lacked the language skills: 'Neither of us are really great at German', a couple explained, 'it is just too much work to sift through all this stuff ... but a friend of ours tells us when we need to sign something.'

I was never a member of the *Baugruppe*, and remained a spectator in decision-making processes. When voting on whether or not I should be granted access, it was suggested that I should not be on the primary email list where most of these exchanges took place. I was only included on a second mailing list primarily used to announce monthly meetings. I did, however, occasionally receive emails when responses were CCed to this second list, or on those rare occasions a particular member wanted me to read their response. I learned to empathize with those who found the emails exhausting. Receiving emails complicated my life: I felt compelled to drop what I was doing, read the content and shift into the required headspace. This building wasn't my future home, but I found the discussions and details exhausting. The technical details, emotions, exchanges and content in the emails forced me to think of the consequences for the *Baugruppe* and for my research. These emails were already shaping the community and making explicit and implicit claims about how people would live together in the future. This was a virtual anticipatory space where the community of dwellers was taking shape.

Despite the fact that I was not on the primary email list, members of the *Baugruppe* often felt it was important to share certain email exchanges with me, so as to allow them to discuss and navigate the intense feelings these emails often prompted. Discussions about these emails showed me the depth of emotion that, for instance, could be attached to how and when future residents should move trash bins to the sidewalk in the future home. These emails had a formal character, but also showed the intensity of emotion that planning home brings to the surface. Sometimes the most formal or technical details could cause an emotional spiral to elevate from the banal to the very heart of the project. A simple message stating that a bench on the rooftop was too expensive could lead to debates about the budget and the central importance of shared spaces for the community and project as a whole. Future homes were being mediated through these emails; those with language proficiency and the ability to strategize a path through the emotional exchanges survived to become planners.

Step three: Learn the lingo

In the 33rd monthly meeting of the *Baugruppe* I found myself trying to decode some of the acronyms that members effortlessly enunciated. WEG, BoP, ARGE, TGA, GV, GF, AG, GBR, KoKo were all seemingly important, but I was lost. These technical terms were learned through participation in the *Baugruppe* and every month the vocabulary deepened. In the 45th meeting we were presented with the pros and cons of different offers from construction firms regarding a proposed insulation solution. After a 20-minute onslaught of information relating to ecological questions of energy efficiency, future risks of insufficient vapour condensation or insulation durability and, of course, costs, the members of the *Baugruppe* had to react to the following text:

WDVS Position 01.03.70, Position 01.03.90, Position 01.02.490, Angebot A60972, abzgl. 0,5% Nachlass ohne Bedingung zzgl. 19% MwSt, VGE023, Stand KoKo 08.

Through attending meetings and following the debates, members could decode this illegible text. They then reacted quickly, voting on this matter of consequence. Those who had read the relevant emails and documents referred to in the code were best situated to make an educated decision. No matter how painful it was to learn how to de-code texts like this, planners had to develop this capacity. Planning the future home was only possible through this technical, bureaucratic and administrative language.

There was a second linguistic modality important for communication in the *Baugruppe*: a discourse of community. Arguments were phrased in reference to what was good for the future building – mediated through technical jargon – but also in terms of what was good for the community. The 3-hour (or longer) meetings offered the time and place to discuss these matters, while the private interests of each resident were largely kept at bay. The most valid arguments would frame a decision around what was good for the community, rather than what was good for one's capital investment in the project.

Accusing someone of treating their apartment purely as an 'investment' was to charge them with high treason. To speak of the building as mere real estate was to belittle the *Baugruppe*'s greater project of producing a community. Similarly, discussions about aesthetic issues of an individual apartment were largely absent from planning meetings. The personal homes were planned individually and in communication directly with the architects and coordinators, but not with the *Baugruppe* as a whole.

Understanding the discourse of community brought me closer to understanding Herr Belking's critique. Discussions of private dwellings and individual investments seemed to muddle, if not pollute the dialogues of the meetings. The way I framed my research interests was misaligned: I brought to the foreground that which was supposed to remain in the background.

Learning how to think like the *Baugruppe* sometimes conflicted with my own predispositions. Having recently read J.G. Ballard's *High Rise*, and with sociological theories of class conflict ringing in my head, I am a little embarrassed to admit that I hoped to find more animosity here. Referring to the two economic models of private and collective ownership, one member of the *Baugruppe* speculated early in my research that perhaps I would find 'gentrification from within the building'. I underlined this in my notes, as it would make a great title for an article. I imagined the welcome reception this finding would receive in publications, satiating my hunger to critically reflect on the values and ideals of middle-class housing.

Fortunately for those involved in the project, this type of animosity was relatively absent during planning. Instead of warfare, there was concerted and collective effort to refrain from antagonism between these groups. During interviews, conversations and meetings, owners told me it is 'good' to 'support' the housing collective. Buying a unit in this building involved voluntarily buying into the economic model of subsidizing the costs of the collective. 'Freely, freely, of course. No one is forced to be part of this project', I was told.

I had hoped that one owner could give me more dirt. Her career revolved around participatory art making and I imagined she would be an expert on critically assessing the practices of the *Baugruppe*: 'I was actually kind of pleasantly surprised with this group, that people are so open to working together.' This kind of discursive framing is a finding being revisited now the building is inhabited as I continue to visit dwellers within the building. The building was supposed to be a 'new proposal for city development', in the words of Herr Belking. And indeed, the *Baugruppe* strongly adhered to ideas of community and working together. For instance, owners also voluntarily made it possible for individual members of the collective to vote on issues that are normally restricted to holders of real estate capital. This effort to extend voting privileges to all dwellers moved beyond the minimum requirements of law in German capitalist society.

These meetings and the process of planning were the closest that most will ever come to building their own physical dwelling. There is something enchanting about a home that is self-built, but physically constructing a house lies beyond the reach of most middle-class urban dwellers. They were working on a particularly large dwelling in a complex urban environment saturated with bureaucratic laws, codes and requirements. This is not a simple Black Forest hut constructed off-the-grid – the *Baugruppe* building was also raised upon a foundation of complexities, architectural norms and finance laws. The technical lingo offered the means to self-build through collectively planning and problem-solving, without requiring a mastery of the skillsets of physical labour. However, the technical language of planning also disenchanted ideas of the self-built home, now an object embedded in stress and bureaucracy. A panacea was found in the discourse of community, which served to ease some of this rationalization of home. The bureaucratic, technical and rational web being spun had a purpose: to engineer a sociable building that facilitated their visions of a future community of dwellers.

Step four: Become active

When first arriving at the 33rd meeting of the *Baugruppe*, I never imagined the often tedious and exhausting monthly events would be so significant for my research. In retrospect this seems very naïve and misguided.

One simple reason I misjudged the significance of *Baugruppe* meetings is that I simply didn't like being there. I have to attend similar meetings at the university and would never have written a research proposal that mirrored the very thing I dislike most about my profession. I am not alone in this feeling: each meeting was attended by 30 to 40 of the 100 or so members. Multiple members of the group estimated that roughly one-third of the membership tried to always attend, one-third visited a couple times a year and another third never attended at all – a reasonable and useful approximation that my field notes reinforce. For at least 3 hours, the lingo engulfed you, interpersonal conflicts emerged, spreadsheets were presented and analysed, old and new crises were discussed, pressure was heightened and subsequently relieved. After having attended these meetings for nearly 3 years, I became socialized into them. I understood the lingo, was familiar with the ebbs and flows of emotions and had a sense of the different actors and their roles. The first crisis I witnessed exhausted me: urgent, argumentative and frustrated voices filled the room and I lacked the background knowledge to understand the debate. I had to try to piece together too much new information: do these two people have history debating against each other, is this topic relevant to everyone, what happens if there is no resolution, will this conflict escalate, how will they resolve a disagreement? Like jumping into a serial novel or soap opera, I lacked context. But over time I learned the rhythms of how crises emerged and were resolved, witnessing each crisis in the context of previous meetings and previous resolved crises.

Attending a *Baugruppe* meeting as a planner involved opening one's self up to the stresses and insecurities of the building and community of decision-makers. It was an invitation to complexity. Staying at home, one could rest assured that there were enough active participants doing the work and making well-informed decisions: the future home rested in good, capable hands. Regularly attending implied that you were the one undertaking the labour of planning the future.

A proficient participant not only attended meetings but also became active in 'work groups' (German: *Arbeitsgruppen*). These were task forces dealing with a specific aspect of planning. Work groups were formed to plan shared laundry facilities or telecommunications possibilities or to reach out to the community in the neighbourhood. Work groups would also plan other work groups: the shared spaces group evolved into five different subgroups. At least 18 groups were active over these two years. No one was paid for this labour. A handful of the most involved members worked over 1,000 unpaid hours as active planners in the *Baugruppe* and its work groups.

Planners were granted certain privileges not afforded to less active members. A work group laboured for over a year to produce a property law contract (German: *WEG Vertrag*) to be signed by all owners in the building. The work group was open to all, met frequently and held a workshop to brainstorm and fine-tune the document. This legally binding contract set out the basic framework of what was and was not allowed in the building, from forbidding satellites on balconies, to limiting rights to change architectural elements, to restricting certain legal but undesired commercial activities, from sex work to drum lessons. Until this document was signed and notarized by all of the 68 owners, no one could move into the building. Producing this document was a complex process. Objections and debates were attached to dozens of subclauses of paragraphs and positions, but nevertheless it needed to be finalized. All but three members had made their peace with this document, but three refused to sign.

During the 52nd meeting, Frau Bachmann presented her case against the contract. Showing mastery of the technical lingo she had a list of six points of contention with citations to specific paragraphs with comments from a lawyer.

- Shouldn't we legislate when the delivery vans can unload at the commercial space to control noise issues?
- How to manage the noises and smells of garbage removal?
- Why can't the key to the wheelchair accessible toilet be available to all?
- How is oil and fat disposed of, if a restaurant moves into the commercial space?
- Can we buy insurance against graffiti?
- How do we legislate the use of one of the shared spaces?

These were all concerns that would affect her sensorial experience of home. She argued that the potential future problems of smells, noises, disrupted visual aesthetics and accessibility ought to be legislated now, as a common and legally binding understanding of what makes a good home.

Frau Bachmann also mobilized the discourse of community to persuade the group of an important point: 'I just think that everyone would be happier if we all had a chance to discuss the contract together, then we wouldn't have these problems.' But Frau Reichel, a highly active planner interjected: 'The work group has been working on the contract for years and we all had plenty of opportunities to join them. You can't now claim that we didn't have a chance.' After a short back and forth Frau Bachmann tried to make it clear 'the main problem is not just the document', but that she felt 'excluded' from the process and 'others must have also felt excluded'. But the reply was the same: 'You should have been active in the work group if you wanted to steer [the production of] the document.'

Frau Bachmann was asking for something significant: to postpone the signing of the contract and, with it, the date from which time the building could be dwelled. The demand for more planning conflicted with the desire for dwelling. She should have been more active, it was argued; now it is too late.

Relatively inactive members were never begrudged, but they were a source of uncertainty for active planners. For this reason, the *Baugruppe* found another way to pass the contract into law by giving the management board the right to sign on the behalf of all. After all, they explained, there were other passive members who represented an unknown factor: 'Someone else could stop the whole process. It could happen. We [who attend these meetings] are a small group of very involved people, but who knows what all the others think!' The most active planners were trusted to work on behalf of the community and to make benevolent decisions for securing future homes. Being active granted more ability to engage in negotiation and even rock the boat, whereas passive members were perceived, in moments like these, as a potential risk for the community.

My own involvement in the *Baugruppe* was relatively passive – I only became 'involved' in select moments, for example, in setting up and cleaning up meetings or helping with a video shoot on the construction site. During meetings, I initially sought to be as unobtrusive as possible, sitting in the back corner of the room. With such a large group, I occasionally disappeared as a researcher, at least for some. All active planners knew my identity, but those who only occasionally visited meetings did not recognize my presence as a non-member. During the 57th meeting, someone I had only seen a handful of times over the 2 years of meetings asked me:

'Which apartment is yours?'

'None actually, I am the researcher from the university, I'm not a member of the *Baugruppe*', I replied.

'Oh you lucky man.'

This member's sense of humour also suggests a difference between the active planners who want to be at the meetings and the less active members for whom the long and detailed meetings are an unfortunate but necessary element of planning, something they prefer to hold at a distance. During interviews with very active members, I was told on a handful of occasions that people actually liked the problem-solving elements of planning. Being involved was 'important', maybe even 'rewarding'. To become a planner, one had to justify this activity as worthwhile while also carrying responsibility for the active production of future homes.

Step five: Embrace shared values

It is unsurprising that when opening up the possibility of planning a future home, a wide array of values come flooding in. The principles guiding what is 'good' for the building and the community are not written anywhere, and may even conflict with one another. Ethnographic research on home might utilize different scales, politics and theory, but most of us agree that one's idea of home is shaped by culturally shared beliefs. The ideas of what 'home' means or what constitutes a 'good home' are infused with values, and in this *Baugruppe*, it useful to think of these in two pairs: (1) participation and community, and (2) fear and trust.

Participation is not compulsory for members, but is a core value of planners. To plan a future home is a unique project that many of us only experience two degrees removed. Apartments in cities like Berlin are both physically built and conceptually planned by professionals. The *Baugruppe* was only one degree removed: they were not physically putting mortar on brick, but were tasked with planning or approving the bricks and mortar used – either in budget approvals or in actually selecting the materials. Making these decisions for the house and community required participation. The kinds of plants chosen, the presence of a sandbox for children and the shared laundry facilities became physical elements to set the foundations for the social universe of community. Participation, like the discourse of community, allowed members to socially engage with one another, before every party has access to their private spaces and the shared building.

Active participants in the *Baugruppe* became planners. They made decisions about what a good building should look like, balancing economics with the values of the community, while keeping some of their private interests at bay. Homes were planned as elements within the larger project of the building and a future community that would offer a proposal for urban dwelling. Planners valued community both within *Baugruppe* meetings and as a model for their future living together. Planners shared a principle: the result of any single vote should not determine your participation in the future. A 'good' planner knew they would not always have personal preferences realized in every vote. Frau Reichel disagreed with the decision to make coated concrete floors standardized for all apartments – she wanted wood floors. She disagreed with postponing a decision regarding the uses of the shared communal room on the roof of the building, but nevertheless, she attended meetings and sat together in work groups with people who agreed and disagreed with some of her positions.

Conflict was part of the process and a planner was willing to 'lose' in a vote, but continue to work with other planners. Members, architects and other researchers told me that this *Baugruppe* is somewhat unique in this way. The architects involved promoted the idea of 'productive' as opposed to 'unproductive' conflict. Before my research began, members of the group were invited to attend a seminar about 'communication in a *Baugruppe*'. Values of community and participation were based on some of the principles learned at the seminar. 'Remember not to get too emotional', or 'I think we are getting caught up a bit too much in an emotional debate' were phrases used to move away from unproductive to productive conflict.

Throughout the first months of my research, my minor conflict with Herr Belking resonated in my mind. I remembered being humbled and taken off my pedestal as an 'expert' on 'home', and this coloured my experience of meetings and subsequent interviews. After an initial 6 months of research, I still felt intimated by Herr Belking.

Growing tired of this situation, I decided to approach him and say something not so different from what is written in this chapter, partly for my own sanity, partly because I thought it was vital for my research. In slightly less articulate German, I said: 'You know, ever since your comments when I first presented my research project, I've been thinking of what you said. As an academic, I am used to hearing critiques and I actually found this helpful. It showed me something I didn't know before, which is good for my research. I was hoping you might be interested in sitting down with me for an interview.' Herr Belking accepted, we met for a discussion and afterwards established a good relationship.

I wonder if this effort to overcome his critique was analogous to learning the values of participation and community. Instead of rejecting his comments, I accepted my minor 'defeat' and continued participating in the project, facing the criticism head-on, rather than avoiding the emotions of the conflict. Learning to overcome my anxiety of Herr Belking and to trust he wasn't malevolently opposing my research was an important part of learning how to think like the *Baugruppe*.

But amidst the 'productive' conflicts, there are tensions that linger. In an interview I asked Herr Kruppe to tell me more about his ideas about what kind of community he envisioned:

> You know the guy who gave you shit on the first time you were there ... so this is a kind of mentality that I don't really fancy, when people get super aggressive for their own needs and claim it is for the community ... Well no, it is not. It is your own private desire to express yourself or present your ideas, or whatever. So these kind of people ... might make it not work, they might really get hard with their feelings and own needs.

Herr Kruppe tells me that this planning process has showed him who he might be friends with and who he might avoid as he dwells in his new home. These comments remained on the sidelines during meetings, coming out in other discussions, or overheard as people would leave the meeting room and walk into the night: 'God, that was exhausting', 'I didn't expect we could discuss a water softener for 30 minutes, a water softener!' or, 'This architect waltzes in here with his architecture theory and gets this damned gate he wants, when I'm the one who has to live with it' are comments overheard at 11:15 p.m. after the particularly long 59th meeting. While sitting together, staged within a meeting, planners performed roles enacting community and participatory values, but after the curtains were drawn and the crowd leaves, the reviews of the performances were not always harmonious. There remained concern, even fear, that the decisions reached might not have been the best possible decisions for the individuals or the group.

Fear and trust are two other values that needed to be learned to become a planner. These values were somewhat contradictory, but nevertheless coexisted. Every meeting was infused with fear. After all there were costly delays – the project was completed 11 months later than planned. The *Baugruppe* estimated that every month's delay brought about 60,000 euros in direct and indirect costs to the group (in wages, rent and mortgage payments, permits, etc.). A misplaced comma in an Excel table 4 years previous led to budget problems.

Rising costs and delays were the results of the past actions of various individuals and firms involved in the project, inciting fears of future problems. In the 39th meeting, Herr Belking told the group, 'As a member of the management board, I have the feeling that things are so complex that we aren't actually steering this. There are so many actors involved, all with their own interests, all trying to steer it.' There was a fear that people with responsibility were not working for the interest of the group, perhaps there was negligence from the architects or coordinators, and there were cases of malevolence from contracted firms seeking higher profits.

In the 52nd meeting Herr Belking told the whole group that 'the management board is not happy with the coordinators'. The conflict was palpable. The two employed coordinators sat with arms crossed tight on their chests, uncharacteristically silent and obviously offended.

At the 54th meeting, Belking initiated a round of applause for the coordinators, telling the group 'we should be thankful that we have them!' The characterization of the coordinators had been radically changed. This was curious, but makes sense in terms of the values of fear and trust. Belking explained that during those 2 months he met frequently with the coordinators, clearing up misunderstandings and double-checking their meticulousness. The fear of rising costs and delays remained, but the coordinators were no longer to blame, we were told. Fear became a motivating factor to double and triple check the work of other planners and a means to reach security: the coordinators became worthy of trust again.

Trust was important for the group as they planned their future homes. After long discussions building in tension and complexity, a planner would often insist that more talking is not the solution, but rather trust. One extreme example from the 55th meeting: 'My god. We can't argue about every little tiny detail or else we will never get this contract signed. We need to be a little more open-minded here and trust that the people who have been working on this [contract] and putting a lot of thought into it!'

These ruptures of fear and appeals to trust served as reminders that members should perceive the group as benevolent: that planners were hard at work for what is best for the building and community. Reminders of the value of trust assuaged fears plaguing the production of home. Fear was one path among many that allowed the *Baugruppe* to finally make the argument that they needed to trust one another; that the community was, at the end of the day, a benevolent one. The future home would be a good home.

There were also parties unable to accompany fellow planners in this transition from fear to trust. Of the three members who actively opposed the property contract, one transitioned from an active planner to a mere member. 'I saw the *Baugruppe* differently after that', she told me, 'for the others, the others are all there together, if you want to join this group, you're actually giving yourself up a bit, and then you're integrated. But if you just want to look into other ideas, you have to weigh that against [being part of the group].' Fear remained but without trust. She transitioned from an active planner to being a mere member, unable to synthesize participation with community values, fear with trust.

Conclusion

The building was delayed by almost 1 year, leading to delays in my research. But this also meant an extra year of meetings that helped me better understand what this project meant for its active participants: it was no less than their attempt to self-build a home within an environment thick with by-laws, codes, restrictions and conditions. The craft learned was not that of a builder or dweller, but that of a planner. Herr Belking and the *Baugruppe* suggested that the building and community ought to be something bigger than a mere container of private dwellings, but the expression of an idea of city development. The carefully plotted out building and community navigated the bureaucratic imbroglio of urban housing laws in order to produce dwelling in the future, both for the community and for individuals.

Beginning this research, I imagined this planning phase would be background for the real work that is underway as I write this chapter: researching dwelling. Yet the home is dwelt not merely by owners and members of the collective, but by those members who transformed into planners over the past years. They actively produced values and an anticipatory sense of dwelling through being active, learning the lingo, surviving the emails and securing membership. Dwellers are a mix of these planners and less active participants. Even this mixture is already being planned: 'We will need another culture, so to speak, as residents not just a *Baugruppe*', says a planner in the 55th meeting, who is organizing the house rules and distribution of labour for the everyday upkeep of the building. The production of home is steeped in the subjectivity of the *Baugruppe* as planners – as nearly every element in the building has been plotted out through active participation. The planned object becomes the lived-in space of dwelling, shared by dwellers who were planners and non-planners alike.

7

Making a home with homeless people

Johannes Lenhard

Alex led me to his niche right next to the Gare de l'Est in Paris for the first time in 2014. It was early spring, still cool outside; most days were dominated by rain, grey skies and a lack of sunshine. But the weather didn't make a difference for Alex; he had no choice but to sleep outside. Alex was homeless. Recently, he had found himself a little square between two pillars just opposite the western entrance of the train station where he felt secure, had enough space for his belongings and enough comfort to sleep at night. Falling asleep was not easy for most of the homeless people [*sans abris, sans domicile fixe*] I worked in Paris during my research between 2014 and 2017. Many of my informants were affected by worries, trauma and violence; home, both in the physical form and as a mental state of well-being and order, was often not easily in reach.

Alex was born in Kosovo but had lived in France for almost a decade before his issues with the immigration authorities started. Despite having been married to a French woman and living with her in Lyon, he had never become a French citizen. Since his divorce in 2013, he had trouble staying in France, oscillating back and forth between Kosovo, Germany and France trying to obtain a right to stay in the country he has considered his home for so long. Since his most recent return in 2014, Alex had been staying in the area around the station. When we met, he had been sleeping in an alcove in one of the train companies' buildings for several months. He was proud of what he had accomplished: neatly cut and folded long pieces of cardboard were perfectly put in place to form a box around his belongings. His two bags – one containing clothes, another one necessary utensils for cooking and general survival – were hidden inside the cardboard covers, as were his sleeping bag and pillows. Everything was perfectly ordered, spaces demarcated for clean and dirty, for food, clothes and utensils, for daytime and night time. At least this little piece of semi-public space, this niche was something Alex had under control, something he felt comfortable coming back to. In this alcove, I encountered what an approximation of *home* was for Alex.

*   *   *

I see the idea of producing order and controlling space at the centre of home and home-making following Brun and Fabos (2015: 12) and Douglas (1991: 289), who explains:

> Home is always a localizable idea. Home is located in space but it is not necessarily a fixed space. It does not need bricks and mortar, it can be a wagon, a caravan, a board, or a tent. It need not be a large space, but space there must be, for home starts by bringing some space under control.

How does this 'bringing space under control' work for my informants and how in parallel do I as a researcher start to make the field – the Paris of a group of homeless people – my home? Are these two operations in fact in tension with each other? This will be the focus in the first part of this chapter. I will think through the complications of my own immersion in the field as a researcher: reflecting on encounters with two other homeless men I met, Mark and Leandre, I will describe how the elusiveness of my informants and our apparent differences made access difficult. As became clear to me retrospectively, at the centre of these difficulties was a second operation of home-making I engaged in at the time: not only did I come to Paris as a researcher who was trying to understand a group of Parisian homeless people, I also had to find my own personal home in this new city. How did these two parallel practices of home-making – as a researcher and as a person – clash on my side?

In the second part of this chapter, I will describe another question which followed on from this issue of my two-sided home-making – that of my responsibility as a researcher. How on the one hand could I support my informants in their home-making efforts but on the other hand not interfere too much and become 'too close'? How could I cooperate more with my informants – to say it in the words of this volume's introduction, 'make a home with them' rather than exploit them or simply dwell in the field? I will describe how I struggled with the power imbalance between my informants and myself and my impulse to help them.

Making homes together and apart

> I have been to the day centre in the morning to get some food. After that I
> went to do some laundry at a different place; I washed my sleeping bag. I helped
> Mama [one of his friends at the train station] to get food and had a late African
> lunch close to Chateau d'Eau [metro station]. Since then I was here [at the Gare
> du Nord] and took care of Mama. I don't know what Leandre [a friend of his] has
> been doing. I expect him to be back here tonight.

Mark had only been in Paris several months when I met him in late 2014.
Originally from Nigeria, he didn't speak French, only English, and he didn't have
a passport. His hope, however, was to move to the UK to 'become a famous pop
singer' – but, since his arrival at the Gare du Nord, he was supporting Mama by
getting her food and following her prayers. Mama, in turn, had taken him in.
She had, over the period of weeks, transformed one corner of the hot air vent
space around the Gare du Nord into a camp for herself, which she shared with
Mark since his arrival. On search for food and other necessities, Mark's typical
day took him through the whole city; he travelled a lot as he describes in the
short vignette above. His day was structured around a central spot – the train
station – but he meandered away from it and his emotional centre, Mama, to
run errands. It was always unclear where he could be found in between food
hunting, visiting homeless institutions, begging and finding acquaintances and
friends to socialize and exchange news as well as goods with.

Like Mark, many of my informants were constantly moving, constantly
switching locations and routines in order to maximize their income and
minimize their involvement with the law. They travelled through the city to
find good begging spots, security, friends and shelter. They usually didn't have
phones and were impossible to contact beyond finding them in person. In Paris,
homeless people often lead flexible lives. On the one hand, public transport was
relatively easy to access even without the money for it; people jumped over the
metro barriers constantly and into the back doors of buses without paying. On
the other hand, neighbourhoods were very diverse – begging was much easier
on the rich Rive Gauche, for instance, but many homeless institutions were
further up in the north, close to the train stations. As a result, people travelled
around a lot. Although I had conducted research into homelessness in London
across the years of 2011–14, it was mostly closed and solid groups occupying
particular territories, streets and even street corners (having 'a spot', which was
very much defended against other people; one had 'a right' to one's spot after

some time – and to the income stream that came with it). In contrast, many of the homeless people I met in Paris were travellers of the city.

Consequently, I often struggled to encounter my informants. I would spend hours walking through Paris – even once I chose to focus my fieldwork on those in the area around the Gare du Nord – searching for my informants without any means of tracking them down. The safest bet was to catch people at their sleeping spots, particularly around the station. For instance, Bitou and his friends – a group of four to six Indian men, who became one of my core groups of informants – had secured a safe spot behind the bars that closed off the central bus station right next to the Gare. The people around Bitou found a closed-off space which they were able to turn into a (temporary) home. They had brought carpets, duvets, pillows, mattresses and other insulating material up the little hill from the train station and arranged them in a wind-sheltered corner at the very end of the bus station. Five to six people could easily sleep in a row next to each other in their shelter which at night was – due to the closed gates – also safe from most intruders. Sleeping spots, such as this one, were – once secured – stable for between some weeks to several months. I met Bitou up here many times after running back and forth through the station on search for my other informants. Being able to find and sit down with Bitou in his niche was beneficial in two ways: it gave me, as a researcher, a fixed point to return to and it made our conversations more stable. Rather than being driven by the constant insecurity of where to sleep, what to eat and where to rest, having even an approximation of a home – a space under his control and order (Douglas 1991) – made it easier for Bitou to reflect and speak to me about his hopes, aspirations and worries.[1] Bitou's successful home-making made my access to the field as a researcher who was dependent on encounters with his informants easier.

In contrast, my own home-making seemed to almost interfere with my access to the field as a researcher. On one, more surface level, there were visible differences between me and my informants evoking distinctions of class, race and lives led and manifested in everyday details such as clothing, speech and mannerisms which were putting some people off. More importantly, however, I had a home and engaged in activities in the city beyond my presence as a researcher in the field. In other words, I was making a home for myself as a private individual in parallel to accessing the field. How was I to delineate this personal home from my field site? These dilemmas emerged in several encounters within the field.

*   *   *

One evening in early 2016, while I was talking to Mark in front of the *Gare du Nord*, he pointed out one of his acquaintances who had just arrived to use the mobile soup kitchen which regularly stopped at the train station. Leandre was very reluctant to speak when Mark tried to introduce us. He shook his head and preferred to stand several meters away from us. He continued to stare at me in a way which seemed to say: 'You don't belong here. You are clearly an outsider in your coat and big scarf and glasses and bag. What are you doing here?'[2] Despite the discomfort I intuitively felt, I eventually approached him and introduced myself; he was very passive, wouldn't face me and only very slowly started talking to me. As our conversation unfolded, he confronted me with the following accusation: 'What are you doing here talking to homeless people? In the end, you just come here, take information from us, write it together, go back and use it for yourself, right?' Beyond his general suspicion, he in particular was weary of me hanging around people like him and Mark: 'You don't speak the code. *Les noirs* [black people] like to stay among themselves.'

The short encounter with Leandre right at the beginning of my fieldwork brought me back to two recurrent questions facing anthropologists : First, how do you access and research a group that you are – along various dimensions – not really part of while also making and retaining your own personal space needed to facilitate reflection? In other words: how do you access the field but also remain your own private person (with your own space, your own clothes, your own views)? Secondly, how do you deal with your informants' sense that your research could be exploitative (and that not only in the postcolonial context, see Comaroff and Comaroff 2003)? While both questions are intricately linked, I understand the first to be more about negotiating access and the second about responsibility – being a good researcher-citizen. Let me dwell slightly more on the first question before approaching the latter one in the second part of this chapter.

Accessing and immersing myself in the field was challenging both because there were differences between my informants and myself and because of the double movement I tried to perform: making a home in Paris as a private individual as well as a researcher of homelessness. In many ways, there were striking differences between my informants and me: I was younger than most of them, didn't share the same ethnicity with many of them, did not suffer from any kind of trauma, had an apartment to stay in and had a job which earned me money. While anthropological thinking has considered differences as helpful for a long time – making the 'strange' familiar is one of the most common aims for any fieldworker[3] – too much difference could lead to a lack of trust and, ultimately, limited access to the field altogether. Over time, I developed several different strategies of how to overcome these initial barriers. Most importantly, volunteering in different trusted organizations helped my informants to lose their suspicion. Once I had established a volunteering presence, people on the street who had encountered me as a volunteer started to see me as a positive, and even useful, presence in a way which countered their suspicion of me being an intruder. The trust I built becoming part of different organizations attached to me as a person beyond the actual context of the volunteering. After several months, I was often identified as one of the good people and my informants started to classify me as a *bénévole* (volunteer) in contrast to their original assumption of me working for the police or the government. This status, together with the snowballing effect I worked off – being taken around different friend groups by my main informants – made access to a variety of groups easier over time.[4]

The problem of establishing my own personal home within – or on the immediate outside – of the field did not, however, become better over time. In a pre-study, I had identified the area around the train stations in the north of the city as an ideal site for an exploration of people sleeping rough in Paris. Both official government (INSEE 2013) and city (APUR 2011) statistics confirmed the prevalence of homeless people in that particular neighbourhood. To stay close to this hub of homeless people and services around them, I picked an apartment in the *quartier* making my closest underground station the Gare du Nord. I used the metro lines starting there on an almost daily basis and regularly the international trains leaving from the Gare to London; I frequented restaurants around the station, picked up bikes as part of the city's bike-sharing program (*Vélib*) and did most of my grocery shopping at a weekly market and in different, often Indian-run, shops right behind the station. My own routines very much unfolded in the area which was also the main living space for my informants. As soon as I stepped out of my flat, I entered my field. With the train station less than five minutes away from what I would come to call my home, my field was truly 'at home'. My observation of the movements of people on the street, and later my conversations with people, usually took place within a ten-minute walking radius from my apartment. Both the train station itself and the streets around it – serving as my most important field site – but then also the day centre, which I volunteered at for almost eighteen months, were handily close. While I found my own ways into the city, I explored and later worked in my field site at the same time.

The proximity, even overlap, of the two was, at different moments, both helpful and something much more ambiguous as an encounter with Barus – in late 2016, just some months before I was to return back to the UK – exemplifies.

Barus was from Bulgaria and had come to Paris to live with his brother who had a secure job in the city. When I met him in 2015, he had been in the French capital already for several years; most of that time, Barus had spent on the street – between begging at the Gare du Nord, shooting up in front of the Lariboisière Hospital, and sleeping at La Défense. His brother didn't tolerate Barus's continuing dependency on substances such as methadone or crack and threw him out quickly after his arrival.

Late one night in December 2016, I was leaving a restaurant with a group of friends close to Pigalle, just about ten minutes' walk from the train station. All of a sudden, I heard a voice asking for money out of a dark house niche we had just passed. My eyes couldn't make out a person at first; there was someone sitting between two houses in the pitch dark, totally alone. While I stepped forward, towards the niche, one of my friends tried to hold my arm at first and walked backward slowly, obviously in fear. I felt responsible to bring the situation under control – wasn't I supposed to know how to deal with people asking for money, even late at night? My other friend grabbed my anxious friend's hand and the two crossed the street, still observing the scene but from what seemed like a more secure distance. Slowly, my eyes were able to make out not only contours but facial features. A smile came to my face when I recognized Barus who himself still didn't know who he was facing. Only when I bowed down, sat next to him and shook his hand, did he look properly and smile in turn. I spent a while chatting to him – he confessed that he had to leave the others at the station alone, he needed to think – before returning to my friends. Their faces had visibly relaxed, too; they were chatting away and laughed when I finally approached them: 'Your research never ends, eh?'

Other instances of this collapse of what I thought of as my private life into the field occurred – often involving friends and family. While the encounter with Barus was the only time fear and discomfort played a role in any of these meetings, I felt that being able to separate the two in some senses was increasingly important to my own well-being. As I had established home as a researcher in the field, overcoming the problems of (initial) access, the struggles shifted towards how to separate my private home from my home as a researcher overlapping with my informants' homes. Making my own social world and home with boundaries to my field had become a way of being stable. Having a different world available, one where trauma and suffering were not the dominating tropes, was important for my own mental health. It gave me space to reflect on what I saw in the field and also the necessary distance to go through two years of intense research.[5]

On the one hand, living close to my informants was very helpful. It let the two sides of my own initial home-making activities – the personal and the professional – coincide. At the same time as exploring the area around my apartment for the nearest supermarket and bistro, I would discover meeting points, sleeping places and begging spots frequented by people who lived on the street. I spent several hours every day, after I first arrived, walking through my neighbourhood. Walking – or tracing routes – as a method of enquiry has arrived in anthropology, most recently, with the take up of de Certeau's work (Certeau 1984) but has also entered studies of homelessness in particular Wolch and Rowe (1992), who use the term *mobility paths*).[6] Unlike Wolch and Rowe, I began not by concentrating on tracing peoples' ways through the city but on observing movements at, to and from certain places. Who used which begging spot around the different exits of the train station? Who slept in which niche, house entrance or bus stop?

On the other hand, the proximity also became a challenge over time. It was complicated to separate field from non-field, professional from private life, for me as a researcher. When – or where – did I stop being a researcher and start being a private person? Was I still doing research when I saw some of my informants on a dinner outing with friends in the area as my friend suggested after the encounter with Barus? The boundary lines with my most important informants where particularly stretched when it came to the other question the encounter with Leandre raised: what kind of a responsibility did I have towards my informants? How much collaborative home-making in the sense of the introduction should I engage in? I will turn to this question in the remainder of this chapter.

Responsibility and home-making for the researcher

Leandre's accusation – you are exploiting your informants – wouldn't really leave me alone. It made me think more about the ethics of anthropological research more generally: how can we make sure that the people we are working with are not research 'objects', but feel supported through our process and are influencing it directly? How much home-making was necessary and good to engage in together with my homeless informants to say it in the words of the introduction? I found three answers to this question in my fieldwork which developed after this very early encounter with Leandre. One and most obviously, I tried to at least protect my informants from damage I could cause myself; I tried to be unobtrusive and ask as few directed questions as possible in my own research. I observed and followed the conversations of the people. Unlike many other anthropologists, I didn't do a single interview with my homeless informants (only with experts) nor did I ever audio-record conversations. Even my questioning was limited; I tried to capture my informants' train of thought as much as possible without pushing my own interests and ideas onto them. Following examples in similar contexts (e.g. Hall 2003), I not only felt that this was the least intrusive way of working with a group as marginalized as homeless people. It also had advantages with regard to data quality. While it made my collecting of data more complicated – quickly typing notes while on the toilet, scribbling words onto pieces of paper while being outside, etc. – I could be more sure about the unstaged nature of the information I collected. By following my informants' thoughts, by letting *them* lead, mostly in an unprompted way, this often left me as an observer rather than participant. As such, the data I collected was less performative addressed towards my presence as a researcher (Bourgois 2002).[7]

The second way I was supporting my informants was connected to my volunteering. Volunteering on an almost everyday basis, I tried to produce situations of mutual benefit based on trust. Overall, I worked in six different homeless organizations – from soup kitchens and day centres to outreach tours and homeless hostels – over the two years of my fieldwork. For all of these organizations, I volunteered my time and helped people to conduct daily activities: going to the hospital, translating from German or English to French, going to the post office, talking to their immigration lawyer, filling out administrative forms, accompanying informants on excursions, listening, supporting them in discussions with social workers, giving out meals and preparing coffee. Overall, I helped the majority of my informants on a personal basis in the above ways and – admittedly in a small but direct way – supported them to move further on their desired trajectory. One such instance of ongoing volunteering highlights the relational and often long-term quality of this volunteering.

I first met Bahija on the street during a street tour I did every week as part of my regular volunteering. Of Moroccan descent, but having lived in Germany for years, she had been on the street in Paris for several month and was struggling. Her skin was bad on her face and on her arms; her eyes looked yellow, a function of a thyroid issue as she explained; she had several suitcases full of things with her. After hearing her story, I told her about the day centre – which would have just been ten minutes' walk away from the churchyard she stayed in at the time – but she never showed up. I only saw her weeks later in the same space and decided to take her to the day centre myself right then. She needed support – at least from the health side of things – as she said herself. As was common practice at the day centre, Bahija couldn't immediately see a social worker but was invited to wash her clothes, shower and obviously enjoy the warmth and coffee in the open space of the centre. After this initial success, Bahija came regularly, at least once a week. We spoke German together because she didn't really speak French. I learnt about how the social services had taken away her children in Germany and evicted her. She didn't want to stay in the mental care facility they recommended so she fled the country. Only recently, Bahija had run out of her thyroid medication but she wasn't in desperate need of the pills. She asked me to come to the hospital with her and be her interpreter. We met two days after in front of the big hospital Bahija had been in before. We didn't have a good experience at the hospital where they straight-out refused to help Bahija ('We don't specialize in glands here.'). We also tried a German pharmacist I was in touch with before without success; we called her bank in Germany to see whether there were funds left that Bahija was promised before her departure. There wasn't anything we could do that day. But Bahija was seemingly less fearful, however; she told me how it helped her to know that somebody was there for her.

While the first contact wasn't easy – Bahija was fearful of institutions in general – we managed to establish a common world of experience and shared concerns. The relationship formed as part of my volunteering activities was the basis for Bahija's trust and her engagement with me. The commonalities we formed by talking, by spending time, were able to replace the initial set of differences I described above and allow for meaningful engagements and support – while obviously not always leading to desired success.

Third, relationships like the one I formed with Bahija – someone I was not able to help at the time – compelled me to at least attempt to use the information I collected on a larger scale to improve my informants' lives. On the most removed but possibly most important level, I feel an obligation to influence the organizational contexts I observed and do what could be called homeless outreach work. This comes in two different ways: first, I am in dialogue directly with the homeless organizations I volunteered in and hold workshops with them to reflect on their practices and my observations and critique of them. In this sense, I see myself as part of the organizational feedback structure, as part of an ongoing interaction to improve the services for the homeless people they are intended for.[8] Moreover, I am interested in engaging the (political) public in a conversation about homelessness. Presenting my work and arguments in non-academic outlets – both in person and as a journalistic writer – is part of this process. While none of these outreach activities are sure to have any actual effect in the short term, I see it as one part of my responsibility as a (publicly funded) researcher to make an effort to take my learnings back into the community and the wider public.

*   *   *

While I attempted to support my informants in the above ways in their home-making activities directly, there were certain boundaries which crept up over time, boundaries of my responsibility that were ambiguous. A later encounter with Pascal illustrated this issue. Pascal had lived all his life in Germany. While he was born in the Democratic Republic of Congo, he moved to Germany as a baby. Unfortunately, his family were never able to get a German passport for him so that at the age of twenty-two, when he got in trouble with the police for not paying a public transport fee (or so he claimed) and spent four months in prison, his right to stay in Germany was threatened. The family didn't know how to keep him in Europe. His father's new wife had just arrived in France and this is where Pascal came in late 2014. They found a Congolese lawyer with a good reputation and within a couple of weeks they had figured out that they needed to 'buy' a refugee story which went as follows: Pascal got into political trouble in the DRC and spent time in prison; his mum decided it was a good idea to leave the country and sent him to France. Voilà: the story of a classic political refugee.

By the end of my fieldwork in late 2016, Pascal was still stuck in Paris, without any housing and with little progress on getting a residence permit. At the same time, he was suffering from heavy pains which frequently took us to the hospital, where I translated from French to German for him. On one of our intense days, I spent four hours waiting for an appointment with Pascal in the hospital; something he admitted he wouldn't have done by himself. The next day, we spent another six hours between the day centre, talking to his social worker, and Nanterre, where Pascal's Congolese lawyer had his office. While I was waiting for Pascal to leave his lawyer's office, I spoke with a friend on the phone, reflecting that I should perhaps invite Pascal to stay at mine for a night. This suggestion made her rather upset and nervous:

> Pascal has an important meeting close to my place tomorrow and I am afraid he will miss it and ruin his chances of getting a European passport.
>
> There has to be a line. Even though you know him and he is German, do you really think you can trust him in that way?
>
> Yes, it wouldn't really make much sense for him to take something from you but you never know.

Was I failing Pascal in this situation, letting him down as a friend? Was this a missed professional opportunity, of getting to another level of fieldwork and being part of the field in a crucial way? Perhaps what my friend saw as a 'too much' was more 'right' or 'necessary'. Researchers such as Alice Goffman or Philippe Bourgois shared their space, their homes and their personal life with their informants. Goffman (2015), who worked with disadvantaged and gang-struck black minorities in Baltimore for almost a decade, lived with her informants. Following around the 6th Street Boys, as she calls them, Goffman observed crimes, drug deals and violence first-hand on a regular basis while living as a viable part of the community of her informants. In fact, she was widely critiqued for this exact involvement (Lubet 2015). Bourgois, in his study of mainly Puerto-Rican East Harlem crack houses in the 1990s, also lived right there with his informants; he studied the crack house on his block and in terms of his methodology followed a similar pattern to Goffman. He goes as far as claiming that participant observation might be the only method of understanding – and accessing – drug dealers and users: 'Most drug users and dealers distrust representatives of mainstream society and will not reveal their intimate experiences of substance abuse or criminal enterprise to a stranger on a survey instrument … in order to collect "accurate data" … we become intimate involved with the people we study' (Bourgois 2002: 9). Can it be necessary to become an accomplice in crime as part of your research, however (Golub 2015)?

Goffman's and Bourgois's research are examples of extremely involved ethnographies which posit not only methodological but legal questions. My own home-making in the field was never legally doubtful nor as involved. The question of boundaries emerged much earlier, however. How can there be something close to 'objective research' when the fieldwork is based (partly) on intimate relationships? But then, how can I research something as intimate as home – not only in its physical but also in its emotional, longing form – *without* learning about it through intimate exchanges? Different relationships – with Pascal, my friend, my supervisor, other informants – overlapped in the process of my different home-making activities – as a researcher and as a person in Paris – and of my informants. They came with competing and, at times, hard-to-reconcile claims which could only be negotiated by continuously thinking through the consequences for everyone involved, and my own ethical stance as a researcher.

In my case, questions of dependency, freedom and desire also emerged. My friend challenged me on the phone: 'If he can't even make his appointment without you waking him up and pushing him basically on a wheelchair to the

Prefecture, do you really think he will make it?' Pascal had not asked me to let him stay over. This conversation forced me to reflect on where my sense of responsibility ended, and problems of dependency, or even force emerged. At what point was my presence altering my informants lives in ways they would not desire? Was my 'support' centred around normative narratives (marriage, job, house), that my informants did not embrace? Where were Pascal's own motivations and desires in this? If he needed so much pushing, did he actually want to go to his appointment? What kept him back?

*　*　*

Pascal didn't stay with me that night but I woke up feeling restless. I tried to call him but was not able to get through to wake him up for his appointment. Was he not able to charge his phone in the hostel? Perhaps he already was on his way and didn't have any reception? At 8:15, Pascal's social worker reached me on my mobile explaining that she was waiting at the Prefecture where his appointment was. Pascal hadn't yet shown up.

I was disappointed. Was the time everyone invested lost? What must have gone on in Pascal's head? What if they were now threatening to throw him out of France? Was Pascal just too young to understand what was going on, that this was a moment in his life in which it was absolutely crucial to stand up for himself, that it was now or never? I was angry with Pascal but I was also angry with myself. Perhaps it would have been – just for the sake of Pascal in this moment – a good decision to not let him leave until I had 'delivered' him to the appointment myself.

*　*　*

Where are the boundaries of the field, of my home in the field and of the home of my informants? What kind of boundaries are necessary – and for whose sake? When I talked to Aline, the manager of the day centre I volunteered at, about my attempts to support Pascal beyond the help provided by the team of social workers, she kept very calm but was very clear in the necessary limits of the work:

> This is not how things work here. Pascal had a chance and we were there to support him – we can't do more than we did for him or anyone else. There are frontiers to the work we are doing and they are both to protect the people and to protect us.

My supervisor back at Cambridge mirrored the day centre's manager's sentiment in a conversation we had after the encounter with Pascal:

> This was the only right decision. You are too involved and should think about coming home. You are losing the necessary distance to the field and to your informants not even thinking about the – even if minimal – possibility of physical harm. You are supposed to be a participating observer.

Aline, my supervisor and my friend, warned me of crossing the boundary between work – the work at the day centre, the work as a researcher – and non-work, between the field and my personal home (and the relationships that come with either). Both were worried about protecting me as well as my informants. As my supervisor indicated, perhaps my field was becoming too much of a personal home. The boundaries were blurring as I became emotionally involved in my informants' lives, as I started to feel responsible for them and in turn made them more dependent on me. I struggled with not being able to support my informants, who were working so hard on making their homes. I wanted to make a (better) home with them in the field.

During the incident with Pascal, my flat became the most important symbol for how to think about the boundaries of the different homes that were part of my fieldwork in France. Admitting Pascal to stay overnight would have been a serious breach of the (literally physical as well as mental) border between my own personal home and my home as a researcher. It would have collapsed my own home-making into Pascal's while I only set out to understand his better through mine. Not only spatially, but also on a level of relationships, keeping homes separate was important both for my informants and myself. In the long term, him depending on me – too much of a collaborative home-making – would have potentially had a negative effect on my informants because I was going to leave again. My home in Paris – both my private and professional one – was only temporary. My other home was in fact in the UK, which is where I was to return to, now that I had started to make too much of a home in Paris, in the field, now that my encounters had almost crossed into an area too intimate to still count easily as research.

Notes

1   Often, it would be the police – or neighbours making the authorities aware of the inhabitants – who moved my informants out of spots, such as the bus station or the parking lot and put them back in a position of uncertainty. While parts of

their elusiveness was born out of necessity – finding the best begging spot, chasing different homeless organizations, visiting friends or obtaining drugs – it was often public 'forces' moving the homeless people around.

2 There was a clear association with my general appearance and demeanour with potentially threatening 'outsiders', such as the police. Me claiming to be a researcher could have just been taken as a trope in such a context by people like Leandre.

3 As a classical argument in anthropology goes: being the outsider, being new to a situation makes you curious, it allows you to be naïve about things that they might potentially take for granted; it makes you wonder about seemingly mundane processes, strategies and behaviours.

4 Access to the groups should not be equated with access to information, however. While people usually trust people working in homeless organizations, certain kinds of information (about drug habits, violence on the street) was not shared widely. Only additional trust building up over time gave me access to these more compromising pieces of information, making my fieldwork particularly long (I spent almost two years in Paris).

5 I recognize that this withdrawal from the situation was not an option for my informants – one of the stark structural differences the absence of home entails. At the same time, such distance felt necessary for my own well-being and my ability to continue my research at times.

6 Particularly from feminist viewpoints, the flâneur methodology has been critiqued heavily (see for instance Peake and Rieker 2013): a city can in fact not be accessed (walkingly) by everyone in the same way. Access of a city – as of many other spaces – is shaped by one's subject position in terms of gender, social status and the like. While this had a major influence on my homeless informants when it came to accessing 'ordinary places' such as the train station, I was tracing an alternative, parallel city around begging spots, soup kitchens and day centres.

7 In fact, Bourgois tape-recorded many hundred hours of interviews and conversations with his crack-dealing and -taking informants; for him the access he had to this accuracy was more important – and more of a protection of his informants – than the anonymity and unobtrusiveness.

8 While it shouldn't be easier for me as a volunteer and temporary outsider to offer this feedback (rather than the homeless people themselves), the power structures I am part of make my voice often heard more easily. This asymmetry is something I am trying to turn to my interlocutors' advantage in this way.

8

A threshold space: Connecting a home in the city with the city

Max Ott

Architecture is moving

By the end of October, it has become cold and windy in Berlin. I have left behind a narrow road, which leads from Köpenicker Straße to the River Spree and thereby passes between two construction sites, an old factory complex from the nineteenth century and three recently completed residential buildings of a housing cooperative. I turn left and take a short walk directly along the river, before I have to move around a low concrete bunker. Next to the bunker there is a small community garden, and behind this garden a pathway runs parallel to the river. On one side it is limited by a metal fence edging a huge piece of overgrown fallow land and the impressive ruin of a former ice factory made of red brick. On the other side and towards the river the pathway is lined with tents. These tents are enclosed by small flower beds and simple rows of cobblestones – indicating tiny front yards and creating a threshold between the pathway and the external skin of the tents, which, for the most part, look like North American teepees. Just a stone's throw away from the river, Frank is waiting under a plastic sheet. Stretched between wooden posts, the sheet protects a table, some preowned garden chairs and two benches from rain and provides shade on sunny days. As I approach Frank, I observe him stepping from one foot to the other. Under his leather jacket he is wearing a turtleneck and an additional sweater and his hands are in fingerless wool gloves.[1]

In 2011, the Berlin Senate Department for Urban Development declared the neighbourhood of Nördliche Luisenstadt an area of urban renewal. Since then, a local newspaper periodically covered the urban planning measures in this part of the city district of Mitte, as well as the people who live there. The newspaper does not judge the different ways of dwelling in the neighbourhood on the basis of any ideal-typical understanding of housing. The editors rather seem to be intrigued by the social and spatial heterogeneity of an area that has been a part of East Berlin's very periphery until the fall of the Berlin Wall in 1989. In April 2015, the newspaper dedicated a short article to Frank's home, calling the squatted state-owned property a 'small tent village' (Steglich 2015).

In the newspaper's terminology, the place where Frank and I meet would be the village centre, where its residents make use of those built structures that express the meaning of a collective space. Next to the sheltered place with benches and chairs, there is a square stage, which is used for film screenings and concerts during summer, and a small pavilion with a shared kitchen. While Frank and I are standing in front of the pavilion, I realize that its outer shell is still under construction, although the kitchen has already been put in operation. 'Who knows?' Frank shrugs. I just ask him when the construction works would be finished and watch Oscar, another occupant, as he attaches small pieces of wood to a façade consisting of waste timber and old recycled windows. 'Maybe never. Maybe we will come up with new ideas of how to improve this building again and again.' Everyone here can continue to shape this collaborative building at any time, Frank adds. 'We are all planners, architects and designers all at once. You just have to be creative."

It might relate to the fact that I have worked in architectural practices for a few years, but this statement attracts my attention. If we take Frank's words seriously, we can assume the occupants of the squatted property to be people who possess and apply both design and crafting skills; they are able to conceptualize their home and to translate a concept into three-dimensional structures. Furthermore, the self-description of being 'planners, architects and designers all at once' transforms a delicate relationship of mutual dependency: how often did we (as architects) wish for more autonomy, when our clients challenged our spatial design proposals? And how often might those clients in reverse have cursed their reliance on professionals, who get paid to make their needs and wishes become reality? Here, on the Spree riverbank, such a relationship seems to be suspended. Instead, Frank asserts a sort of hybrid subjectivity, which might favour a more self-determined way of creating a home. This also implies the possibility to arrange space and time in a specific way: Once you are your own client, the question of how long collective design processes should take may be negotiated differently. Indeed, it may also be kept open.

'Everything is temporary', Frank says, as we sit down on a bench beside the river. Then he adds, laughingly: 'And so are we.' Since he arrived three years

ago, the whole area has changed completely, Frank explains. Only two or three
of the first teepees still exist, whereas everything else has been 'relocated (and)
rearranged' repeatedly. The result is an ever-changing spatial appearance of
the squatted property, something I could experience myself over the course
of one year of fieldwork. It is based not only on constant adaptions, but also
on the replacement of whole components of this settlement: whenever an
occupant leaves the small community of roughly twenty people, his or her tent
is subsequently torn down and when a new person joins the group, a new one
has to be built. 'It just happened that way', Frank tells me, 'and that's good.' Thus,
everyone has 'his own tent', and at the same time 'every tent looks different'.
Eventually, it was also the naming of the informal settlement that evolved from
this practice of building, demolishing and rebuilding. Frank tells me that after
the occupants had experimented with different construction methods for a
while, more and more tents resembled the architecture of teepees. Since then,
the occupants call their home TeePee-Land.

Frank and I have spent several hours outdoors, when we part. It is already dark
and I pass by the brightly illuminated windows of the cooperative's buildings with
mixed feelings. On the one hand, I am impressed by what Frank showed me and
by what he spoke about. It inspires me to reflect on the processual character of
dwelling – when people get together, appropriate a place, and gradually develop
ideas of its qualities as a shared home; when they start to translate those ideas into
a built structure, which they experience as a dynamic arrangement, produced
but also changeable by their creative actions. Didn't I just get a good impression
of this reciprocity between materiality and sociality that makes TeePee-Land a
'moving project' (Latour and Yaneva 2008: 80)? Such qualities confront me with
the conditions of dwelling within 'my own four walls' and the limitations these
walls entail. The old residential block where I live appears to me as rather 'a
static object' (Latour and Yaneva 2008) and the possibilities for modifications
are constrained. The complex, located in an inner-city district from the late
nineteenth century in Munich, is managed top down and not by its occupants;
the house regulations forbid activities like laying out flower beds in the joint
courtyard or any bigger self-initiated reconfiguration within the apartments. I
also wonder how much the physical characteristics of my apartment on the third
floor may contribute to this notion of immobility. Now and then, I rearrange
my furniture or paint a wall, but a massive wall is not easily broken through,
let alone moved. Maybe not only the house regulations prevent me from setting
things into motion here. The place where I live is lacking something that is at
the core of TeePee-Land: the ephemeral and bricolage character of architectural

structures made of light materials that are easy to change and to redesign. Or the close proximity between private interior and collectively appropriated exterior spaces, separated from each other only by a few centimetres of sheets.

Perhaps it is due to the cold and the contrast between the illuminated residential buildings and the increasing darkness on the squatted property – but on my way home, other thoughts cross my mind as well. Is it not true that Frank's statement 'You just have to be creative' gets another meaning, once it is getting dark or when it starts to rain heavily? When the warm season ends and the days are getting cooler? Or whenever TeePee-Land's occupants need fresh water? As much as I have linked his phrase to the idea of a self-determined design in the first place, I look at it differently when considering questions of daily reproduction on a property without running water and electricity. Here, creativity does not just appear as a magic potion, which gives people the power to materialize their desires. Where it is not possible to switch on the heating quickly or to call a craftsman, but where *to dwell* means to think about everyday things and to find solutions, creativity also becomes an imperative. You just *have* to be creative – isn't this actually an interesting play on words?

Depending on the perspective we choose, the notion of creativity thus gains an ambivalent meaning: we might see it as an individual disposition that allows someone to give shape to his or her own ideas of dwelling. But we can also approach creativity as subject to the external conditions upon which someone has to dwell. And it strikes me that the same seems to apply to 'temporality'. The architecture of tents made from recycled waste wood, collected branches and sheets, differs not just in terms of physical durability from the residential buildings in the neighbourhood. Besides this visible aspect, they both have a completely disparate legal basis. While their neighbours may refer to rental contracts or even ownership titles, the squatters' right to dwell on an abandoned state-owned property is not anchored in any legally binding agreement. It is solely depending on the goodwill of Berlin's municipality. Seen from this angle, TeePee-Land is not only a 'moving project' because it is kept moving by its residents' specific ways to shape space. It is also subject to external influences, which are able to put an end to such a process by forcing TeePee-Land's occupants to move on. 'Everything is temporary', Frank says. 'And so are we.'

In the light of such reflections, I suggest we are well advised to see the physical materialization of ideas of dwelling not as a sole expression of creative freedom, detachable from existing power relations. This would be superficial. But we need to address the socio-material complexity of 'self-other relations' (Moore 2011: 10–16) in a wider sense and combine it with an understanding of the physical structure of space as an element of ethnographic experience, which we should link to the observations from encounters with our interlocutors. Therefore, as soon as we take into considerations the old industrial ruins, the fallow land as well as the many new buildings and construction sites surrounding TeePee-Land, the squatted property is no longer a 'small tent village'. It is one component of the ongoing transformation of a former industrial neighbourhood, which later became no-man's-land within the GDR border strip, and has by now turned into a central area of a city under enormous pressure of growth. Such pressure increases the competition for spaces still open to further development and it threatens especially those who do not own the land on which they dwell. Here, the appropriation of a property cannot be justified by reference to the legal system of property ownership. Other modes of legitimizing its use are required. 'It's better to have your neighbour as a friend than as an enemy', Frank explained to me, while we were talking about the temporary status and open future of TeePee-Land. We should ask about the effects of this conflictual situation on the practice of making a home in TeePee-Land, as well as the necessity for its occupants to find allies. These questions bring me back to the beginning and the low concrete bunker I passed by on my way to meet with Frank.

Creating thresholds

When I first came to Berlin in summer 2015 to do fieldwork on collaborative architecture, it wasn't my aim to study a squatted property. I was interested in the adjoining cooperative housing project. Back then, with my observations of TeePee-Land still to come, I tended to reduce the notion of making a home to the process of building houses – conventional houses, one could say, with walls, doors and windows, several floors and rooms, a staircase and a roof. As an architect, I had spent countless hours on drawing floor plans or detailing multi-layered façades for such buildings. I was trained in focusing on their physical aspects but also curious about the social dimension of housing, especially in projects that were designed in participatory processes by architects and future residents and draw on ideas of collectively living together. One year before I started fieldwork, I had come across the three cooperative buildings on the Spree riverbank in an architectural magazine. A drawing displayed their spatial context, and above the bunker, located on the cooperative's property, the word 'boathouse' was written. Nonetheless, I paid attention mostly to the pictures of three huge shared apartments, each providing space for more than twenty members of the cooperative. I live together with three flatmates, but apartments for such large groups seemed exceptional to me, compared to an average of new residential construction that focuses on singles, couples or families with two children. I really wanted to see one of these apartments from the inside to learn about how its occupants organized their cohabitation. But when I was actually standing in front of the buildings, I became painfully aware that I had never really thought about how to put this wish into operation. I didn't know anyone who could have given me access to the houses. And I didn't dare to ring the doorbell, as I didn't expect any resident to invite a stranger to enter his or her most private rooms. I walked around between the buildings for a while. On ground floor level, each building has one large room, generously glazed and four and a half meters high. The cooperative calls them option spaces (*Optionsräume*) – they are open for changing uses, such as spontaneous meetings of larger groups for lunch and dinner, joint workshops or public events. Besides the entrance of one of the option spaces someone had put a poster. It announced the 'innovators club', a monthly meeting in the boathouse concerned with 'innovative concepts for a good neighbourhood'.

One week later, I enter the building for the first time; steps lead me downward and I push aside a heavy steel door. The door gives access to a low room, open to the river and extending about half a meter onto the water surface. A U-shaped platform encompasses a small pier and the long sides of the platform stretch out towards ceiling-high sliding windows. Their thin steel frames strengthen the impression that the planks covering the floor and the water surface are touching each other. This visual effect appears somewhat ironic considering the original function of the boathouse. It was never meant to create connections, but to stabilize divisions; from here, the National People's Army of the GDR sent patrol boats to secure the border territory between East and West Berlin. After the reunification of Berlin and the successive destruction of the border fortifications, the boathouse had lost its purpose. For years it was left untouched, until in 2004 the fallow property, which later became the cooperative's building site, was turned into a public beach bar and the boathouse became a dance club. This informal appropriation lasted seven years and left a visible trace on an inner wall of the boathouse: 'We have to take, what we need' is written on the wall in large black letters.

It is Robert who has drawn my attention to the history of the inconspicuous building on the Spree riverbank. I just started to feel uncertain about what to do next, as he came up to me, asked me who I was, what I did, and if I had already heard about this place. Now, we are standing at a window in the evening sun. Behind us, there is a large table with some sheets of paper, a couple of coloured markers and a note that invites everyone to write down ideas about 're- and upcycling' of objects found at the riverbank. Robert is a member of the cooperative and started the innovators club with two goals in mind: on the one hand he believes that a lot of people with 'ideas of improving things' live near the river. In his opinion it would be a pity, if 'we just keep talking, instead of trying to do something together'. On the other hand, Robert speaks of the boathouse as an 'ideal location' not only for the cooperative's members to come together. Instead, the innovators club could also provide an opportunity for old and new neighbours in the area to get to know each other.

While Robert is talking to me, two people join our conversation. I shake hands with Martin, an architect, who lives in a shared apartment and runs a network agency on the ground floor focused on improving the preconditions of collaborative housing projects. Then, Robert introduces me to Frank: 'He lives right next to us in TeePee-Land. Have you already been there?' Martin and Frank start talking about the dynamics of spatial change along the River Spree, and Frank mentions the planning of a pathway and the importance of developing a strong proposal. As I ask what Frank was referring to, Martin explains that the city of Berlin has been intending for many years to create a public riverside pathway for pedestrians and cyclists on a longer section of the southern riverbank. It now looks like this plan will be realized with the support of public funds, and before a mandatory architectural competition can be organized a participatory workshop shall take place, where the residents of the concerned area may introduce their own ideas. The public pathway will lead through both the cooperative's land and the squat. Since the squatters fear their replacement and the sale of the rest of the property to a private real estate investor, who has already bought the adjoining fallow land, members of the cooperative and occupants of TeePee-Land have decided to promote their idea of what Martin calls a 'pathway through history and culture'. In Frank's view, this includes a design informing everyone about the specific history of the area – a history of creative and bottom-up ways of appropriating abandoned spaces for which the boathouse is just one example among many. However, the riverbanks should not be perceived as a 'museum' but as a 'place that is alive', Frank elaborates and gives some examples: he mentions public film screenings and concerts in TeePee-Land, the communal garden next to the boathouse, taken care of by members of the cooperative and TeePee-Land, and a regular stand-up comedy event in the boathouse, organized by his fellow occupant Oscar. 'We hope that we can convince the city administration of our ideas', Martin says.

The intentions of Berlin's urban planning administration do not only affect a discussion between neighbours, who come together in a boathouse. They also have a visible impact on how TeePee-Land's residents design their home. Although the official plans show quite plainly the temporary and fragile status of the squatted property, the complexity and length of planning as an institutionalized process of decision-making also offers them opportunities to a creative appropriation. While the administrative staff was still organizing the procedure of finding ideas for the design of a riverside pathway, Oscar started to tackle this issue in summer 2015 and began to redesign the section of the unpaved pathway that runs through TeePee-Land. He used regular cobblestones to create a solid surface, which resembles the result of a professional road construction work. Oscar refers to the city's yet unredeemed project of improving the public accessibility of the Spree riverbank: 'As far as I know, Berlin has been wanting to create a riverside pathway in this area since 1904. And yet not much has happened.' He is well aware that the squatted property is 'public land' and everyone has the right to cross it. Now, TeePee-Land's residents are paving this pathway themselves and for free, Oscar explains and describes this activity as a gift to the city, which otherwise would be compelled to spend tax money. Then he exhibits the expertise of a planning professional: 'By the way, this path is two meters wide, according to the legal standards.' Frank, in turn, relates the new design of TeePee-Land's pathway to his broader understanding of the accessibility of the squatted property: 'We are open to the public 24 hours a day', he says. 'This is our way of showing that we have nothing to hide and that anyone who passes through will be able to pass through safely and will not be harassed.' Everyone should feel welcome in TeePee-Land, regardless of his or her origin, appearance or political belief. Oscar is convinced that this stands in contrast to many other squats he has already experienced: 'If you are not dressed like a communist, you may never belong there.'

Notions of home often include various dimensions of space, sociality and time. When people say: 'My home is my castle' they might refer to a building or a flat that both protects individuals from the outside world and provides a sense of empowerment and independence. But they might also consider themselves as dwelling in broader and mutual social networks and spatial scales, while speaking of 'my neighbourhood' or 'my hometown'. I believe a sense of being at home is influenced by and can change with experiences of these different dimensions as potentially related, and the possibilities to shape them in that sense. For instance, as much as I like the relative anonymity of living in a large inner-city residential complex, I also appreciate the opportunity to chat with my neighbours, to empty their letterbox and to know they will water my flowers in exchange. I learned that the possibility of creating relations is particularly important in TeePee-Land, where Frank addressed the relevance of having 'your neighbour as a friend' against the background of the informal settlement's fragile status. One such neighbour is a housing cooperative, which understands itself as an 'alternative statement' to the valorizing of properties on the Spree riverbanks, and has members like Robert or Martin, who stand up for experimental practices of producing urban space. Such thinking comes with a kind of recognition that allows TeePee-Land's occupants to extend their radius of action in varied ways. On the one hand it gives them access to spaces of significance for everyday reproduction: they get timber and firewood from a wood workshop in one of the cooperative's option spaces and they are invited to fill up their water cans and recharge their electronic devices in another option space close to the boathouse. On the other hand, it is exactly this boathouse where Frank and Oscar can move beyond such basic activities. The building provides the possibility to host a public stand-up comedy, a 'cultural event' as Frank calls it, where TeePee-Land creates itself a 'place that is alive'. And it produces a threshold in a broader sense, because here and together with others, Frank discusses the history of the Spree riverbanks, tries to shape its present, and imagines its best possible future. One example for such an imagined possible future is associated with the project of a public riverside pathway. Even if paving a pathway might seem like a small act, it is nonetheless of great importance: Oscar pointed out that TeePee-Land's property is indeed public land and by adding a pavement surface its occupants actively increased its practical value. They produce a tactile demonstration of their willingness to take care of a once-abandoned property, to connect it with the city, and to welcome everyone who enters the place where they dwell. This finds a positive response also from those who have the legal power to determine the future of the squatted property: Until today, the district government of Mitte has waived the right to evict its occupants and instead, in Frank's words, 'silently agrees' to tolerate TeePee-Land at least until a plan for a new riverside pathway will be realized.

When a temporary home is a public space

In the previous sections, I suggested an understanding of making a home that regards both people's creative means to translate ideas of dwelling into physical space, as well as their broader socio-spatial context not as separated fields of action – they always intersect, and they may challenge each other. As a consequence, rather than to focus on the distinction between home as an alienated or unalienated domain we should think about the tension between those domains and the effects it has. My depictions of the spatial practices of dwelling on the Spree riverbank aim to contribute to this consideration: As much as TeePee-Land's occupants may create temporary structures in accordance to an ideal of a self-determined way of dwelling that values constant renewals, adaption and replacements, it is in reverse the temporary status of a squatted property within an area of transformation that questions their home and increases the pressure to legitimize it. And then again this pressure influences specific creative actions, which might signify – and here I quote from the introduction of this volume – a 'degree of creative alienation'. Such tensions have an important effect, which also produces frictions: If you live on the squatted property, your temporary right to stay rests on your will to accept that it is actually a public space and to act accordingly. A lot depends on your capability of incorporating this dimension and its implications into your notion of home and to understand it as part of your 'ethics of dwelling' (Zigon 2014), as my last observation shall illustrate.

'I had a boringly ordinary life: average consumer, eight-hour day, paying the rent, paying off the car. And in the end of the month: broke. … I could no longer be bothered. So, I sold everything and packed my bags.' In 1983 Frank left Luxembourg and since then he was 'always on the move'. Roughly three decades later, he found TeePee-Land by chance: during a party on the roof of the former ice factory, he spotted the place and met some squatters and then decided to join them for a while. When I asked him in October 2015 if TeePee-Land was now a place where he could imagine he could stay, Frank hesitated for a moment before he answered: 'I would say yes. As long as everything here is progressing. … If it stopped to develop further, I would look for something else again.'

A good six months after entering the boathouse for the first time, I visited the innovators club again. Five people were sitting at a table, playing a board game, and I spotted Robert and Oscar, who were standing together at an improvised bar counter. Frank was not present. Oscar was talking with Robert about the riverside pathway and told him that he was sceptical about the prospects of their joint proposals. There was no 'real participation', he said, where everything could be discussed and questioned. To him, it seemed that the administrative departments had already decided not to listen to the occupants' ideas. As I asked about Frank, Oscar told me that he had left TeePee-Land about one month ago and did not plan to return. 'He lost faith', was Oscar's laconic answer to my question about Frank's reasons. At first, I was surprised because I did not think about the person who had told me that he was 'always on the move' but about someone who had spoken enthusiastically of his idea to build a large teepee to host guests in TeePee-Land next year. But then, Oscar described for at least fifteen minutes some recent conflicts and disagreements between the occupants; he talked about who was selfish or not, who was responsible for what and who contributed how much to the design and the networking of the informal settlement. 'Are you losing faith, too?' I asked Oscar and he answered: 'Maybe I am. Otherwise you would not have the chance to hear me expressing my thoughts on our conflicts so openly towards you.'

Half an hour later, Oscar and I are standing at the entrance door to the boathouse, smoking a cigarette. He tells me that many residents in TeePee-Land sooner or later complain about the fact that the squatted property is completely accessible for everyone and at any time. Some occupants have left TeePee-Land because they couldn't bear this situation, others have left because they were annoyed by the repeated quarrels resulting from it, and Oscar mentions that he himself might soon become one of the latter. If someone wanted to live in TeePee-Land, it is in Oscar's view not enough that he or she only *accepts* its public character: 'You have to want it like that', he says. 'It is something you chose, when you decided to join the squat.' Oscar thinks of TeePee-Land as a conscious experiment for a really open community, something that had by now become nearly impossible anywhere other than in Berlin: 'Do you know a place, where you can still live like this in the middle of the city?' he asks. But instead many squatters would argue that not everyone should be allowed to enter, because this was their own home. Then Oscar adds something – it now occurs to me sometimes when I am entering my apartment and makes me think about this action as a short moment in which I am free to create a connection or to reproduce a boundary: 'Home', Oscar says. 'That word illustrates the problem. It sounds to me like something you can lock with a key. But this is not the case here.'

Note

1 The empirical material used in this article was collected through participant observation and semi-structured interviews. In the article, I quote statements made during visits in TeePee-Land (13 September 2015, and 28 October 2015) and my participation in the innovators club in the boathouse of the housing cooperative 'Spreefeld' (3 September 2015, and March 2016). I use pseudonyms to ensure the anonymity of the persons quoted.

9

Making a home on a volcano

Adam Bobbette

I have begun writing this reflection about home-making in a *gubuk*, a simple Javanese wooden structure without walls, wood floor platform, and red clay tile roof. It is most commonly built in rice fields so that farmers can find some respite from the sun or rain. This *gubuk*, however, is not in a rice field but a small patch of forest adjacent to fields of chilies, rice, tomatoes and a small sand mine. Due east is the mouth of Mount Merapi, a volcano that every decade or so ejects boiling hot clouds that descend through here and onwards into the lowlands. If not exploding with superheated clouds, landslides of boulders and hot mud fall and earthquakes make the entire mountain tremble. Otherwise it sits quietly and releases white vapours from its jagged stone mouth. Sometimes people say that the crater looks like hands held together in prayer.

This evening, though, from the *gubuk* there is no sign of the crater; I am instead surrounded by, or better yet submerged in, the sounds of *sonten*, that crepuscular time of day when the light transitions between saturated aquamarine blue, orange and peach, to black; the mosques in the villages begin their call to prayer and the polyphony of insects and field animals rises to a roar. There is a structure to this evening chorus: insects unheard throughout the day begin to sing then soon give way to the rise of a different crescendo of drones, clicks and screeches. I haven't yet learned the names for the insects that create these songs, just as I'm only now learning the names for each of the trees and plants in this 1,000-square-meter piece of forest. So I listen, watch the night fall, take notes, and wait until some other time when a friend is nearby and I can ask them to teach me their names.

This *gubuk* was built two weeks ago. It was disassembled from a field and carried here by my friend Ade and five of his friends. It is on loan for some undefined period of time until we decide to return it. He therefore only paid for a few replacement tiles for the roof. I arrived the week after it was built from

Yogyakarta where I usually rent a room in an old colonial house far too expensive for many Indonesians but affordable on my foreign postdoctoral salary. On this two-month-long stay, I have been spending weekends on the volcano, in the forest, preparing the land with Ade to make a home, and the *gubuk* is the first structure built so that I had a place to sleep.

The day after the first night in the *gubuk*, Ade and I began to clear trees with an *arit*, a sickle with which you strike downwards at the trunk until the weight of the tree cracks at the wound and it topples over. Most trees were no thicker than a leg and not much more than four years old. The majority of what we cut down were andra trees, from *Calliandra calothyrsus*, a species native to South America which was imported when a few Dutch colonial foresters brought two seed samples to Java from Guatemala in 1936 (Powell 1997). They hoped to use it as a shade tree on the expansive coffee plantations, that, along with tobacco and tea, spread across Java and fuelled the Dutch colonial economy. It transpired that the tree was highly aggressive in disturbed sites and rapidly colonized areas exposed to volcanic eruptions, landslides, earthquakes and mining. They grew faster and in greater number than other species and shaded them out. Hence their presence on this piece of land with the *gubuk*, because it too is disturbed.

Ade bought the land after he returned from operating heavy machinery in Bornean plantations. Some of the world's largest plantations are there and they provide the fruits that are crushed and processed into our cooking oils, shampoo, skin cream, chocolate, soap, make-up and processed food. I have flown over them before and they stretch to the horizon: sublime monoculture grids in monuments to modernist consumption. Martin Heidegger, in the 1950s, described the Western conception of resources as the transformation of nature into a 'standing reserve', meaning the transformation of the world into a thing that is there for our use and because of which it can have no other meaning (1977). This is the epistemology of what is described as extractivism (de la Cadena and Blaser 2017): a plantation is a radical reduction and simplification of what a palm tree can be and do, it can produce oil, and any of its other capacities and relationships are not as significant as this.

Ade, like many young rural Javanese men, left home to work on one of these plantations. He acquired a licence to operate heavy machinery and worked for a company levelling land at a gargantuan scale for the creation of a new plantation. It was his introduction to the exhilarating and bewildering scale of environmental transformation for the sake of human production and consumption, and a direct experience of what modernization meant. Ade described to me how overwhelming it was to see nature transformed at such a scale by humans. He didn't last long, after he'd made enough money to become flush – by village standards – he returned 'home to Merapi'[1] as he put it, to buy land and apply his expertise in land-moving to the rehabilitation of disturbed sites. One of those pieces of land was the land with the *gubuk* now on it – where I am writing this.

In the early 2000s, the land had been a mining site for stones and sand used in local construction. Houses in the area are often finished with stones from the volcano and the volcanic sand is mixed with concrete into their walls. The top half-meter of the land had been pushed aside to expose the larger more valuable stones beneath and, because of this, the land steps down from one border to the next. It was mined because the value of the stones far exceeded the value of rice, chilies, tobacco or other vegetables grown on these cold and wet upper slopes. It is important to keep in mind too that all of this material *is* the volcano. At 6 kilometres from the caldera we are at an altitude of roughly 2,000 meters above sea level and all of the stones and sand comprising this land has been deposited, blown, rolled or thrown down from the mouth of the volcano. The larger boulders, the size of basketballs or larger, traversed those 6 kilometres in waves of mud that swept down and flattened forests and filled the deep river beds that in some spots sink as low as 50 meters deep. Some of that material is from the cataclysmic eruption in 2010 when hundreds of thousands of people became refugees for three months. Otherwise, material can also be from the eruption in 1930 which flattened and killed most of the people in the village 1 kilometre away. It was never rebuilt, though elderly people have told me that they sometimes see it in the middle of the night, a ghost village, still operating, with women cooking and cows wandering the streets. If the mined material was not from those two eruptions, it could have been from the continuous eruptions between 1902 and 1913 or from a number of eruptions between 1915 and 2008 (Kusumadinata 1979; Voight 2000).

Follow the narrow concrete canal at the edge of the property as it ascends through rice paddies. Cross a hillock of chest-high grass, jump the canal, follow another. Walk along the narrow concrete edge because it is easier than struggling through the tangle of shrubs and young andra trees. The water rushing through the canal is coming from the river canyon, and flows down to the villages where it is used for washing. As you approach the edge of the canyon, the sounds of crushing and scraping intensify. The clinking of stones falling into the flatbeds of trucks and the revving of their engines fills the vast space of the river bed. At a clearing of trees the view opens onto large front-end loaders digging away at the giant river; a few of them are placed at the canyon walls that tower above them. An army of empty trucks descend into the river then ascend full of sand and stones, making their way down the potholed roads, twisting down the volcano, through villages, until they shift north, headed for the ports in Semarang and Surabaya where they load their goods onto freighters. They carry the material to Singapore, mainland China, Bali or Jakarta, where the material becomes cement in condominium walls or 'land' below luxury apartments (Bobbette 2018). On this long journey, money passes through the hands of corrupt local officials, police with greasy palms, poorly paid local politicians looking to pay their children's school fees, farmers looking for fast money, and itinerant workers, like Ade once was, who circle throughout the Indonesian archipelago hustling for work they can't find in their own fields and towns. Much of this chain is held together by illegal means. In 2015, I helped Ade document illegal mining so he could make a case to the local authorities – they shut them down a few months later. In 2016, looking from this same clearing, there were no machines in the valley. But 'like a boxer who you punch in the face and he keeps getting back up', was how Ade described the mining. The police sweep in, arrest a few people, call in the press to make a spectacle of it, and a few months later the trucks and machines come back.

Not only does the mining support this political ecology of local corruption and regional geopolitics and material flows, it is also perilously shortsighted. Miners see the volcano as a resource to be extracted, a standing reserve, and this produces disasters. The river valleys on the volcano do not just transport the massive amounts of materials that spew from the mouth – sand, ash and stones – they mitigate its impact. In previous years, the local government had issued mining licences under the auspices of riverbank maintenance. The logic was that the removal of high-cash-value 'debris' would be good for the flow of the river. However, in the next eruption, the wider and cleaner banks of the river will allow more material to flow further and faster, endangering distant villages with runaway floods of hot mud. An undisturbed volcanic river bed on Merapi is full of young and old tree species like andras but also banana, bamboo, teak, pines, giant ferns, sago, hibiscus, mindi, and albizia, in a pattern of succession, a term which is used by ecologists to describe the process of landscape growth from the first grasses to the maturation of large trees. The greater the density of this material, the more resistance it creates for the avalanches of mud or the swooping of hot clouds by slowing down its movement. The denser it is, the better the work it does to protect lowlanders. A denuded river valley with straight, clean walls is like a pipe; it accelerates material towards the columns that hold up the bridges that cross the rivers. These bridges support a relentless daily load of traffic from nearby cities; in 2010, concrete bridge pillars 15 kilometres away from the volcano were torn apart like soggy paper.

It is because of this tension between an extractivism that transforms nature into a passive object for human use and the volcano as an active, unpredictable, and restless agent that I will sleep in the *gubuk* tonight. This tension between transforming the volcano into a commodity by impoverished and often precarious workers, the local and international economy of owners, builders, and others that support them, and the struggle against mining by activists like Ade, is one way that this volcano is made into a home, fought for and defended against. It is a struggle over the meaning of what the volcano is; in other words, it's ontology. But at the same time, the volcano too is an active material agent in itself as it shakes, erupts, and erodes. The volcano is the subject of human projects, ideas and values, but it is also beyond them and irreducible to them. It has an agency and capacity to act that exceeds what humans think or want of it. Because of these tensions I have decided to join Ade and others who make their home here and sleep in this *gubuk* tonight as the cicadas scream like buzz saws and strange, sometimes terrifying, noises pierce the darkness. I recognize these tensions; they are in certain ways familiar. The logic of extractivism on the volcano has also built the cities I grew up in and have called home. It has caused the vast environmental transformations that I have witnessed through my lifetime and has caused effects to reverberate throughout my culture and the culture of those living on the volcano as it radically transforms nature and has to negotiate and make sense of new environments.

I have come to understand this small area of land on the volcano as an intersection of concepts and materials, a meeting point or zone of encounter between values, ideas and material forces that are both caught up in those concepts and values and exceed them. This includes my own concepts and the histories of their formations that I bring to the place and have to negotiate as they encounter, are transformed by, and transform others, like Ade, in the process of making a home here. It also means understanding the partiality and contingency of our concepts of places and home as they encounter and negotiate others, confront and are transformed by others and the more-than-human world's capacity to transform how humans think. This is to occupy the fraught process of making a home with others, being changed by them, and changing our neighbours, in turn.

Creeping to the edge

This indeed is what a home is. More than a built structure, or an architecture, it is an assemblage of parts. These parts are often heterogeneous fragments – of values, ideas, wills and matter – that don't always fit smoothly together. Making a home on the volcano meant being in the centre of this assemblage and its contradictory forces. I came to understand that making a home there meant negotiating ideas about nature and spirituality, but also the volatile agency of the volcano.

I first met Ade in 2015 when I was embarking on my fieldwork for my PhD through a contact in the city of Yogyakarta. I was invited to Ade's village, Keningar, to meet Sukmadi, because he mediated between people in the village and spirits in the volcano. Ade was one of the first people I met in addition to Sukmadi when I was trying to understand what it meant to live so close to the peak of a volcano. I came to understand that in Ade's village there were people who felt that living with such an unpredictable force required negotiating with the spirits and ghosts who lived inside the volcano and along its flanks. For Sukmadi, the volcano wasn't a resource but a living being that demanded of humans that they pay attention to it, give it offerings and communicate with it. The volcano had ideas of its own and acted on them. When it erupted it was speaking with the people who lived there, and as I came to understand from Sukmadi, when the volcano shuddered or released a landslide through the canyons it was because humans were exploiting it. To live with the volcano meant undertaking an ongoing negotiation with a living being that, as much as humans interpreted it, was considering and reflecting on human action itself. When people died they went to the volcano, not only to its interior but they hid in its trees, stones and rivers. For some, too, the inside of the volcano was a Keraton, an Islamic sultanate that mirrored the sultanates that used to rule Java. The volcano had a king, retinue, soldiers and a market. It was a social being with a social structure and eruptions were not the effect of plate tectonics but the action of the sultanate going to war, expressing disdain with human politics and corruption, or sometimes just having a party. Making a home with a volcano meant understanding how its events, its liveliness, was a process of social commentary.

Making a home with a living volcano required encountering and negotiating yet another cosmos, the one from the lowland state scientific volcano observatory which was charged with protecting and ordering the evacuations of people from Ade's village and other villages at similar altitudes. Both scientists and shamans on the volcano were trying, and continue to try, to make a home on Mount Merapi, along with more than one million other people trying to live there. This, it seemed to me, could have a lot to teach us about what it meant to live with a nature that is unpredictable, the kind of nature that in the age of climate change and the Anthropocene is increasingly becoming the norm for the rest of the world.

But what was important was that people didn't agree about what they were on. They had very different notions of where they lived and their different notions created different ways of making a home in different cosmos. The scientists in the observatory had a modernist understanding of the volcano. According to them, it was the product of plate tectonic activity in the Indian Ocean about 500 kilometres away to the south where the Australian plate was crashing into and subducting below the Indian plate at about 10 cm a year. As the Australian plate plummets below the other it melts under the intense pressure and increasing heat as it descends into the lithosphere. The rocks liquefy and float back up to the surface; along the way they meet resistance until it turns into the explosive mix that creates volcanoes. This narrative only became orthodox in the 1960s in global geology and according to this story Java, and the Indonesian archipelago, is some of the youngest land on our lithosphere. This is why there is so much volcanic activity in the region – the earth is building itself anew here.

For Ade and Sukmadi, making a home on the volcano meant negotiating these different cosmos. They do not occupy just one single cosmos but are in-between them, between many different volcanoes at once: the volcano that is the sultanate and full of ghosts, the volcano that is the effect of plate tectonics, the volcano that is a resource, the volcano that is rumbling, and the volcano that deserves protection. They are also in a home that is between the mouth of the volcano and the lowland cities, where modernist state scientists work in their laboratories and the government exerts its influence. To make a home in Keningar, in the simple sense of staying put, required leveraging of tensions between these cosmos against one another. Holding one's ground here, as I came to understand, demands a creative process of strategic negotiation with these multiple cosmos, of leveraging a living volcano against its transformation into a resource or an effect of plate tectonics.

I was invited to a ritual dinner by Sukmadi, a *selamatan*, a common event held for big or small events ranging from a circumcision to moving into a new house. I spent the evening in the kitchen with Sukmadi and his wife, among pots of curried chicken, bags of fruits and vegetables, and platters of intricately cut and wildly coloured deserts. One of the mainstays of a *selamatan* is the *tumpeng*, a serving of rice shaped in the form of a volcano. Everyone would eat a portion of the rice volcano as a collective communion, eating the rice volcano made of rice grown on the slopes of the volcano, transforming the outside into the inside, performing the link between the sustenance of the body and the land that produced it.

When everything had been prepared we moved the food into a black pickup truck and, with a dozen others, drove along the potholed road into the forest before turning and descending down into the canyon. We stopped in the middle of a concrete bridge where the most intense sand mining was taking place. It was evening and many of the miners had returned home but a few large machines were still gnawing at the banks and men were hauling shovels full of dirt into trucks. We laid a mat in the centre of the bridge, closing it off to oncoming traffic while people descended onto the bridge with bamboo torches and more food. As darkness fell, the moon lit the stream of water coursing through the canyon. More food had been piled into the centre of the mat, enough to feed a banquet, and Sukmadi said a prayer in high Javanese to the spirits living in the river and the volcano asking for their support in preventing the mining. Off to one side of the bridge, a small group of men had lit incense and said their own prayers. They left a miniature figurine in a package of clove cigarettes, a few fruits and scattered rice and rose petals around it. Back in the centre of the bridge, everyone had begun to eat, first taking a piece of the rice volcano, then bits of chicken, fruit, steamed vegetables and crackers. Elderly women wearing *kain*, a kind of traditional female sarong, or still in their work clothes of track pants, T-shirts and rubber boots, shared with men in sarongs smoking unfiltered clove cigarettes in one hand and nibbling at dinner with the other. All the while the miners were in view and we, on the torchlit bridge, in view of them. At the end of the meal the leftover food was gathered up and thrown over the south side of the bridge, away from the miners and into the river as an offering.

The miners would have known what we were doing. They would have known that we were invoking local spiritual powers and a cosmos in which the volcano is alive. The following day when more miners returned, they would have seen the offerings, and they too would know that they were operating in a field in which the volcano was not only a standing reserve, a resource lying in wait to be hauled out and transported away. It is not as if this act caused the miners to stop their work; nor do I think it was ever imagined that way by Sukmadi and others. It was rather part of a process of resisting the transformation of the volcano into a resource. This was a kind of possession. The meal was partly meant to bring out the doubts that the miners themselves had about what they were doing, to amplify them from within their own understanding of the world. It is certain that the miners would have been very familiar with the fact that the volcano was a living being and that the *selamatan* was an offering to spirits because such an event is a common occurrence across Java and they would have grown up with them. It was a kind of possession in the sense that spirit possession, as it is practiced here on the volcano by Sukmadi, is a process of seeing from another point of view (De Castro 2002; 2014). Often, villagers in Keningar became possessed by the spirits of animals or of the dead but also by spirits from the volcano that speak through the person and allow Sukmadi to understand the point of view of the volcano, what it wants, is upset by, or thinks about human activity. This kind of possession is a way to see from a point of view that can't normally be accessed. The invocation of spirits that night in front of the miners was in this sense an attempt to have the miners see the volcano from the point of view of the volcano, that it was more than a standing reserve, that it could speak, had ideas, that it too was alive.

Why didn't I do this at home?

After I had finished my fieldwork, then my dissertation, I was lucky enough to be awarded a position that would bring me back to Java. I was to write a book but I had also decided that I wanted to dive more deeply into the many conflicted worlds of the volcano. I felt I had more to learn about what it meant to make a home in a place in which the cosmos and nature are plural. My own life as an academic has been itinerant, settling on four continents in little over a decade in a to-ing and fro-ing that may not abate anytime soon. When I thought about creating some stability, that middle-class imaginary of permanence that I was raised with but never trusted because it suggested a kind of closing off and retreat, it made the most sense to escape it by learning how to make a home in a place that was defined by the intersection of multiple cosmos. Certainly every home is multiply constituted but it was the volcano that allowed me to understand that. Moreover, on the volcano the problem of how to co-exist with volatile nature at the intersection of many ideas and concepts is more intense than anywhere I had known before and because of this I understood that making a home there could also teach others about what it meant to make a home in the Anthropocene. Living on a volcano had wider lessons about living with an unpredictable nature that intersected with multiple worlds, plans and projects. It could potentially teach me how to live with volatile nature.

I proposed to Ade that we collaborate and build a home that would be a platform. It would be a place of rest for itinerant curious people like me, but it would also be a platform on the edge of a volcano to bring people together who want to try and understand the relationship between people and nature, geology and politics, the earth and cosmos. It was an idea of home as a kind of ongoing research centre, home as a mechanism for study and understanding. As an environmental activist concerned with mining and its social and natural consequences, Ade could use the space to host seminars and retreats to learn about the mining. It could be used to monitor the mining activities over long periods of time and build cases against it to bring to the authorities. Journalists, ecologists, geologists, and anyone else interested in learning about the mining and helping to facilitate its eradication could stay there. It could plug in to the burgeoning environmentalist movement in Java and be a meeting place for members of the movement to share stories and strategies. But it could also be a place of exchange between city people and communities that live on the volcano. Many young leftists in nearby cities have little connection with rural people and especially people that live on the volcano. Ade and others call them 'metropolitans' and think they are often snobbish and dismissive of rural political and environmental issues. Urbanites often romanticize rural people, especially those on the volcano, because they imagine that they hold onto and continue to practice traditional Javanese conceptions of nature that are disappearing in the cities. But these practices are under threat because of the entrenchment of conservative Islam throughout Indonesia that pits animism as backward or polytheist. As Ade and I discussed this, the home would be a physical structure to house exchanges between sympathetic uplanders and lowlanders that could potentially build solidarity between them.

No doubt, the risk is high. Landslides and hot clouds have descended on this land before and they surely will again. Though, for those familiar with volcanic activity on volcanoes like Merapi, these events rarely come without warning. Earthquakes and small eruptions that remain confined to the peak are precursors, sometimes unfolding for months before a large and truly dangerous eruption occurs. Because of this people know when it is time to leave and they can descend to safety before they are exposed to harm. This also means that one can never build anything too permanent or costly without accepting the high risk that it may be destroyed. It also means that the land is inexpensive as the property market has been shaped in part by the risk of exposure to eruptions. Traditional Javanese architecture was developed in view of the many volcanoes that transect Java and the ongoing shuddering and shaking they create. Built of wood columns and beams with clay tile roofs, they snap together like a kit of parts, fastened by wooden pins rather than metal nails. When the ground shakes the entire structure is flexible enough to sway with the ground and should some tiles come loose or a beam or two detach, they can be fitted back together again. Because of this, we too will build structures informed by the traditional Javanese style and if it is all destroyed, we will piece it all back together again until the next time. In this way, the house becomes the most flexible and nimble kind of platform, a meeting space between social and material life that creates encounters but can never dig its heels in too deeply. It finds ground and stability in the lightest of touches.

As a foreigner in Indonesia, I am not allowed to own land. The reasons for this are too complex to explore here but it has practical consequences for building a home on the volcano. It nevertheless accords with my collaboration with Ade. I never wanted this project to be about my ownership of a place, or a way of staking ground from which I could either shut out or control the world. It was always a way to engage and produce encounters in which control and authorship is always in negotiation, always a complex and reflective process. I never wished for the project to be about being pure or right or beyond reproach, and Ade and I will produce all sorts of unexpected failures which we will have to work on. Regardless, the postcolonial property ownership laws of the Indonesian state ensure that I cannot own land but must enter a partnership. Because of this I have entered into new layers of the social fabric on the volcano, meeting carpenters and people selling old pieces of Javanese furniture, doors, and windows. The five men building the first small house, a *joglo*, an open plan room without walls and a roof that looks like a farmers hat, are all Christians and drawn from Ade's family circle and friends. They are revealing the interconnected Javanese Christian community woven across the Western slopes. When the first structure is finished we will have a pig roast to celebrate, smoking it on a spit in the forest, the smells of which remind me of where I grew up and will be a rare, and an almost transgressive event in a predominantly Muslim place. Making this home is precisely this process of an ongoing revealing and facilitating of new relationships that are not only social but that cross the borders of the human with non-human relationships with things, plants, rocks and more. It means navigating the histories of property ownership and its genesis in the colonial and postcolonial histories of Indonesia, ideas of nationalism, but then too, of religious politics of navigating and negotiating these relationships in terms of what they make possible and what they exclude. In order to understand what it means to live on the volcano, it wasn't enough to simply take part; it required making a home, and in doing so navigating the multiple cosmos and weaving new relationships between them and myself.

One day when Ade and I were working on the land – I was pulling weeds and he was chopping wood to burn in his kitchen – he asked me why I didn't do this at home. Why didn't I build a house in the forest there? Why would I travel halfway across the world and build a house with people that aren't my family? Why not build a research centre in a place where I grew up, in a culture and language that was my own?

I didn't have a good answer. I said that I always wanted to leave the rural place I grew up in, I always looked elsewhere, I was never curious about my own culture, rarely felt like celebrating it and nationalism wasn't something I understood. The Canadian, working-class culture that I was raised in wasn't something I respected or romanticized or wanted to protect; instead, I often felt persecuted by it and that it required moving elsewhere – becoming a foreigner and an outsider – to feel at home, to feel that I could make a home. Perhaps because it wasn't a matter of settling in to an environment in a way that it became invisible to me but a matter of being able to remain distant as I settled, to be inside and outside at the same time. Certainly, as I now understand, this is what it takes to make a home anywhere; we all watch ourselves as we make our homes, reflect on the process, take distance, but I needed a more radical displacement to feel at home, where making a home could feel strange so that I could understand it more clearly. This is because our basic decisions seem all the brighter, with more contrast, and we can't so easily pretend that we understand things. What I came to realize was that we all live on a volcano, but it took a roundabout way for me to understand this. It took moving between continents and learning new languages to understand that we all live in spaces that are in flux at the intersections of multiple cosmos. It was only due to my own ignorance that it took so long to understand that making a home anywhere is to make it among an assemblage of conflicting ideas and a nature that doesn't succumb to them.

As the writing of this chapter is coming to a close I am preparing to leave the volcano and Indonesia and return to my office. The Christian builders have finished the structure and roof of the *joglo* but it will not be ready for me to inhabit before I leave and I won't return for another five or six months. They will finish it a few days after I board the airplane. But in the meantime a group of young artists and activists from the city interested in learning about the politics of mining, plants, and the music of birds and insects have made plans to stay in the *joglo* while I am away. We have also planned to publish an annual journal from the Lithic Garden (the name we have devised for the place); it will be a collection of writing and documentation. A home as a platform for encounters – with or without me there – it is happening.

Note

1   Merapi is the name of this particular volcano but also means 'volcano' – and any volcano can be and often is called Merapi. More conventionally, this volcano might be rendered specifically as 'marapi', but this specificity thins out the complex ways in which *home* on Merapi was thought about.

10

After the eviction: Navigating ambiguity in the ethnographic field

Farhan Samanani

On a warm day in November 2014, I showed up, with a flyer in my hand, outside the offices of the nonprofit company which managed the social housing on the housing estate on which I lived. The 'Caldwell'[1] estate was made up of hundreds of homes, in looming tower blocks and in rundown terraces, the majority of which were once social housing – that is, housing owned by the local council and allocated to citizens on low income at low rents. Citing the age and deterioration of these buildings, however, over the past decade the council had spearheaded an ambitious 'regeneration' programme, replacing the old buildings with newer ones. To fund this, they had adopted a strategy of selling off the land and development rights to private developers, presenting this as an investment opportunity. Having discovered that the area was much less dense than the London average, the council offered the developers the right to build a 50/50 split of socially rented and private housing. The developers,[2] would take over from the council in providing social rents – receiving public subsidy to help them do so – while they were free to retain the full income from the rental or sale of private units.

By that time, I had been conducting ethnography in the London neighbourhood of Kilburn for five months. Encompassing the Caldwell, alongside some of London's most affluent streets – and with everything in-between – Kilburn for me was a site for trying to understand how Londoners imagined and built particular forms of community in the midst of growing 'superdiversity' (Vertovec 2007). As part of this work, I had been following a large group of activists who mobilized around ongoing cuts to national social services, and who recently spun-off a housing-specific campaign group. Several of my interlocutors from this group were involved in planning the housing demonstration, and had urged me to show up.

To my surprise, however, I arrived to find a group of around a dozen unfamiliar faces, and was almost immediately pitched into a series of confrontations. As I nervously introduced myself, Zoe, a senior employee of the housing management company subcontracted by the council to manage the estate, emerged from the locked-off offices, annoyed at the disruption. Zoe had been introduced to me a few months prior, and up to this point had been warm and helpful, talking me through the politics and policies surrounding the regeneration. Seeing me among the protestors, however, she shot me a look of betrayal, and asked me what I was doing there. I tried explaining that as a researcher, I simply wanted to understand these issues from all sides. She responded sceptically, turned and retreated into the office.

Realizing that Zoe and I knew each other, the protestors turned to question me: what exactly were the motives of my research? This time, I had a bit more of an opportunity to explain myself. After some back and forth, it was decided that I could stay and talk with those who were happy to share. By my third conversation, however, I hit resistance. A pair of protestors resented what I had said to Zoe. I was 'overcomplicating' things, they said – this was a straightforward matter of injustice, and there were emphatically *not* multiple sides to the issue. They would only consent to take part in my research if I acknowledged this.[3]

In the midst of this exchange – which was threatening to boil over into an argument – I heard someone call me by name and took the chance to extricate myself. Sitting in a corner of the occupied office lobby was Jane, whom I knew from previous meetings of the housing campaign. At some distance from the boisterous protestors, in a nervous hunch, she seemed keen to withdraw from the protest. Yet she was arguably the main reason everyone was here in the first place.

*   *   *

In her younger days, Jane was a professional athlete, and as she grew older she shifted into making a living from freelance fitness instruction – yoga, dance and general-fitness. In Kilburn, demand changed quickly and studios, gyms and community centres were often unreliable hosts. So, when the offer of a permanent fitness-instructor job at a spa resort in the Philippines came her way Jane was thrilled but wary. She was used to things falling through, and the job had a six-month trial period followed by a stringent evaluation. As she packed her bags to set off, she decided to hold off on saying anything about possibly moving abroad to the local council, who owned her socially rented flat.

As a 'secure tenant', Jane had the right to hold onto her council flat during her six-month stint abroad.[4] Ever since the regeneration project had begun on the estate, however, rumours had swirled about social tenants suddenly losing their tenancy rights, or being forced to move outside of the area, or even outside of London, in order to remain eligible for social tenancy. During my research, I was never able to confirm those rumours that suggested social tenants were being systematically displaced. However, I did encounter a number of instances where tenants who wished to remain in the area had to first endure a range of convoluted and disruptive procedures. For instance, tenants whose buildings were being demolished were sometimes told that they would need to move away for a period up to two years before there would be space available for them to return. Against this background, Jane herself was apprehensive as to what might happen if she informed the council that she would be away for an extended period – and so she remained quiet. To keep an eye on things while she was away, Jane took in one of her friends as a subtenant. Again, this was within her rights. However, in this case, subleasing was only permissible with advanced agreement from the council.

Things came crashing down following a plumbing leak. When her friend called to tell her of the leak, Jane phoned up the council to arrange a repair. When doing so, she mentioned that she was abroad and was having a friend look after the flat. Unbeknownst to her until later, following that call, the council immediately opened an investigation. A few days later, Jane's manager called her into her office and informed Jane that she had just received a call saying that Jane was under investigation for benefit fraud and that, unless she was able to resolve the matter immediately, she would be terminating Jane's contract. In a panic, Jane phoned the council herself and, after navigating a maze of redirections, finally spoke with the caseworker assigned to her investigation. The caseworker accused her of exploiting her social tenancy for private gain, and informed her that the council would be pursuing eviction. Insisting that she had done nothing wrong, Jane argued that she was simply having a friend tend to the flat while she was away. With the council unwilling to drop the case, and with her job already in peril, Jane quit and returned to London a few days later to tackle matters herself. After a long struggle, which started out as a procedural battle but eventually went to a court tribunal, a final decision was made: Jane would be evicted.

What sort of home was lost on that day? And what would it mean to reclaim it, or begin anew? In this chapter, I offer an account of Jane's shifting hopes and plans in the lead-up to, and aftermath of, her eviction. At the same time, I present this as an account of some of my own ethnographic practice, dilemmas and ethical struggles, in miniature. As Jane grappled with what it meant to lose or rebuild a home, her story prompted me to reflect on what it meant to build relationships and commitments – both personal and analytical – in the ethnographic field.

*   *   *

Jane had never really accepted the verdict of her tribunal and was determined to fight. Reaching out through friends and local charities, she was directed to the housing campaign group as a potential source of help. Despite this, from the first time she attended a group meeting, she seemed to radiate palpable discomfort at particular moments; while she was comfortable sharing the details of her story, she seemed much less so discussing tactics and questions of how to apply pressure on the council. After getting acquainted over the course of several meetings, Jane agreed to meet me for coffee. Over a few hours she shared her story, but also her anxieties for the future. She had lived in her flat since her early twenties when it became clear that whether as an athlete, a teacher or some combination of the two, she had an uncertain financial future ahead of her – prompting her to apply for social housing. For the past seventeen years, her council flat – affordable, comfortable, hers – had been a source of security against more changeable fortunes. And, despite the insistence of the council and the verdict of the tribunal, she was certain she had not done anything wrong – not really. Throughout our conversation she paraphrased several instances where council officials, and even the presiding judge at her trial, acknowledged that she had violated the letter of the law much more than the spirit. She had made a mistake, it was true – and she emphasized her own willingness to admit this – but it was not made with malicious intent. Nor was it significant: had she simply informed the council of her travels and sublet in advance, she would have been fine. With the eviction grounded in her failure to perform this simple act, she remained hopeful that an exemption might be made.

The roots of this hope seemed to reach in different directions. As she told her story, she also recounted what she had learnt about the recent shifts in council policy over the past two decades. Despite many of these changes being ones she disapproved off, the fact of changing policy and practice over time gave her hope that there could be other shifts yet to come. She argued her case in the language of current policy, citing the council's desire to be seen as 'building community' in the midst of the regeneration. Surely then, she insisted, it didn't make sense to evict and displace those people who knew the area best – who, like her, had been a part of the community their whole lives.

Jane also seemed to find hope in being able to tell her story, and in seeing others respond. As we talked, she frequently quizzed me as to whether I understood and agreed, and when I responded affirmatively, she would light up: 'So you see!' she would say, talking excitedly about how things might still change. My affirmation seemed to stand in for the potential affirmation of others, including council caseworkers, who were also people after all. Right up until her eviction, Jane would insist on trying to arrange face-to-face meetings with different officials, in the belief she might convince them, if only she could meet them individually. She saw the autonomous judgement of officials, hidden behind a façade of ostensibly inflexible rules, as a sort of 'black magic' and recognized its double-edged potential, to both save and condemn. Nonetheless, she held out hope. Following her eviction, Jane was barred from re-entering her flat and collecting her things. A few days later, we found ourselves outside of her building's front door, strategizing. Glancing at the frowning guard planted at the entrance, she remarked: 'Maybe I can sweet talk him into letting me go up, you know? If they're keeping an eye on me?'

These tempered forms of hope, in the malleability of policy and in human recognition, were cross cut by a different sort of hope in organized political pressure. For Jane, the housing campaign group embodied this hope most clearly. At meetings, she would ask veteran activists whether they thought this was a winnable campaign – whether it was embarrassing enough for the local council, or capable of generating enough public attention to prompt a reversal in the decision to evict. At times she would grow animated through the talk of protests and placards, obstructions and slogans. In other instances, however, she seemed to withdraw uncomfortably, as plans were made around her. After one such meeting, as we walked back to the Caldwell together, she gave voice to this anxiety. After the protest at the local council offices, another was being planned in the lobby of the central council building. Jane fretted as to whether this public spectacle would serve to apply effective pressure, or only cast her as unsympathetic and bothersome.

As Jane moved between both possibilities, I found myself at a loss as to how to respond. If my fieldwork had taught me anything, it was that her odds were slim, regardless of approach. Sweeping budget cuts, emerging from the British government's programme of austerity, had left council officials scrambling to find savings and remove claimants from the benefits ledger. Against this context, I had seen protests and other disruptive challenges break through the routinized logics that were used to squeeze out claimants, and I had also seen disruptive behaviour used as an excuse for caseworkers to refuse to deal with claimants. 'Ought I to share any of these stories?' I wondered. 'What good would they do?'

Before this second protest could materialize, Jane found an envelope through her door giving her a date for when the bailiffs would show up to evict her. Rapidly, energy shifted to organizing a barricade outside of her flat. Within the campaign group, as plans were discussed, members shared stories of past anti-eviction actions, as a way to reflect on tactics and drum up optimism. And yet, with talk of eviction in the air, members also began talking about the costs of such actions. In the past, such actions had led to some members winding up in police custody, while others incurred financial debts that were never repaid. Ribs were bruised and friendships were strained. While no one suggested that the protest at Jane's ought not to go ahead, a few did explicitly question the efficacy of such tactics overall, given both their personal costs and their failure, thus far, to create more systemic change.

On the day of the eviction, a large crowd gathered in the hallway of Jane's tower block. Members of the housing campaign group were joined by friends and supporters from other left-wing and anti-austerity campaigns across North West London, and by members of other Kilburn community groups. In the hall, protestors chanted and sang protest songs. They set up a table with tea, chocolate, fruit and cake, and invited Jane's neighbours to join them and to discuss questions of housing. Meanwhile, both Jane and I found ourselves shrinking away, hoping not to be seen by whoever eventually arrived. Recalling my earlier encounter with Zoe – who hadn't spoken with me since – I had begun to worry whether today would involve burning another bridge with another one of the few council officials happy to talk with me. I wanted to support Jane – who I personally believed had been treated unfairly, and who had become a friend in her own right – but I found myself anxiously making excuses to stay away from the front of the barricade. Jane too spent much of her time with a small group of personal friends, also towards the back, or in her flat itself.

I can't speak for Jane, but my own anxious ambivalence bubbled up from a series of demands and desires that seemed impossible to reconcile: I wanted to maintain access and trust as a researcher working with the council; I wanted to show solidarity and commitment towards the activists and community figures gathered outside Jane's flat, and to continue conducting research with them as well; and I wanted to be able to offer Jane, who seemed to be nervous about both the impending eviction and the boisterous barricade, some semblance of reassurance.

The source of our feelings may have varied, but my anxiety seemed to mirror Jane's, perhaps even to feed off it; when the bailiffs showed up, and were halted in the barricaded hallway, Jane was nowhere to be seen.

* * *

It wasn't until five months later that another attempt was made to evict Jane. Occurring without any warning, official or otherwise, this time it was successful. I found out a few days later through a text message. Along with a (mutual) friend from the housing campaign group, Jane was coming to see if she could get some of her possessions out of the flat – beyond the single case she was allowed to leave with at the time. Although the council promised to deliver the contents of her flat to her forwarding address, the set delivery date was far away. Jane was also worried that the council-hired movers would fail to collect some of her less-obvious belongings – the mounted bathroom mirror, the carpet she had bought and laid herself, or her slow cooker, which had leftovers in it at the time of the eviction. She hoped to recover a few items and to do an inventory herself. I lived in the next tower block over from her former flat, subletting a room in one of the two privately owned flats in the building. When I called her up in response to the text, she asked me if she could keep some of her possessions at my place, until she settled somewhere else. I quickly thought through how I would negotiate this with my flatmate, and then tentatively agreed. Jane's old building was due to be demolished, and had been emptied out. When we arrived outside, the guard watching over the empty property refused us entry, and we left empty-handed.

After we parted ways, I paced around the estate with a feeling of anxiety. During our excursion to recover her furniture, Jane had spoken hopefully about finding a place nearby. With the building due to be demolished, moving back to her old flat was no longer an option. But the eviction had made her officially homeless, and she thought there might be a chance for her to be rehomed nearby, still on the estate. Her asking me to keep hold of her furniture – near to her old flat – seemed indicative of this hope. While Jane was explaining this I responded encouragingly but afterwards I found myself with an uneasy feeling, wishing she would let go of the idea of returning – which, although I couldn't bring myself to say so to her, had come to feel increasingly unrealistic – and make a fresh start. When fighting her court case, she had incurred a significant debt, and now the council wanted to charge her for unpaid rent for the months between the first eviction attempt and now. These debts made it feel unlikely that the council, or anyone within it, would suddenly turn helpful. More than this, however, they felt menacing: a reminder that you could lose your home, be denied access to almost all your possessions, and still have further to fall. I wanted to tell Jane to cut her losses before things got worse. Walking back and forth, I fiddled with my phone, turning it over and planning what I would say to her – but I couldn't bring myself to call.

Several weeks later, Jane texted again, asking if I was at home. She explained that she had managed to negotiate with the council to move her possessions herself. She was still prohibited from entering the building, but the hired workers had brought the furniture to the tower block's front door, and from there she and a friend had loaded it into the friend's van. She felt that this arrangement would give her a greater ability to try and ensure everything was gathered. She had dropped most of her possessions off with other friends, but had left a few items of furniture on the street for me to hold onto.

Meeting up a few hours later, we found the furniture still where she had left it, and we began to dismantle it, to make it easier to carry. With what felt like endless trips back and forth, we managed to move it, piece by piece, to my flat, placing some into storage, setting other items up in my bedroom. As we did so, Jane mused on what she might do to find a new, long-term place to stay, and recounted her frustration with the movers emptying out her flat. They seemed insistently unable to find certain items, no matter how careful her instructions were. The worst of it, she said, was they claimed they did not see her slow cooker anywhere. She wondered if it had been thrown out.

That evening, I sat down, exhausted, to write up my field notes. Under my bed was the old, folding chair I had previously used. Now, instead, I perched on the edge of the sturdy office chair Jane had entrusted me with, hunched over my notebook, reluctant to fully settle in. It felt like an emblem of a stubborn hope – one I did not know how to handle.

*   *   *

While still in the field, I remember struggling with these events, both personally and as an ethnographer. How was I to make sense of them? Where was I to follow them? What stories could I tell? What could I do? Incensed by the seeming injustice of what had happened, and familiar with how other ethnographers had confronted exclusion and displacement, I could feel a tug towards the municipal archives. In those documents – and perhaps also in talking to officials and in observing how others encountered them – there was the promise of assembling a critical account of power and interest, of liberal governmentality and late capitalism, which would expose this story not as a case of personal wrongdoing, or of rotten luck, but as symptomatic of a deep and systematic inequality. This story was compelling, resonant with so much else happening on the estate that pointed to how the estate was transforming from being seen, managed and experienced as a concrete social safety net, to a high-risk, high-potential investment. I knew as well that this sort of story – of how the privatization of public goods shaped new forms of exclusion, conflict and subjectivity – was one that was familiar and valued within the academy; it was not just a narrative I found compelling, but one that others would recognize and respect. When writing up my field notes in the evening, I often found myself musing about what I could do – how I could search for documents, whom in the council I could talk to – to capture this narrative.

There were other things, however, that tugged in different directions – towards different, competing stories. After Jane's eviction, there were other protests in her name, but Jane herself no longer took part. Throughout the time I had known her, she had been ambivalent about her case being turned into a cause for mobilization. Given this, I wondered, might it not be worth asking what motivated the activists themselves? Where and how did they see 'the political' and what did such readings neglect? Re-reading my notes from the day when the first attempt to evict Jane was successfully resisted, my writing now seems to bristle with irritation. While there, I moved through the crowd, asking those assembled about their lives, their histories of activism, about why they felt motivated to be there that day. Writing up these exchanges, I returned frequently to contrasting the confident, grand narratives of change and revolution, of people, power and community to the anxiety that I saw Jane as embodying (and which I clearly felt myself!). I found myself asking what it meant to believe – as I had been told by the protestors at the estate management's offices – that there was only one story about housing on the Caldwell to tell.

Then again, there was this question of recognition – this idea that Jane held onto that if she was simply able to tell her story, to make herself known as an individual and not as a case, then she may be able to effect a different sort of ending. This hope was tested against security guards and caseworkers, and even in court, and yet never seemed to break. It also seemed to be mirrored in the attitude of officials like Zoe, who seemed to believe that it was important to support individuals personally, even within the framework of a standardized system. I might have investigated how such beliefs in recognition were fostered, and how they came to sit alongside other political claims. Or, yet again, I might have kept closer to my original intentions for my ethnography as a whole and focused in on questions of community: how it was deployed as an ambivalent and contradictory resource, by redevelopers and council officials as well as protestors and Jane herself, towards different trajectories of change and resistance.

Truthfully, I pursued all of these questions at different moments and in different ways. Yet I did not do so freely and without cost. The richness and complexity of everyday life that ethnography claims to capture does not exist sui generis, but emerges through the tracing of particular relationships and not others. In assembling ethnographic accounts, we commit to particular relationships, and modalities of relating, and discard or disavow others. These acts of assembly are never confined simply within moments of ethnographic writing and analysis. Rather, the social and ethical commitments that we forge in the field are already acts of analysis, and they inevitably constrain what we are able to see and speak about later on. Put simply, to tell different stories, we must first commit to actively following them, within our own lives as fieldworkers.

Jane's stubborn hope left me facing the question of how to respond: to account for Jane's eviction as a product of governmentality would parse Jane's ambivalent hope in a particular way – as partly captured by this governmental logic, and partly in excess of it; to focus on Jane's desire for recognition might instead suggest a focus on the intersubjective dimensions of hope; to focus on how certain matters were rendered political would be to commit to imagining a division between what was political and what was not, regardless of how much this relationship shifted and varied. Any one of these accounts would require me as an ethnographer to learn to recognize a particular relational logic, to come to embody it myself, and to follow where it led. And so, drawn by these different accounts at different moments, there were inevitably questions I did not ask, forms of 'evidence' I did not pursue, relationships I failed to recognize.

Each of these accounts tugged down different paths. I, meanwhile, committed to none of them – at least in this case. For months after leaving Kilburn, I would think through Jane's story, and the material I had collected on it, and feel frustrated that I had nothing more decisive to say about it: that I couldn't use it to tell a powerful tale of inequality in twenty-first century London any more than I could use it to work up a counterintuitive but revealing glimpse into the way the 'political' was constructed by activists. Had I failed to attend to this as a good ethnographer? What choices had I actually made in the field?

*   *   *

Not long after helping move Jane's furniture, I got in touch with Phil. Phil worked for a Somali community group, as a full-time caseworker, helping people manage their bills, benefits and legal troubles. Facing language barriers and precarious circumstances, within a context of ever-changing migration policy, it wasn't uncommon for Phil's clients to have incredibly complex cases. In Kilburn, Phil had built up a reputation as perhaps the area's most knowledgeable caseworker. And so, following a conversation with a friend involved in an anti-debt campaign, it was suggested that I put Jane in touch with Phil, as the individual with the best chance of seeing a way through the tangle she faced.

After her eviction, and after staying with a friend for a month, Jane had moved to a squat in Holborn. Two months after we last met, we arranged to catch up over coffee at the British Museum, not far from her squat. During our conversation, Jane recounted the advice Phil had given her when they had met: her debt was a problem, he said, and the council would be reluctant to house her as a social tenant if she still had significant arears with them. But if she could afford to at least start paying a little bit each month – she could, she acknowledged – then he felt confident he could make a good case for her being granted a new social tenancy. He warned her, though, that the location would be difficult to manage. Increasingly, new social tenants were being housed all over London and beyond. It was possible to eventually move back to a desired area by swapping properties within the council's allocation system, but making the right exchanges could take several years.

As we spoke, Jane confessed that moving elsewhere would perhaps not be the worst thing. Over the last two months she had let most of her teaching in Kilburn wind down. Facing a commute to teach classes in Kilburn, she had decided that either she would look for more work nearby – or else that if she were going to commute, there was no need to prioritize Kilburn, which had come to feel a bit trying and sad for her. Meanwhile, she continued to talk fondly about elements of the neighbourhood, and about her old flat. In fact, reviving the subject from our last conversation, she spoke in particular detail about her slow cooker: she had in fact finally located it among the possessions that had been returned to her, but it appeared to be missing its inner pot. Noting that there was food in it that would have gone off by the time the movers arrived, she speculated that the pot was likely thrown away. She told me how important it used to be to her to structure her day, enabling her to eat healthily while also maintaining the flexible schedule working as a freelancer often demanded. It gave her a sense of order and control. 'It used to be easy for me', she remarked, 'it's tricky now.'

That evening, I spent some time online while exchanging text messages with Jane. Unable to find a replacement pot from any vendor, I instead found a similar model of slow cooker to the one Jane had described and was pleasantly surprised at how cheap it was. I offered to order it as a pre-emptive housewarming gift for wherever she settled. Jane thanked me for finding the replacement cooker and said she would order it herself.

Jane's eviction left me with a feeling of lingering guilt over not being able to do more. I had to remind myself that I was unable to take her in – that I already lived as someone else's subtenant, and that we already had my flatmate's brother sleeping on our living room couch. Likewise, although the two of us got along well, there was something about her situation that made my research feel exploitative; to me, it felt clear she looked to our conversations as a way to vent and seek reassurance, and I worried that these needs made for an unfair exchange, no matter how upfront I was about my presence as a researcher.[5] Being able to connect her with people like Phil, better equipped to help her navigate her complex circumstances, helped take the edge off this guilt.

A few months later, when Jane, as a favour to a friend, agreed to teach a series of age-friendly fitness classes back in Kilburn, she suggested that we meet up a few hours before one of her classes. Before our meeting, I checked in with Phil to see how things were going with getting her back on the social housing list. With some bafflement, he remarked that while Jane had seemed initially enthusiastic about their agreed plan, she soon fell out of touch and had yet to send him anything on a debt plan that he might be able to use to persuade the council.

When we met, I tentatively asked Jane what had happened with Phil. She readily admitted that she wanted to sort out her income and secure some less sporadic work, before thinking about housing. Perhaps she wouldn't want to be under the local council at all but would move to where good work was, she mused. She wasn't sure. In the next breath, however, she confessed that she had also found herself reluctant to go look for new teaching contracts. She felt as if she wasn't ready and that she wasn't sure how to rebuild:

> But I don't even have my mirror back, you know. And it's a full-time thing – building the contacts you need to be a freelancer. I've lost all these years of work that I've done in the area, and now I have to start again, you know, but it's only worth it if I know I can take it seriously. You can't do it half-heartedly … and I want to move on but it almost feels like my head's in one place and my soul's in another.

As we continued the conversation, however, she seemed to shift perspective, and mused about potentially leaving London altogether – perhaps even attempting to move abroad once more:

> Now's the time I should really be looking at some big things I've been meaning to do, because now's the time where I can make those changes, you know? Like

what have I got to lose? But then I've got to make time for them. I can't keep thinking about whether my solicitor owes me money or all these little things, you know? And I've probably got to stop teaching this class [in the area] you know? It's hard, because they're my regulars, and I know they won't go anywhere else, but it takes time, you know, every time there is a class that's for a couple of hours, and if it's only for a few people – it ties you down!

As we argued in the introduction of this volume, home is often imagined as an unalienated domain – as a place where one's essential self reposes. Home grounds who we are, within a world of flux. Ethnographers have problematized this image of home, through revealing the labour, imagination, tension and even violence that can make up the home, but they have also reproduced it through dominant conceptions where doing ethnography is equated with immersion into a particular social field, or set of lives. What happens though, when we look closely at a life and realize that there is no singular point, or trajectory for immersion? What happens, as in Jane's case, when home itself is a state of flux, characterized by cross-cutting doubts and uncertainties? How do we understand the meaning, the location, the feel or the materiality of home, when our interlocutors themselves face dispossession or social and material insecurity, and may struggle to imagine a present or future home themselves?

Michael Herzfeld, in developing his notion of 'cultural intimacy' (2016), argues that ethnographers ought to occupy a 'militant middle ground'. He develops this notion in relation to his analysis of how states construct narratives of collective identity. He argues that official narratives of cultural identity often rely on evoking everyday forms of resistance and creativity for the air of authenticity that they lay claim to. Conversely, these everyday assertions of identities that exceed the frame of the official, the national or the collective, are nonetheless voiced in reference to it. A middle ground emerges, then, between fixity and fluidity – which Herzfeld also traces as a space between 'empiricism and speculation, infinite regression and the most crass form of scientism, rejection of language as peripheral and its excessive adulation as the defining code for all human ways of making meaning' (2016: 187). Put simply, this middle ground is located between accounts of the social as settled and concrete, and those which cast the social as open, indeterminate and in continual flux. For Herzfeld, this is the space where ethnography ought to unfold – following everyday attempts to navigate between the given and the possible.

Herzfeld's vision is helpful, but he is also able to locate this middle ground in more definitive terms, because of his focus on the construction and contestation of singular national identities. The grounding becomes much more perilous, however, the more we bring diversity into the picture. In Kilburn, throughout my time there, I encountered different narratives of British, Londoner and neighbourhood identity, which overlapped and tugged apart in different ways. These different visions not only were distributed across inter-group or inter-personal differences, however, but could be embodied by single individuals. Jane, with her competing visions of home – her contrasting, irreconcilable hopes and uneasy tensions, which proved animating in one moment and paralyzing the next – embodied this diversity even in the intimate domain of home. For her, home – lived or ideal – was far from a place beyond alienation, but rather a domain of competing possibilities that generated alienation and belonging simultaneously. For Jane, then, the middle ground between the given and the possible emerged not between the creativity of her own life, and broader, more structured narratives, but as a space of indeterminacy within her own attempts at holding onto or recovering a sense of home.

In the field, I did not think of this problem in terms of Michael Herzfeld, diversity or middle grounds. Rather, it emerged as an affective tug – a feeling of connection and commitment I struggled to name, but felt guided by nonetheless. I was stuck with a persistent feeling, a whisper which suggested that the fact that Jane had all these stories to tell about home – all these hopes, all these dilemmas – mattered more than just picking a singular account and committing to it. That was certainly the case when we talked. As much as she seemed to ask for reassurance or for my opinion, she did so in a speculative voice, and with a strong, nervous sense of the dilemmas she faced. Rather than closing down this speculation in any definitive way, there was a request here, to stay with the trouble, the indeterminacy, the speculation she evoked – to dwell in the difficult middle without resigning oneself to it. If for Jane, home was both hope and loss, both possibility and injustice, then as an ethnographer and as a friend, the best I could offer was to navigate this space together.

Notes

1   The name of the Caldwell estate is borrowed from Zadie Smith's novel *NW* (2012), which inserts the fictional estate into the otherwise true-to-life geographies of London's NW6 postcode – where I conducted my own fieldwork.

2   Or third-parties brought on-board as partners to manage buildings after construction.

3   This is the most I have, or will, write about these individuals.

4   For more on these regulations, see http://england.shelter.org.uk/legal/security_of_te
    nure/secure_tenancies/what_is_a_secure_tenancy#4

5   Of course, this level of 'need' on Jane's part is likely not as marked as that between a
    great many anthropologists and their interlocutors. Although not the primary focus
    of this chapter, I would note that although much has been written about the political
    considerations and the considerations for reflexive writing that emerge out of such
    asymmetry, there are far fewer ethnographies where this hierarchy emerges as a clear
    and important detail within ethnographic accounts themselves.

11

Acts of 'homing' in the Eastern Desert – How Syrian refugees make temporary homes in a village outside Zaatari Camp, Jordan

Ann-Christin Wagner

For thousands of years, the Azraq wetlands, east of Amman, the capital of Jordan, have been an important stopover for bird migrations between Europe and Africa. Species with poetic names – honey buzzards, little crake marsh harriers, cranes and white-eared bulbuls – have bred in the oasis or rested after an exhausting journey over the Sinai and the Arabian Peninsula. In the twentieth century, though, growing water consumption in the burgeoning metropolis nearby depleted the Azraq Basin. By the early 1990s, all surface water in the wetlands had disappeared – through continued water pumping, the water reserve has since been restored to a meagre 10 per cent of its original size (RSCN 2015). According to a faded poster at the Azraq Museum, the number of migratory birds in Jordan went down from more than 300,000 in the 1960s to 1,200 at the beginning of the new millennium.

Derek Robertson, a Scottish painter, has explored the connections between the migratory journeys of birds and humans in Jordan's Eastern Desert. Like birds, humans are border-crossers, although they risk getting stuck. In 2016, the closure of the Syrian-Jordanian frontier disrupted longstanding regional mobility circuits of all sorts: labour and educational migration, trade, but also the exchange of spouses within kinship and ethnic minority networks. One of Robertson's watercolour sketches, *The Desert Is Full of Promises*, shows a bee-eater, stranded in the Jordanian desert because it mistook an abandoned blue bus for a lake. A group of Bedouin children gathers around it, pouring the tiny bird water on a saucer. The drawing highlights the capacity of animals and humans to make temporary homes in inhospitable environments – and the importance of solidarity for the survival of the displaced.[1]

What birds and humans have in common is their sensitivity to changing habitats and their mobility-based survival strategies. When birds' flight patterns are rerouted, it indicates environmental change. In similar ways, human flows are reshaped by natural and man-made disasters, perhaps nowhere more so than in Jordan. Since its independence, the country has welcomed several waves of refugees, including Palestinians, Iraqis and, most recently, Syrians. The UN High Commissioner for Refugees (UNHCR) currently records over 650,000 Syrians in Jordan, although the 2015 governmental census gives figures more than twice as high (Ghazal 2016). Zaatari Camp, located 80 km northeast of Amman, has become emblematic of Syrian displacement in the Middle East. Aerial imagery from the camp has dominated the news around the globe; seen from the nearby highway, its white containers gleam in the sun. To cope with the mass influx of Syrian refugees, Zaatari Camp opened in 2012. With almost 80,000 inhabitants in early 2019, it has since turned into Jordan's fifth biggest city. That does not make it representative of Syrian displacement, though – more than 80 per cent of refugees live outside camps, including in locales on the fringe of the desert (UNHCR 2019). In urban areas, Syrians get by through a combination of work in the informal economy, humanitarian assistance and remittances from relatives in the Gulf or Europe (Wagner 2019).

This chapter speaks to existing research in Forced Migration Studies on home-making in protracted displacement and legal limbo (cf. this volume's introduction). Exploring parallels between bird and human flight, it uses the concept of 'homing' to study the entanglements of home-making and mobility among Syrian refugees in Zaatari Village, a small settlement on the doorstep of Zaatari Camp. Only a stone's throw away from the Syrian border and Jordan's most important humanitarian hub, these refugees have managed to survive largely under the radar of national authorities and aid agencies. The Oxford Dictionaries define 'homing' as 'relating to an animal's ability to return to its territory after travelling away from it' (Oxford Dictionaries 2019). For the study of refugees, I prefer 'homing' to the more frequently used 'home-making'. First, it captures the seasonal nature of homes and processes of temporary home-making that are stretched between various locations. Although the protagonists of this chapter are far from leading nomadic lives, an analysis of 'homing' in Jordanian exile brings to the fore that home-making is not necessarily bound to one place or even linear movement.

Second, I understand refugees' acts of 'homing' as a form of resistance to processes of 'othering' in the host country. Since the onset of the Syrian conflict, the Jordanian state has constructed Bedouin kinsmen and former labour migrants as 'refugees'. Imposing new forms of humanitarian documentation, the tightening and eventual closure of the Syrian-Jordanian border between 2014 and late 2018 and restrictions on Syrians' freedom of movement and right to work have all challenged my interlocutors' pre-war and more recent ways of belonging to Zaatari Village. Looking at Syrian displacement through the lens of "homing" foregrounds multiple *acts of navigation*. To find refuge, jobs and housing in exile, they capitalize on pre-war transnational support networks and migration experiences between Homs, their city of origin in western Syria, and Zaatari Village in north-eastern Jordan.

This chapter looks at the different roles that Syrian refugees occupy in the village: as temporary *guests* within a securitized nation-state framework; as *kinsmen* who are bound to their Jordanian hosts by translocal ties; and as low-skilled foreign *workers* within uneven regional labour markets. It draws on a total of fourteen months of fieldwork in northern Jordan in 2016–17 that I conducted for my doctoral thesis. For most of this time, I lived in nearby Mafraq, a mid-sized provincial town where I volunteered with a small European NGO. In December 2016, I befriended Dr Hussein, a young Jordanian researcher at Mafraq's Al al-Bayt University who had recently completed his PhD in Scotland. On a gloomy winter day, he invited me for a very British cup of tea into his home in Zaatari Village, a place that I had briefly visited a year earlier together with a (now-defunct) French organization. What was supposed to be a courtesy call turned into a day-long excursion into Syrian and Jordanian homes. Insights in this chapter come from a series of interviews with five Syrian families, as well as from information provided by my Jordanian host.

Guests

When Dr Hussein offered to give me a tour of Syrian households in Zaatari Village, he had a specific idea of 'home' in mind. The polished version of Jordanian hospitality and peaceful coexistence between refugees and hosts that he wanted me to see reflects the country's raison d'état. In Jordan, hospitality has become a major feature of post-independence national identity, to the extent that its commodified version figures prominently in the heritage industry (Shryock 2004). But it also informs an increasingly restrictive refugee response. Like many of its neighbours, Jordan is not a signatory to the 1951 United Nations Refugee Convention. While the term 'refugee' was long reserved for Palestinians, Iraqi and later Syrian refugees have been received as 'guests' (Achilli 2015; Mason

2011). A recent news article exemplifies the extent to which the guest discourse has permeated policy and public talk about displacement: 'Population stands at around 9.5 million, including 2.9 million guests', a headline of the *Jordan Times*, Jordan's English daily newspaper, ran in January 2016 (Ghazal 2016). Since 2014, new governmental regulations have restricted Syrians' access to public services and freedom of movement across the border and in urban areas, increasingly forcing them to live in camps (Achilli 2015). Without access to Jordanian citizenship and sustainable livelihoods, 'guests' can never truly be 'at home'. And yet, Mahmood, a young Syrian man with scarce material resources, managed to build a career and even a house in Zaatari Village, despite increasingly hostile refugee-reception policies.

In December 2016, my first stop in Zaatari Village took me to a single-story cement house on the outskirts of town. As I got out of the car, dust rose in the strong winter winds. In the distance, I could distinguish the fences of Zaatari Camp. Dr Hussein and I quickly made our way into the cozy living room of Mahmood, a Syrian man in his early thirties. Once we were comfortably seated on cushions, with a cup of hot tea to warm our hands, my Jordanian host gently nudged Mahmood to tell me his story.

Mahmood was a simple man. Born into a Bedouin family, he grew up in the al-Bayada neighbourhood in Homs, Syria's third-largest city before the war. After fifth grade, he quit school to assist his father with the family business: selling milk and sheep. At the onset of the Syrian conflict, Homs was among the first cities to rise against the Assad regime and subsequently the victim of a brutal two-year siege. Al-Bayada, Mahmood's area, was one of the opposition strongholds and frequently shelled by army troops. By the end of 2013, over half of Homs's pre-war population of 800,000 had fled within the city or beyond its confines – al-Bayada was one of the neighbourhoods most affected by displacement (UN HABITAT 2014). In early winter 2013, Mahmood illegally crossed into Jordan. After only five days, he left Zaatari Camp.

In Zaatari Village, he now worked as a tiler, earning as little as 10 Jordanian dinar (ca. US$14) a day. At the time, this was the standard rate for low-skilled day labourers in the informal economy in northern Jordan. Sometimes, he also found employment on the nearby fields. Moving to a bigger city, or even Amman, had not occurred to him. 'In the village, we are all from Homs.' In the meantime, he had also begun to remake other parts of his life. Mahmood proudly gave me a tour of the house that he had built with his own hands. As I learned that day, a house like his cost around 10,000 Jordanian dinar (ca. US$14,100) – not a small sum in a country where the average monthly salary stands at US$637 (Azzeh 2017) and the monthly income of Syrian workers is usually below Jordanian minimum wage (Yahya, Kassir and El-Hariri 2018). He led me through two rooms with kitschy wall decorations, a TV and mattresses, and into his new kitchen, still under construction. Clearly, all that was missing was a loving wife, and indeed Mahmood hoped to get married soon. Sadly, a match with a Syrian cousin in Lebanon had failed to materialize when she did not receive permission to travel to Jordan. Now, he was looking for another spouse close by.

What makes Mahmood's living conditions so extraordinary is how they compare to Syrians' struggles in nearby Mafraq and other urban sites of displacement in Jordan. In both locations, the number of inhabitants has doubled since 2011. In Mafraq, the UNHCR statistics count 84,000 refugees (UNHCR 2018), although the town's mayor estimated their number at closer to 100,000 at the time of my fieldwork (personal communication, 2016). Zaatari Village, home to 12,000 Jordanians before the crisis, has welcomed an equal number of newcomers (Omari 2014). But this is where the comparison ends.

In the streets of Mafraq, the presence of labour patrols was a threat to Syrians who made a living in the informal economy without official work permits (Human Rights Watch 2017). The prospect of deportation to the camps or even Syria fuelled a variety of avoidance strategies: men often went into hiding or worked at night. It also encouraged child labour. Syrian women and children were the frequent target of bullying, as locals blamed overcrowded schools and hospitals on the newcomers. By way of contrast, labour patrols and harassment were literally absent from Mahmood's life in Zaatari Village.

On the other hand, Mafraq was home to numerous aid agencies, NGOs and faith-based charities, and most Syrians received assistance from more than one. Driving through Mafraq and other Jordanian cities, one could not help notice the mushrooming of NGO labels on buildings, street signs and even bodies – many aid providers gave out clothes with their logo, especially to Syrian children. While Mahmood had duly registered with the UNHCR office in Mafraq, a precondition for freedom of movement in Jordan, he had never signed up for aid with any other organization. Odd jobs, easy to come by in the village and not putting him at risk of deportation, provided him with a stable income, enough to build a house and make provisions for his future family.

Most importantly, Mahmood had a place to call home. In a 2017 survey, only 1 per cent of Syrian respondents outside Jordanian camps claimed to own their domicile. Two-thirds were drowning in debts, and housing costs were the most important burden on their wallets (Tiltnes, Thang and Pedersen 2019).

As I could observe in Mafraq, most Syrians lived in overpriced, substandard apartments and under congested living conditions. Struggling to pay the rent, they were frequently evicted by impatient landlords. Clearly, Mahmood was among the more fortunate even in Zaatari Village. Later that day, Dr Hussein took me to a makeshift tent city on an empty square, the size of a football pitch, inside the village. As it started to rain, the inhabitants of these tents rushed out to offer us shelter and hot tea. They also greeted Dr Hussein enthusiastically. One of them was Abu Mohammed, a man in his fifties. Although used to living in concrete houses, he and his family now shared four tents. Inside, the barren ground was covered with thick carpets, and curtains separated the kitchen from the main sitting area. In a corner, a traditional tea service was on display. Outside, the men of his family had built provisional toilets. According to a Jordanian member of the International Red Cross, 50 per cent of refugees inside Zaatari Village lived in tents like these. And yet, Abu Mohammed was not unhappy. His tents had electricity and he made a small income from a makeshift supermarket that he had opened in a shack nearby. How did people like Mahmood and Abu Mohammed manage to carve out a living in such a remote corner of a foreign country?

Kinsmen

When Mahmood argued that 'they were all from Homs', he meant two things. On the one hand, he was referring to the tight-knit Syrian community in the village. A five-minute drive away from his home, Dr Hussein led me into a compound, made up of a handful of cement houses similar to the one that I had just left. In one of the dwellings, I met Um Ahmed, a woman in her thirties with four young children who had come to Jordan four years earlier with her neighbours from Homs. In 2015, Um Ahmed's husband had returned to Syria to take care of his own mother and sisters. He once sent her 200 Jordanian dinar (ca. US$282) but mostly left her to fend for herself. For a while, the International Red Cross had supported her with food vouchers, but the aid had stopped in mid-2016. Sometimes, Um Ahmed found work in the greenhouses in the Eastern Desert, picking and sorting tomatoes for a meagre 6 Jordanian dinar (ca. US$8.50) a day. And Um Ahmed was not the only single mother I encountered that day. Others had left elderly husbands behind. These women and their children only survived because their old and new Syrian neighbours gave them food and even built them cheap houses.

On the other hand, Mahmood was also referring to his Jordanian *hosts*. In fact, Syrians and Jordanians in town were adamant about the fact that they all belonged to the same Bedouin tribe, the Beni Khaled. As Dr Hussein told me, Zaatari Village had been founded in the 1960s by a Syrian family. In exchange for developing the place, they were granted Jordanian citizenship. (I never managed to verify his story.) But however shady their common ancestry, Mahmood was confident that he shared with Dr Hussein 'the same dialect and the same family'. Um Ahmed's female friend, herself a single mother who had not spoken to her husband for half a year, confirmed: 'They [the Jordanians] are Bedouins like us.' Abu Mohammed was quick to point out that cross-border kinship ties used to be upheld through frequent visits and intermarriage. Long before the war, he had visited Zaatari Village on his way to Saudi Arabia where he was hoping to find work as a shepherd, and his aunt had married a Jordanian relative from the village in the early 1990s. Another old man in his tent insinuated that this was not the first time that Jordanian villagers had helped them out. He and his family had come to Zaatari Village 'in the 1980s'. From what I understood, it was a subtle reference to the massacres that the Syrian regime had committed against the Muslim Brotherhood, but also ordinary civilians, in Hama, close to Homs, in 1982. It was at least conceivable that previous waves of violence had pushed conservative Sunni Muslims – and potential activists – to seek refuge across the border.

In the present, transnational kinship networks translated into more secure legal status, material resources and livelihoods for Syrian refugees. To begin with, most Syrians that I met in Zaatari Village had spent no longer than a couple of days inside Zaatari Camp – Jordanian relatives played an important role in getting them out. Dr Hussein's brother himself served as a sponsor for various Syrian families. In the early days of the camp, many Syrians had left through informal channels and subsequently managed to transfer their UNHCR registration to an urban centre. This prompted the Jordanian authorities to forbid the UNHCR from providing documentation without proper sponsorship. In 2015, the bail-out process was suspended altogether (Achilli 2015). Abu Mohammed explained to me how villagers had assisted him. Before coming to Jordan, he had phoned his relatives to notify them of his travel plans. When he arrived, they were waiting for him at the gates of Zaatari Camp, ready to complete the paperwork. He was able to leave immediately.

In the village, *Jordanian* relatives also provided their Syrian kin with material goods – for example, with cheap electricity. In the tent city, Abu Mohammed tapped into his neighbours' grid and paid them a meagre 10 to 15 Jordanian dinar (ca. US$14–21) a month. In return, this allowed him to open a small supermarket where he sold chips and sweets to Jordanian children. This way, he earned ca. 30–40 Jordanian dinar (ca. $42–$56) each month.

Most importantly, men like Mahmood and Abu Mohammad were allowed to settle on Jordanian ground for free. Only in Azraq town in north-eastern Jordan, similar patterns have emerged. As in Zaatari Village, Syrian refugees constructed cement houses on their relatives' land (Kamel Dorai, personal communication, 2015). And the dwellings that they erected went far beyond emergency shelter. Lovingly furnished houses and tents like Mahmood's and Abu Mohammed's testify to Syrians' ability to build more permanent homes, in direct contradiction to Jordan's attempts at framing their stay as temporary. They also speak of refugees' 'homing' skills, that is, their ability to navigate displacement and regain familiar ground abroad, and to reactivate older ways of making family across borders.

Therefore, the comparison of a mid-sized town and a village, Mafraq and Zaatari Village, reveals that *where* Syrians seek refuge and how well they fare in exile depends on the type of pre-war transnational connections that they could resort to during conflict. Naturally, much of Zaatari Village's greater success in integrating newcomers in the local economy and housing market can be attributed to the smaller influx of refugees, the lesser pressure on public services and the – beneficial – absence of Jordanian authorities. Yet it remains that refugees with strong family ties in the host country sought shelter in villages, rather than more anonymous urban areas. In villages, strong support networks then allowed them to rebuild their lives more quickly and become economically self-sufficient. By way of contrast, refugees in Mafraq, originally from central and northern Syria, disposed of weaker employment linkage. They benefited from their knowledge of local labour markets and employers, rather than tangible financial support, free housing and land provided by relatives.

Employees

However, Dr Hussein's warm words and friendly relationships with his Syrian relatives in the village did not obliterate the strong class differentials between refugees and hosts. While Mahmood and other Syrians lived in brick shacks and even tents, local Jordanians inhabited bigger and more sumptuous houses. The more prosaic truth is that Jordanians in Zaatari Village were not only tribesmen, but also *employers*. Digging into the backstory of pre-war Syrian labour migration to Zaatari Village sheds a new light on these striking inequalities. Since the 1980s, several of the older Syrian men that I interviewed had come to the village as unskilled labourers. Pre-war migration was highly gendered, and usually male. Some women like Um Ahmed, who had never visited the village in person before the war, recalled her father's travels to Zaatari. After returning as *refugees*, Syrians continued to work informally for their better-off Jordanian kin. Mahmood, for example, was one of the artisans decorating Dr Hussein's splendid villa. The latter proudly pointed out to me that his Syrian relative was allowed 'to enter the house'. I could not help noticing the contradiction, as we had just spent an entire day popping up unannounced at Syrians' doorsteps. As Mahmood told me, other Syrians tended to their hosts' sheep. While Syrians thus received support from their Jordanian kin – documentation, land, electricity and jobs – they also provided a valuable resource in return: cheap foreign labour. Their role in the informal economy has to be understood against the backdrop of Syrians' pre-war migration experiences and Jordan's hostile immigration policies.

While the Arab world lacks strong supranational organizations and policies, transnational labour migration has achieved de facto regional integration *from below*. But the lack of institutional frameworks and restrictive national immigration policies have produced a deeply fragmented 'pan-Arab labour market' (Thiollet 2017: 30). Jordan is a case in point. Long before 2011, its immigration policies were designed to frame Syrians' and other migrant workers' stay as temporary and push them into the informal sector. This 'non-policy of migration' (Van Aken 2005: 118) helped keep a struggling rentier state afloat (De Bel-Air 2008). In the 1970s, remittances from Jordanian white-collar workers in the Gulf had led to considerable upward social mobility of Jordanians back home and to the outsourcing of manual labour, especially in agriculture and construction. In the 1980s and 1990s, however, the return of Jordanians and Palestinians caused soaring unemployment rates of up to 30 per cent. Structural adjustment policies and the shrinking of the public sector put additional strain on Jordan's labour market, provoking the tightening of immigration policies and the restriction of foreign labour to certain low-skilled sectors. As a consequence, Abu Mohammed's and other Syrian men's pre-war circular mobilities are largely absent from official Jordanian immigration statistics. Before 2011, legal Syrian migrant workers made up a tiny percentage of legal work permit holders in Jordan. As the country lacks national asylum laws, Syrian refugees after 2011 were still subjected to the same asymmetrical migratory policies as other foreigners. Within the framework of the 2016 Jordan Compact, the host country offered to employ Syrians in so-called Special Economic Zones and to issue at least 200,000 work permits (Bellamy, Haysom, Wake and Barbelet 2017), but its impact was slow to trickle down to the countryside: by late 2016, I had not met any Syrians with work permits in either Zaatari Village or Mafraq.

Hence, the case study of Syrian refugees in Zaatari Village illustrates more than one type of cross-border dynamics. On the one hand, it highlights how Syrians capitalize on highly specific, *translocal* connections between a single neighbourhood in Homs and a tiny village in the Jordanian desert to deal with conflict-induced displacement. Reactivating older notions of tribal identity that predate the emergence of postcolonial states in the Arab world allowed them to subvert state logics of containment. Syrians' celebrations of 'family' also played on shared sentiments of Bedouin hospitality and, in more contemporary terms, pan-Arab solidarity.

On the other hand, though, Syrians' translocal mobilities were embedded into broader regimes of labour migration in the region. Therefore, the chapter goes beyond a narrow focus on conflict-induced displacement by drawing attention to wider processes of joint 'migrantization' and 'precarization'. In their study of mobilities in the aftermath of the Tunisian 'Arab spring', Garelli and Tazzioli (2017) define the latter as 'the processes of transformation that concern the economic and social condition of some people and that make it more difficult for them to stay in a certain place or to move' (p. 72). Finding employment in the informal economy in Zaatari Village was nothing new to my male Syrian interlocutors who had occupied a marginal position in Syrian society long before the war. But the conflict in their home country and the (temporary) closure of the border interrupted men's customary migrations and put them at the mercy of their employers, on whom they now depended not only for jobs, but also for secure legal status. Displacement also changed the gendered demographics of Syrian migration to rural areas in northern Jordan: after 2011, many former migrants brought their wives and children, and occasionally abandoned them in the village. Power and wealth differentials between refugees and hosts thus limited the extent to which Syrians could make homes in Zaatari Village. Nowhere is this more obvious than with regard to the ambivalent nature of the 'gift' of land. I was surprised that Mahmood, despite his considerable financial and emotional investment into his new homestead, was adamant about going back to Syria as soon as possible. In a similar vein, Dr Hussein explained: 'They [the Syrians] don't have *mulk* [private ownership]. In five years, they will go back.'

How Syrian refugees assess temporalities of displacement reveals their *personal* aspirations, both in the short-term and in the more long-term future.

To me, building concrete houses seemed to betray intentions to stay. However, Syrians' plans for return suggest that not all homes are built for eternity, and that different homes might fulfil different purposes. Mahmood, for example, lovingly equipped his kitchen with pots and pans to make it look acceptable to a potential spouse. In this regard, the material house was meant to help him obtain a specific – social – version of 'home': a family of his own. But mobility and acts of border-crossing were factored even into his strategies of family-making. He explored ways of importing Syrian women from other places in the Levant and was planning to take his family back to Homs in the not-so-distant future. Time and again, his 'homing' ability allowed him to conceive of old and new homes in the Middle East – and to find ways to get there.

But the temporary nature of Syrian settlement in Zaatari Village also has an important *political* dimension. Rumours of 13,000 new cement houses in the village sparked a controversy in Jordanian media and forced the local mayor to issue a denial. He clarified that only a few Syrians had received land from their Jordanian brethren, pointing out that the practice clashed with municipal plans for urban development. Much of the land allocated to Syrian refugees was allegedly bookmarked for agricultural purposes (Omari 2014). Shivering outside Mahmood's house, I found it hard to imagine olive trees in the barren desert. But in a country where land is a precious commodity – less than 5 per cent of Jordan's surface is arable – urban development has long been at the heart of power struggles between the Jordanian government, Transjordanians, Palestinians and, more recently, Iraqis and Syrians (Hughes 2016).

Earlier in 2016, I had accompanied a UK-based researcher to the office of Mafraq's mayor. We had a cordial conversation in formal Arabic about the humanitarian response in town until we asked about the land that Zaatari Camp was built on. The room fell silent. Clearly, the land that Mahmood's house was built on is valuable not only because it might be converted into an olive grove, but also because of its proximity to Jordan's biggest camp – a camp that is already transforming itself into a proper town. In 2017, a UNHCR representative was quoted as: 'Certainly, one would imagine that in some form, Zaatari will remain. But we hope as soon as possible it ceases to be a refugee camp' (Jaafari 2017). The emergence of a vibrant informal economy, epitomized by the camp's main shopping street which was ironically dubbed 'Champs-Elysées', has been taken as a sign of the gradual urbanization of the camp, as has been the appropriation of shelter. Dalal (2015) finds that refugees from different parts of Syria furnish their caravans differently. Bedouins from Homs, for example, have added tents to demarcate their space. Refugees on both sides of Zaatari's fence engage in 'home-making' in the desert. It might well be that Syrians in the village will have to cede ground if their Jordanian hosts rediscover the value of their 'gift': an empty patch of land, but now right next to a sprawling urban centre.

Home-making in transitional spaces

Another sketch by Derek Robertson bears the title: *For the Wayfarer That You Meet*. It blends together drawings of yet another richly coloured bee-eater, a carpet rolled out in the desert, adorned with tiny coffee cups, and blue road signs from the border region that demarcate Jordan's location as a regional crossroads. To Robertson, the painting speaks of 'the generosity of the Jordanian people … both at a personal level and nationally, in giving shelter to millions of refugees'.[2] To me, the little bird captures the unruly mobilities of my Syrian interlocutors. As the poet Wisława Szymborska points out, birds signify the possibility of movement and transitions. 'Even if it be a sparrow – its tail is abroad, thought its beak is still home. As if that weren't enough – it keeps fidgeting!' In a similar vein, the different meanings that Zaatari Village, along the route of migratory birds, has acquired for Syrians and Jordanians are closely related to complex forms of mobility. For the refugees that I interviewed, displacement is not simply a one-way street but embedded into more longstanding and circular migration trajectories and plans for future travels and homes.

This chapter did not seek to romanticize transnational connections as a panacea for displacement and dispossession. A scrubby outpost on the edge of the desert, Zaatari Village is home to a couple of thousand refugees who live in substandard accommodation and work in the informal economy, often under exploitative conditions. Relationships between Syrians and Jordanians are fraught with power differentials between citizens and refugees, middle-class employers and unskilled day labourers, landowners and those who erected their dwellings on borrowed land. Brick houses, tents and villas stand side-by-side. That these homes are far from unproblematic leaps to the eye. And yet, a shared sense of tribal identity, much older than the frontiers of the Jordanian nation-state, as well as more recent translocal practices of family visits, intermarriage and labour migration bind the refugee and the host community together. Cross-border family bonds have allowed Syrians to bypass humanitarian infrastructures such as the nearby camp, but also to remain largely under the radar of Jordanian authorities. However, to grasp Syrians' and Jordanians' understanding of the temporalities of home-making, one needs to factor in the formers' mobility-based survival strategies. As migrants and refugees, Syrians have not come to stay – but rather to come and come again. Like birds, they are able to adapt their travel routes in times of crisis and to devise new ways of making more or less permanent homes.

Syrians' experiences of loss and acts of navigation on the edge of cultivated land deeply resonated with me because I, too, had just lost a home. After a devastating break-up, I had fled into the 'field'. In Mafraq, a Jordanian family took me in and like my Syrian interlocutors, I tried to find common ground with my hosts. We bridged tremendous cultural, religious and linguistic gaps by emphasizing not shared ancestry, but shared middle-class aspirations: higher education, a white-collar job, an educated spouse. After some months, my host parents offered me to use their family names. As for Syrians in Zaatari Village, my social status in the border town was thus secured by a tribal affiliation. Like them, I also had to find ways to deal with social inequalities, although in my case the power balance was reversed, and sometimes ambiguous. As a German national with funding from a British university, I had the right passport and sufficient financial resources to come and leave not only Mafraq, but also Jordan, as I pleased. Borders that were closed to Syrians, but also many Jordanians, remained open to me. I also inhabited a more sumptuous 'home': while my five-person host family shared a flat, I had a three-room apartment to myself. Privacy, I soon learned, was a luxury in the desert. On the other hand, I knew preciously little about local customs and place names, let alone the Bedouin dialect, and relied on my ever-patient host mother to instruct me. Because she taught me how to behave at weddings and funerals, I could demonstrate belonging to the local community and my Syrian friends. While refugees in Zaatari Village knew what to expect, to me, home-making in nearby Mafraq was first of all a never-ending learning process, and one that still continues long after I officially finished my doctoral fieldwork in summer 2017. At times, it felt like a tightrope act. One thing, at least, that I had in common with my Jordanian and Syrian acquaintances was the love of birds. In the early morning, I often lay awake, listening to the birdsong and crowing of roosters, over the muffled sounds of bombings across the nearby border. In Mafraq's souq, I admired the tiny creatures that merchants kept in cages outside shops and restaurants. As for Syrians, songbirds have an almost mythical presence in their everyday lives and poetry, and many refugees bought canary birds, which came in many colours, to entertain their children.

On a final note, the provisional nature of refugee home-making in Zaatari Village suggests that place-based solutions to displacement might miss the point. A common approach in humanitarian action aims to restore refugees to formerly sedentary existences, through return or resettlement elsewhere. As the example of Syrians in northern Jordan serves to show, this risks overlooking returnees' longstanding mobility histories, but also ongoing insecurity and violence in their places of origin (Monsutti 2008; Scalettaris 2009). While a recognition of refugees' mobility-based survival strategies has been written into aid agenda's more recent plans for protection, for example UNHCR's 2009 urban refugee policies, host states like Jordan tend to control and securitize the movements of foreign populations on their territory (Long and Crisp 2010). In October 2018, the reopening of the border started a new chapter in Syrian-Jordanian relations. Would being mobile again in the Levant allow Syrians like Mahmood and Abu Mahmood to rebuild their lives more quickly? In the context of diminished refugee protection worldwide (Crawley and Skleparis 2017), this chapter aimed to put Zaatari back on the map: not as a humanitarian facility in a wasteland, but as an inhabited place where people have long nurtured different types of belonging. As the Global North and Zaatari Camp are getting more fenced off, one should not forget that Zaatari *Village*, a site of refuge in the desert, has been constituted by acts of movement and border-crossing.

Notes

1 For more of Derek Robertson's work on birds and refugees in Jordan, see www.creativepastures.com/migrations

2 Derek Robertson, 'For the Wayfarer That You Meet'. *Creative Pastures*, 2019. https://www.creativepastures.com/migrations

12

A house divided: Movement and race in urban ethnography

Melissa K. Wrapp

The promise of democracy has lost its shine in South Africa. More than twenty years after Nelson Mandela took office, the country is still widely considered one of the most unequal in the world.[1] Racial tensions roil just beneath the surface of a landscape scarred not only by segregation, but by 'spatial apartheid'. Young South Africans, facing near 50 per cent unemployment and desperate for opportunities, have become increasingly frustrated with the slow pace of change. But rather than labor, it is land that is a central idiom through which South Africans voice the untenability of racial inequality in the country, and calls for radical economic transformation in popular discourse are coupled with the constant refrain that whites must 'give back the land'.

In his inaugural State of the Nation Address in 2018, President Cyril Ramaphosa hailed a new dawn in which South Africans must put aside negativity, division and lack of trust. Much more controversially, he also suggested that a program of land expropriation without compensation be initiated in order to generate growth and make more land available to the people for cultivation. This has sparked a firestorm of debates around land reform, with some more dramatic commentators prematurely marking the 'end of private property as we know it'. Though historically such debates have centered on the redistribution of rural land, where racial disparities in ownership are most severe, there is a growing sense of recognition that urban property in South Africa is also fraught with the legacies of dispossession.

Houses in black urban townships are invariably written of disparagingly as 'matchboxes' by journalists and academics alike, ostensibly the wreckage of an indifferent apartheid state. Yet for many Xhosa residents in Cape Town these buildings are *amakhaya* (homes, in the isiXhosa language) – places of affective and ontological rootedness – and often a family's only asset. I lived in South Africa for a year, while studying property and experimentation with sustainable urban design practices in Cape Town. I quickly became immersed in a multitude of conflicts over family home ownership that my interlocutors were involved in mediating. As a researcher, navigating spatial apartheid and understanding these conflicts meant making home in multiple sites throughout the city. For my interlocutors, I soon learned that the divisions cut much deeper.

In this chapter, I explore the politics and practicalities of making home as an ethnographer in a context of extreme inequality and urban spatial segregation. In many ways this chapter is about movement – about moving house, and moving through space; about who has the power to move, and who is powerless in being moved; about how people come together in movement (and in movements), and about what remains fixed, what persists, amidst that movement. Through foregrounding the history of one interlocutor's struggle to return to his family home, I unpack the legacies of dislocation that shape the contemporary Capetonian housing milieu. By weaving in my own challenges with negotiating the place-based politics of recognition in the city, I not only address the complexities of my personal experience of living in the field, but also speak to the deeper cultural significance of home in South Africa.

Displacement

It was nearly 9 p.m. on a crisp spring night in Gugulethu, a township on the outskirts of Cape Town. Dozens of people had gathered in a local church for a biweekly community meeting to discuss housing issues, but after four hours their patience was wearing thin. As soon as the closing prayer finished, most attendees scrambled into the dirt lot outside to vie for a lift from the few scattered drivers rushing to their cars. A small crowd pressed forward towards the meagre altar, seeking answers from the community leaders, personal assurances that their 'cases' would be taken up.

Sandla and I were alone in the back pews.[2] As I finished up my field notes and checked a few of my isiXhosa translations with him, he began to tell me the latest developments in his family's ongoing housing conflict.

Born in the early 1980s, Sandla has fond memories of growing up in his paternal grandparents' home in Gugulethu, known as Gugs. After five years of living on NY 11 (NY is short for 'Native Yard', as the streets are named in Gugs), his parents were allocated a house by the government some fifteen kilometres away in the newly developing township of Khayelitsha.

The history of township development in Cape Town is a history of overcrowding and excess, of the municipality allocating too little space to black residents confined therein and residents inevitably spilling out into the surrounding land. This flow of concentration and diffusion was shaped by a core contradiction in the colonial and apartheid governments' policies, in which they both depended on black labor and imposed strict 'influx controls' on the number of African people permitted into the province. Though conventionally associated with the apartheid era, many of the key policies effecting racial segregation and dispossession in South Africa predate the Afrikaner Nationalist Party's rise to power in 1948. Thus, rather than being introduced all at once, these policies gradually ossified over the course of decades. Crucially, in 1902 the Native Reserve Location Act authorized the government in the Cape Province to establish residential areas for Africans outside of towns. In 1923 urban areas were nationally legislated as white, and provisions were made for land to be set aside for African 'locations'. Then, in 1934, the Slums Clearance Act licenced the forcible removal of black people in areas deemed to be slums. Finally, in 1950 the Group Areas Act compelled the creation of separate residential areas based on race and prevented people from buying property or living in an area of another racial group.

Gugulethu first developed in the 1950s as an emergency camp for the city's slum clearance program. Gradually, over the course of many years, black people were forcibly relocated there from more central parts of the city. Sandla's grandparents were moved to Gugulethu in 1962. Over time, the camp was formalized into a township conceived as a 'family life settlement' for Xhosa residents. As in the other, older black townships then, houses in Gugulethu are believed to be *amakhaya*, family homes (frequently juxtaposed to *izindlu*, mere 'houses'). Residents treat these homes not as private property in the conventional commodity sense, but as the inalienable, collective property of the family. Given that black South Africans were barred from property ownership, however, from the municipal perspective these houses were considered 'rental stock', leased to occupants and administratively passed down through generations but ultimately the property of the state.

A few decades after Gugulethu, Khayelitsha was developed, again to relieve overcrowding and preserve the Group Areas system of racial segregation in Cape Town. Residents from neighbouring townships like Crossroads and Nyanga were forcibly relocated there. Aptly named, in terms of Sandla's personal history, Khayelitsha means 'new home'.

Sandla struggled with the transition to his new neighbourhood. When he eventually dropped out of high school, a period of what he described to me as 'troubles' began in his life. It was a sore subject that I could tell he was both deeply ashamed of and eager to discuss, never fully going into details, yet continually obliquely referencing them. I never pressed him to share more than he offered. But there were hints. He took a keen interest in assisting other young people suffering from drug addiction and sometimes alluded to his own recovery process. There were also euphemistic references to 'playing with cars', which I understood to mean car hijacking. But as he grew older, Sandla also dabbled in local community politics, assisting anti-eviction activists in various campaigns to return people to their homes, usually in instances of bank repossession.

Sandla shared his history of political engagement with me one afternoon as we waited for a community meeting to get underway. Everyone was busy discussing a letter threatening eviction that one elderly person had received from the municipality. Speaking of his youth, Sandla reflected, 'What [the municipality] were doing was wrong, chasing people out of their houses. Where are they going to stay? Why can't there be another resolution for their problem, instead of being chased away? I didn't like that.' He also confessed he was enjoying himself. 'To us it was fun! Young boys having fun. We were happy to throw stones. We wanted to be out there. Fighting. *Toyi-toying* [protesting]. Burning things. Being chased by the police. It was fun because we were young and wild, you know?'

Trouble followed Sandla. In 2008, he finally fled back to NY 11, where his grandma was living alone. After another night of fun, the police were coming to Sandla's parents' house in search of him, and he was desperate for somewhere to hide, somewhere to rest. 'I just wanted to sleep, Melissa.' His grandmother took him in, but Sandla found himself shocked by her living conditions. She was in her seventies, no longer fully able to care for herself; the warm home he remembered from his childhood was filthy. Sandla never planned to move back to Gugulethu, but a few weeks of caring for his grandma turned into years. Cleaning the house, fetching groceries, and cooking became a kind of rehab for Sandla, and a relief for his grandmother.

After several years, this comfortable routine of mutual support came to an end, when his grandmother became too old for him to care for, and she left to live with an aunt. At the same time Sandla's younger brother Lucky was tiring of Khayelitsha. He came to live in the shacks at the back of the house, and soon they fell into partying again. Late night binges turned to petty squabbles by day. Eventually Sandla's mother, fearful of her sons' fighting, arranged for Lucky to move into an uncle's house across town (who himself was staying elsewhere with a girlfriend). Sandla continued on partying at NY 11, until one day a few months later his father's sister showed up unannounced and threw him out. 'You think this is your house? You think you can act this way in my mother's home? You must pack your things and go!' he remembers her yelling.

Sandla was indignant. While he recognized that the house didn't belong to him, he felt it was his right to stay there as a member of the family. This logic is consistent with a general belief among Xhosa people that every family member has a right to return to their *ikhaya*, whether for a brief visit or a longer stay to get back on their feet. Without consulting the family elders, his aunt unceremoniously tossed him out and installed her son in the house in his place. Once again looking for refuge, Sandla turned to his mother's family home, across Gugulethu on NY 84, where he moved into his cousin Sox's shack at the back of the house. I arrived in Cape Town a few months later, as Sandla continued to spar with his aunt.

His maternal family was outraged at what happened to him, and also perhaps a little anxious about finding space for him in their home. One cousin had heard about local meetings on housing issues taking place at the church up the road and suggested Sandla attend. To his surprise, the meeting was filled with people experiencing similar challenges: family members kicking them out of the house, disputes over title deeds, arguments between siblings over whether to sell a home, and more. 'When I listen to their problems', he once shared, 'it makes mine feel like it is not so big.' He kept attending each week, not only in the hopes of finding assistance for his issue, but also to get involved in what he saw as injustices taking place in his community. Animated by his own sense of persecution at home, Sandla felt that in attending these meetings, offering words of support and participating in actions to reinstate people in their family homes, he was doing something concrete to rectify the wrongs he saw around him. 'You are helping people, but sometimes it's like therapy for *your* problems', another man in a similar situation told me.

That night at the community meeting where we sat together in the pews, he was fresh from the latest series of confrontations over the house, these pivotally occurring at his grandmother's funeral.

'So … what does this mean?' I asked after he finished recounting the story. His eyes flickered with anticipation and waggish energy, and he declared, 'I think it means war.'

Becoming known

Sandla and I met during my first month of fieldwork. In the initial phase of my research, I interned with a local NGO that upgrades informal settlements through collaborative community design processes. On the weekends, I spent my time hanging out with activist friends in Gugs. Although we first met five years ago when they were working for the Anti-Eviction Campaign, they had since formed their own grassroots human rights advocacy movement known as *Abemi* (roughly 'citizens' in isiXhosa, with connotations of autochthony). Abemi recast itself several times over the years, first forming as something of a labor movement, then organizing around the rights of backyard shack dwellers (or 'backyarders'), before transforming again into a platform for mediating housing disputes.

Conflicts were intensifying as the city ramped up its title transfer program, aiming to hand over the title deeds for thousands of municipal rental properties, especially those built in the apartheid era. Given that these properties have been occupied for decades, there are generations of claimants attempting to participate in the *nikezela* ('hand over'), often pitting family members against each other in the struggle to secure houses. To address this challenge, Abemi held open community meetings during the week; over the weekend, they were invited to come to houses where families were fighting (usually over home ownership, but also often over interpersonal issues). And so a group of thirty or so community members would convene at the KFC in the center of Gugulethu every Saturday and walk from house to house, listening to disputes, examining legal documents and seeking to find peaceable resolutions. It was a heady blend of more conventional mediation, anti-apartheid activist organizing and Xhosa forms of communal deliberation.

Early on, one of the more senior leaders watched me fumble to take notes and follow the proceedings. He barked at Sandla, who was accustomed to being ordered around as a 'youth member', to help translate. As the group departed from one house, where the grandchildren were fighting over the title deed, to head to the next, Sandla and I lagged behind. While we meandered through the streets, a friendly debate about the details of the case evolved into a broader discussion about the significance of family homes.

'There are certain rituals you need to do at your family home', Sandla explained. 'It depends on the situation. Sometimes ancestors can come to you in a dream. You go to the elders to interpret it, and they tell you to make a ritual at your family home.' Such traditional ceremonies take place over the course of several days, and involve the extended family gathering at the home to sacrificially slaughter an animal, brew *umqombothi* ('traditional beer'), and communicate with the family's ancestors. They are held to mark key life events, like the birth of a child or a child's transition to adulthood, to offer thanksgiving or to seek guidance. For Xhosa people, the ancestors act as an intermediary to God, so performing rituals not only affirms a person's identity in relation to their kin, but also is a way of practicing spirituality and regaining physical and emotional well-being. 'You must go to the home of your father – your family home linked with your clan name [*isiduko*]', he continued. 'That is where your family is rooted. That way the message goes to them.' Someone walking near us interjected, 'It's like if you swap [cell phone] SIM cards – the message can't go through. Your ancestors can't get the SMS if you go to a different house!'

Sandla fell silent for a moment and then confided, 'I actually need to do a ritual. You see my leg?' I looked down and noticed for the first time that he was walking with a limp, stiffly rolling off of his heel with each stride. 'Two years ago, I was shot.' It was back when his brother was still with him on NY 11. One late night at a *shebeen*[3] he got a phone call, and when he ducked outside to escape the sound of blaring house music, he was shot in his side. 'It was dark. I think he thought I was somebody else. Mistaken identity.' He never saw the shooter, since he quickly lost consciousness, but onlookers later told him that the man jumped on top of him to 'finish the job'. He repeatedly tried to shoot Sandla, but first he missed, then the gun jammed, and the guy finally gave up and ran off. At the hospital, doctors were unable to remove the bullet lodged near the base of his spine, the cause of Sandla's limp.

He looked up at me with a touch of wonder in his face. 'The ancestors must have protected me, ne? I think I must make a ritual to thank them. That's why I need to get back to my grandfather's house.' I nodded solemnly, beginning to understand the true depth of the cultural significance of *amakhaya*. It was not only out of economic desperation that people were fighting, and sometimes literally dying, over these houses. Although such customs have relaxed to a degree in urban areas (perhaps primarily because of limitations on space and the dearth of housing, but also because of the influence of Christian norms), they are still vital to Xhosa people's sense of self, spirituality, and their connection to kin. In the context of the trauma of dispossession and forced removal, being known by and connected to one's ancestors through ritual performances of attachment to a family home is an essential means of reproducing rootedness, belonging and identity.

At that time, as Sandla and I strolled through the streets, I did not yet understand that walking would soon become a sort of ritual I would practice in order to become known in my field site. For I was also seeking to find the most appropriate, safe, and productive housing for myself. My plan, devised before getting to the field, was to live with a friend in a shared house in the city while working for the NGO; from there, I would explore whether moving to Gugulethu was possible while I was working with Abemi. Living 'in town', as people say in reference to the city center, made sense for a lot of reasons. It was close to the civic center, where many of the municipal officials I wanted to interview were based. The provincial government archives were just a short walk up the road. An abundance of cafés made scheduling interviews easy. Crucially, it meant traveling against the stream of interminable traffic that congests the city's highways to get to the NGO's office in Khayelitsha. As a woman, I was ostensibly safer navigating alone in town.

Given that 'town' was legislated as a 'white area' under apartheid, it is also strongly associated with the wealthy white minority that continues to dominate its swanky skyscrapers and well-kept inner-city suburbs. The further enmeshed I became in my relationships with Abemi, the more untenable my living situation became. The people we were encountering, and the activists themselves, were facing bitter housing disputes, being evicted, making do without basic services, living in shacks and overcrowded homes on the urban periphery. As I was meeting people, inevitably they would ask where I was living. In Cape Town, the question 'where do you live?' is a loaded one. The city's geography of segregation remains largely unchanged, and in the patchwork of townships and suburbs sprawling out from Table Mountain a Capetonian can instantly filter you into a racial and economic category the moment you reply. And my interlocutors' reaction to my reply, '*eTown*', felt quietly devastating. A knowing nod. A momentary flicker of assumptions confirmed across their faces, as if to say, 'Of course you do.' A subtle feeling that a bit more distance had crept in between us; perhaps I could only then see the distance that was there all along.

How could I expect people to trust me to open up and share their stories, then blithely return to the safety, comfort and privilege of the city? I resolved that moving not only would be beneficial in terms of the technicalities of conducting my research, but was also ethically necessary. And so one day when my closest interlocutor, Mr. Thole, called to tell me a room in the backyard of his sister's house had opened up, I was overjoyed; without further thought, I told him I would be moving in. He was my oldest friend in Cape Town, and I loved his family members, fourteen of whom lived together in Gugs a few blocks over from his sister's house. Living as a 'backyarder' would mean that I would have a degree of privacy to escape each day to recharge and work on field notes. My rent money would also contribute to the family's income without my becoming a burden and taking up space in the house. As an added bonus, their family home was on NY 84 next door to Sandla, who had quickly become a trusted friend.

When I got home later that day, I absentmindedly googled the address and my stomach dropped. The house wasn't in Gugs, but a few blocks over in an adjacent neighbourhood called New Crossroads. Technically, it was in Nyanga, a notoriously violent township known as the 'murder capital' of South Africa. I panicked. I had committed to renting the room, and Mr. Thole was already texting about how excited his family was; I also knew him well enough to trust that he wouldn't put me in a dangerous situation. He was an older man, well known as a respected PAC[4] activist who had been involved in more militant forms of struggle under apartheid. I knew in his mind his reputation would be enough to protect me, but surely one person's influence could only go so far? I frantically called my partner in the United States to talk things through, and I'm grateful he supported me in following my better instincts to trust Mr. Thole.

Learning what, and who, to trust about safety in South Africa is challenging. The levels of violent crime are staggering, but I also always felt much of the advice I received was strongly colored by racial paranoia. I would ask someone about taking the train alone for example and, flabbergasted, they would describe what sounded like a post-apocalyptic war zone. Another would answer that the train was a mundane part of their daily commute. As I started casually floating my moving plans to test the waters, some people were excited, but most (including Gugulethu residents themselves) were anxious and concerned. I was repeatedly asked if I would be buying a gun. One friend in construction made an earnest, elaborate proposal that I build additional walls and security bars into the room to give myself 'more time' in the case of a break-in. When I tried to politely say this seemed like a bit much, he countered with plans to wire in a security system.

In the end, I decided to rely on social relationships instead. I signed up for further Xhosa language classes. And, recalling Mr. Thole's assertions when we first met – 'I am *known*. No one will lay a finger on you.' – I pitched an idea to him: 'What if we walked around the neighborhood together a couple of days each week before I move in?' To my surprise, he loved the idea, so every few days I would pop around to go for walks.[5] Walking soothed Sandla's leg pain, so often he would hear us from next door and tag along too. We made a motley crew, waving and chatting with puzzled neighbours as we strolled along. Children were always the most curious. A group of men who played dominos out on the corner, a few houses away from the local *shebeen*, were a permanent fixture on the street. Everything was a difficult balancing act in impression management. Be friendly without putting out an 'invitation'. Be humble without looking like a victim. Be respectful but mind your business and move along. But ultimately, in helping me to become known in the area, these walks were crucial in smoothing my path, and soothing my nerves, before the move. They also became a chance for Sandla to update us about his case, which was about to intensify again.

Intestacy

After moving to Nyanga our walks continued, usually at the insistence of the women in Mr. Thole's family. But eventually I went from an oddity to uninteresting, at least for the people in our area – children's shouts of '*umlungu!*' ('white person!') still sometimes followed me down the streets elsewhere in Gugs. I adjusted to collecting water each morning from a tap in the yard, learned to tune out the booming bass each night from the shacks next door, and became more deeply enmeshed in Abemi's cases. As with the Tholes themselves, I spent much of my time between meetings and interviews hanging out at the family house on NY 84, watching Zulu soapies with aunties and playing with their two-year-old grandchild.

One morning, just as the children left for school, Sandla's aunt shuffled in from next door and announced that his grandmother had passed away in the hospital. It took days before I finally saw him, crossing paths in the yard, and was able to offer my condolences. He thanked me, but seemed strangely elated. 'Things are happening Mel! I think I might be going back home.'

Xhosa funerals in the townships are held *ekhaya* ('at home'). During the week, a rented marquee tent materializes in the front yard of the house, usually overtaking a portion of the street, where the metal stakes are driven into the asphalt. Sandla had been scarce because he was immersed in pre-funeral preparations, family gatherings and prayers. The elder men in his family were apparently unaware that his cousin had overtaken the house. In one boozy, late night meeting, Sandla regaled them with stories of his confrontations with his aunt and one encounter in particular, in which he claimed she threatened that the house would no longer be 'a Jola house' (Sandla's clan name). In other words, she would claim the home for her husband's clan. Maintaining the 'legacy' of a home was a crucial factor in many of the disputes I had witnessed. I wondered if he was playing up to their patriarchal sense of ego, but he thought it was tipping the scales in his favour. Some denounced the aunt for circumventing their authority and expressed support for his right to move back home.

That Saturday I joined the Tholes for the service on NY 11. None of us knew Sandla's grandmother, but we decided it was important to make a show of supporting him. We arrived shortly after 9:30 a.m., as the program was already well underway. More than fifty people were packed into the uncomfortable plastic folding chairs lined up under the tent, with a few dozen more scattered on the sidewalk behind them. The scalloped edges of the white plastic tent draped sadly over the edge of the roof, shading the dirt yard below where close family members were sitting around the coffin and listening to a pastor preach fire and brimstone. He flowed between isiXhosa and English, his sentences punctuated by declarations of 'Yes Lord!' from the crowd. A few young men hustled around us, carrying red Coca-Cola crates filled with 'cool drinks' (glass bottles of orange Fanta, Coke, Sprite and Stoney ginger beer). After hours, we piled onto a pair of buses that shuttled us to the graveyard, where the coffin was interred, before heading back to the house for lunch.

I collected meals off the back of a truck for myself and a couple of aunties and wove my way through the crowd to the folding chairs they had snagged. It was standard funeral fare – a styrofoam takeaway container filled with samp, carrots, potatoes and chicken – something I sadly knew was 'standard' since attending funerals had unexpectedly become a regular feature of my fieldwork. As we ate I finally spotted Sandla, who rushed over to greet us in between handing out cool drinks. While somber, he was still brimming with excitement. He told us simply being back inside the house felt like a victory, like it was some kind of positive sign, even if it was only for the funeral.

We did our best to perform respectability on Sandla's behalf, dressed in our Sunday best and politely chatting with various relatives and neighbours. The event was the culmination of months of his trying to sway his family's perceptions and prove he had 'really changed'. He was going to church, volunteering with Abemi, and working part-time organizing youth activities for a local non-profit. Though his father had been distant after Sandla left Khayelitsha, they were at least on speaking terms again. After hearing about the conflict week-in and week-out, I half expected there to be some fireworks at the funeral. In the end it was somewhat anti-climactic; we left late in the afternoon as things fizzled out. I had to wait until the community meeting the following week for the news.

The real discussions about the fate of the house took place behind the scenes, during 'after-tears' drinking later that night. Sandla pled passionately for his right to return home, energized by months of dialogue over other people's cases at Abemi meetings. When family members seemed ambivalent, he appealed to their sense of cultural pride and propriety, insisting that he must come home to make a ritual for the ancestors after his shooting. 'I won't be myself, I can't be Sandla, until I'm able to come home!' He even proposed sharing the house with his cousin or occupying the shacks at the back. All for naught. Despite the men's earlier outrage, his aunt shut the discussion down. Sandla described her as 'more financially able' than the rest of the family, and she was able to bully the others into acquiescence. Once again, he was spurned.

Later at the meeting, as we sat together in those pews, I waffled at his 'declaration of war'. The decision was a devastating blow. 'But, what else can you really do?' I asked. 'Wouldn't continuing to fight only alienate you from the rest of your family?' I also secretly wondered if he was healthier living with his mother's family on NY 84, and less prone to falling into old habits. 'You seem to be doing so well … won't opening this up again get you off track?' He considered my questions briefly before dismissing them, 'I don't have a choice; I have to fight.'

A few weeks went by. I got lost in fieldwork. The next time I saw Sandla I was rushing to court – a man I had interviewed about the municipality renting out his family home to someone else had been arrested when, out of desperation, he decided to occupy the property by force. Hearing me shout out to Mr. Thole that we were running late, Sandla materialized in the yard, clutching a stack of papers. 'Mel! Can you read something for me? I want to make sure the English makes sense!' Before I could respond, he triumphantly shoved the stack into my hand – a copy of his ID, a death certificate for his grandmother, and a handwritten letter describing his life on NY 11 (with his departure and the family's decision about the house conveniently omitted). With each document I scanned, my confusion gave way to clarity: Sandla had decided on his next battlefield.

The title deed for Sandla's family home was in his grandfather's name. As with most people in the townships, his grandmother died without a will. Perhaps his family assumed the fate of the property was settled by virtue of their meeting, or maybe they were unaware of the issue of title altogether. Sandla, it seemed, was now going to try to wrangle control of the house by registering the property with the Master of High Court (the branch that deals with deceased estates), obtaining the title deed, and evicting his cousin. I lingered on the letter, keenly aware both that I was troubled by the omissions and also that almost nothing about the formal legal processes I had encountered in my fieldwork mapped neatly, or equitably, onto what was happening 'on the ground'. I answered the only way I felt comfortable – yes, the English did make sense.

Going home

I later confided in Mr. Thole about the letter. He was well-versed in intestate succession, having accompanied many people to the Master's court. Part of me suspects he privately advised Sandla to go the 'legal' route. His initial attempts to mediate the dispute when Sandla was first thrown out were something of a nonstarter, since the aunt outright refused to attend any meetings. When I asked, Mr. Thole deflected from answering questions about the plot to secure the title deed, only remarking vaguely about the difficult life Sandla has led. However, over time I sensed he was starting to side with the family's consensus on the house. Maybe it was inadvertent; maybe it just got lost in the shuffle; but in the end, he repeatedly delayed in taking Sandla to the Master's, and the papers collected dust in cousin Sox's shack. Another anti-climax.

For his part, Sandla enrolled in classes to begin working on earning his matric (South Africa's GED equivalent). With less time for Abemi meetings, I started seeing less and less of him each week. He was still living on NY 84, though disagreements with his cousin had forced him out of the shack and onto the couch in the living room of the house. Every so often we crossed each other's paths late at night, and when he walked me home to New Crossroads we would catch up. Although school had pushed it to the back burner, Sandla still talked longingly about one day going home.

Like so many other conflicts I experienced in the field, it would be easy to chalk up Sandla's fight with his family as an isolated personal problem. But to reduce these experiences to individual idiosyncrasies is to obscure the broader structural conditions, and deeper history of displacement, that have shaped present-day conflicts. The intergenerational trauma of dislocation reverberates in Sandla's story, from his grandparents' forced removal from the city of Cape Town to his parents' relocation to Khayelitsha. Decades of being forced into overcrowded living conditions with unclear tenure arrangements and no alternatives have created a context ripe for conflict. However, so too echoes a strong history of mutual aid, solidarity and activism. And the motivations behind his struggle to return home are as multivalent as 'home' itself: a form of shelter, an economic asset, a place of spiritual rootedness, a connection to family, a site of past belonging and future aspiration.

Discourse around post-apartheid urban transformation often centers on bridging the gap between black and white Capetonians. As a researcher, overcoming that divide in order to understand the impact of contemporary spatial planning regimes meant living in multiple sites throughout the city.

And yet ironically, dwelling alongside Sandla, in similar housing albeit for dramatically different (and differently constrained) reasons, offered me insight into much deeper forms of fragmentation. Sandla's story reveals that the violence of segregation lives on, not only between social groups but also in the fractures within families forced to make home within apartheid's constraints. It also complicates straightforward narratives about property transfer and economic justice; a title deed, though essential, cannot paper over the wounds of centuries.

*   *   *

The last Saturday before I left the field, I went, as always, to sit on the planters outside KFC to meet up with Abemi members. Before the house visits got underway, I spoke with as many people as possible to say goodbye. It was an emotional morning. Several women warmly questioned if I really had to leave. Once again, Mr. Thole helped to smooth my path.

'Of course she has to leave', he cut in. 'That's how it works. Everyone has to go home.'

Notes

1 This claim is often made based on the measure of income inequality, a metric known as the GINI coefficient.
2 The names and exact locations in this chapter have been changed to protect my interlocutors.
3 A *shebeen* is an unlicenced bar, common in South African townships and often run out of someone's home.
4 PAC is an abbreviation for the Pan Africanist Congress political party.
5 In fact, when I moved out and a Zimbabwean couple took over the room, they begged Mr. Thole to walk around with them too so that they would be seen together by the neighbours. Only later, as I encountered multiple newcomers to the area who were assaulted and mugged, did I realize how vital our walks were.

Bibliography

Abrahamian, L. (2007), 'Troubles and Hopes – Armenian Family, Home and Nation', in D. Tsypylma and W. Kaschuba (eds), *Representations on the Margins of Europe: Politics and Identities in the Baltic and South Caucasian States*, 267–81, Frankfurt/Main: Campus.

Abu-Lughod, L. (1986), *Veiled Sentiments*, Berkeley: University of California Press.

Achilli, L. (2015), 'Syrian Refugees in Jordan: A Reality Check', *Policy Brief*, European University Institute. Available online: http://cadmus.eui.eu/bitstream/handle/1814/34904/MPC_2015-02_PB.pdf?sequence=1 (accessed 1 January 2019).

Ahmed, S. (1999), 'Home and Away: Narratives of Migration and Estrangement', *International Journal of Cultural Studies*, 2 (3): 329–47.

Ahmed, S. (2004), *The Cultural Politics of Emotion*, Edinburgh: Edinburgh University Press.

Allerton, C., ed. (2016), *Children: Ethnographic Encounters*, London: Bloomsbury.

APUR (2011), 'Sans-Abri à Paris – La Présence Des sans-Abri Sur Le Territoire Parisien et l'action de La Collectivité Pour Aider à Leur Réinsertion', *Atelier Parisien D'Urbanisme*, January. Available online: www.apur.org/fr/nos-travaux/abri-paris-presence-abri-territoire-parisien-action-collectivite-aider-reinsertion (accessed 21 March 2019).

Azzeh, L. (2017), 'Kingdom's Average Monthly Salary Stands at $637 – Report', *The Jordan Times*, 7 April. Available online: www.jordantimes.com/news/local/kingdom%E2%80%99s-average-monthly-salary-stands-637-%E2%80%94-report (accessed 31 March 2019).

Bellamy, C., S. Haysom, C. Wake and V. Barbelet (2017), *The Lives and Livelihoods of Syrian Refugees*, HPG Commissioned Report, London: Overseas Development Institute. Available online: www.odi.org/publications/10736-lives-and-livelihoods-syrian-refugees (accessed 1 January 2019).

Benston, M. (1969), 'The Political Economy of Women's Liberation', *Monthly Review* 21 (4): 13–27.

Berlant, L. (1998), 'Intimacy: A Special Issue', *Critical Inquiry*, 24 (2): 281–88.

Birdwell-Pheasant, D. and D. Lawrence-Zúñiga, eds. (1999), *House Life: Space, Place and Family in Europe*, Oxford and New York: Berg.

Bloch, E. (1995), *The Principle of Hope*, Boston: MIT Press.

Bloch, M. (1993), 'Zafimaniry Birth and Kinship Theory', *Social Anthropology*, 1 (1b): 119–32.

Bloch, M. (1995), 'The Resurrection of the House among the Zafimaniry', in J. Carsten and S. Hugh-Jones (eds), *About the House: Levi-Strauss and Beyond*, 69–83, Cambridge: Cambridge University Press.

Bobbette, A. (2018), *Cultures of Forecasting: Volatile and Vulnerable Nature, Knowledge, and the Future of Uncertainty*, PhD dissertation, School of Geography and the Environment, University of Cambridge, Cambridge.

Borneman, J. and H. Abdellah (2009), *Being There - The Fieldwork Encounter and the Making of Truth*, Berkely: University of California Press.

Botticello, J. (2007), 'Lagos in London: Finding the Space of Home', *Home Cultures*, 4 (1): 7–23.

Bourdieu, P. (1970), 'The Berber House or the World Reversed', *Social Science Information*, 9 (2): 151–70.

Bourdieu, P. (1976), 'Marriage Strategies as Strategies of Social Reproduction', in R. Forster and O. Ranum (eds), *Family and Society*, Baltimore: Johns Hopkins University Press.

Bourdieu, P. (1992), *The Logic of Practice*, London: Polity Press.

Bourgois, P. (2002), *In Search of Respect: Selling Crack in El Barrio*, Cambridge: Cambridge University Press.

Bowlby, S., S. Gregory and L. McKie (1997), '"Doing Home": Patriarchy, Caring, and Space', *Women's Studies International Forum*, 20 (3) (1 May 1997): 343–50.

Brun, C. (2015), 'Home as a Critical Value: From Shelter to Home in Georgia', *Refuge*, 31 (1): 43–54.

Brun, C. and A. Fabos (2015), 'Making Homes in Limbo? A Conceptual Framework', *Refuge*, 31 (1): 5–17.

Capo, J. (2015), '"Durable Solutions," Transnationalism, and Homemaking among Croatian and Bosnian Former Refugees', *Refuge*, 31 (1): 19–30.

Carsten, J. (1997), *The Heat of the Hearth: The Process of Kinship in a Malay Fishing Community*, Oxford: Clarendon Press.

Carsten, J. (2003), *After Kinship*, Cambridge: Cambridge University Press.

Carsten, J. (2018), 'House-Lives as Ethnography/Biography', *Social Anthropology*, 26 (1): 103–16.

Carsten, J. and S. Hugh-Jones, eds. (1995), *About the House: Lévi-Strauss and Beyond*, Cambridge: Cambridge University Press.

Castro, E. V. (2002), 'Perspectival Anthropology and the Method of Controlled Equivocation', *Tipiti: Journal of the Society for the Anthropology of Lowland South America*, 2 (2): 3–22.

Castro, E. V. (2014), *Cannibal Metaphysics*, Minneapolis: Univocal.

Christou, A. (2002), *Narratives of Place, Culture and Identity: Second-Generation Greek-Americans Return 'Home'*, Amsterdam: Amsterdam University Press.

Cieraad, I. (2006), *At Home: An Anthropology of Domestic Space*, Syracuse: Syracuse University Press.

Cieraad, I. (2006), 'Dutch Windows: Female Virtue and Female Vice', in I. Cieraad (ed.), *At Home: An Anthropology of Domestic Space*, 31–52, Syracuse: Syracuse University Press.

Clark, I. and A. Grant (2015), 'Sexuality and Danger in the Field: Starting an Uncomfortable Conversation', *Journal of the Anthropological Society of Oxford*, 7 (1): 14.

Clifford, J. (1983), 'On Ethnographic Authority', *Representations*, 2: 118–46.

Clifford, J. and G. E. Marcus, eds. (2010), *Writing Culture: The Poetics and Politics of Ethnography*, Berkley: University of California Press.

Collier, J. F., M. Z. Rosaldo and S. J. Yanagisako (1987), 'Is There a Family? New Anthropological Views', in J. F. Collier and S. J. Yanagisako (eds), *Gender: Essays Toward a Unified Analysis*, Stanford: Stanford University Press.

Comaroff, J. and J. Comaroff (2003), 'Ethnography on an Awkward Scale', *Ethnography*, 4 (2): 147–79.

Crapanzano, V. (1985), *Tuhami: Portrait of a Moroccan*, Chicago: University of Chicago Press.

Crawley, H. and D. Skleparis (2017), 'Refugees, Migrants, Neither, Both: Categorical Fetishism and the Politics of Bounding in Europe's "Migration Crisis"', *Journal of Ethnic and Migration Studies*, 44 (1): 48–64.

Crockford, S. (2017), '*After the American Dream: The Political Economy of Spirituality in Northern Arizona*', PhD dissertation, Social Anthropology, London School of Economics and Political Sciences.

Dalal, A. (2015), 'A Socio-economic Perspective on the Urbanisation of Zaatari Camp in Jordan', *Migration Letters*, 12 (3): 263–78.

Daniels, I. and S. Andrews (2010), *The Japanese House: Material Culture in the Modern Home*, London: Berg.

Day, S., E. Papataxiarchis and M. Stewart (1999), *Lilies of the Field: Marginal People Who Live for the Moment*, Boulder: Westview Press.

De Bel-Air, F. (2008), 'Circular Migration to and from Jordan: An Issue of High Politics'. *CARIM AS* 20, European University Institute. Available online: http://cadmus.eui.eu/bitstream/handle/1814/8341/CARIM_AS&N_2008_20.pdf?sequence=1 (accessed 1 January 2019).

De Bel-Air, F. (2013), 'Composition of the population', in M. Ababsa (ed.), *Atlas of Jordan – History, Territories and Society*, 246–52, Beirut: Presses de l'Ifpo.

de Certeau, M. (1984), *The Practice of Everyday Life*, Berkeley and London: University of California Press.

de la Cadena, M. and M. Blaser, eds. (2017), *A World of Many Worlds*, Durham: Duke University Press.

Deleuze, G. and F. Guattari (1994), *What Is Philosophy?* New York: Columbia University Press.

Denzin, N. K. (1997), *Interpretive Ethnography: Ethnographic Practices for the 21st Century*, London: SAGE.

Derrida, J. (2005), 'The Principle of Hospitality', *Parallax*, 11 (1): 6–9.

Desjarlais, R. (1997), *Shelter Blues: Sanity and Selfhood Among the Homeless*, Philadelphia: University of Pennsylvania Press.

Dittmar, H. (1992), *The Social Psychology of Material Possessions: To Have Is to Be*, New York: St. Martin's Press.

Doná, G. (2015), 'Making Homes in Limbo: Embodied Virtual "Homes" in Prolongued Conditions of Displacement', *Refuge*, 31 (1): 67–73.

Donzelot, J. (1997), *The Policing of Families*, Baltimore: Johns Hopkins University Press.

Douglas, M. (1966), *Purity and Danger: An Analysis of Concepts of Pollution and Taboo*, New York: Praeger.

Douglas, M. (1991), 'The Idea of a Home: A Kind of Space', *Social Research*, 58 (1): 287–307.

Dovey, K. (1985), 'Home and Homelessness', in I. Altman and C. M. Werner (eds), *Home Environments*, New York: Plenum Press.

Dupuis, A. and D. C. Thorns (1996), 'Meanings of Home for Older Home Owners', *Housing Studies*, 11 (4): 485–501.

Duyvendak, J. W. (2011), *The Politics of Home: Belonging and Nostalgia in Western Europe and the United States*, London: Palgrave Macmillan.

Easthope, H. (2004), 'A Place Called Home', *Housing, Theory and Society*, 21 (3): 128–38.

Emerson, R. M. (1981), 'Observational Field Work', *Annual Review of Sociology*, 7 (1): 351–78.

Fabian, J (1983), *Time and the Other: How Anthropology Makes Its Object*, New York: Columbia University Press.

Fabian, J. (1990), 'Presence and Representation: The Other and Anthropological Writing', *Critical Inquiry*, 16 (4): 753–72.

Gardner, K. (1993), 'Desh-Bidesh: Sylheti Images of Home and Away', *Man*, 28 (1): 1–15.

Garelli, G. and M. Tazzioli (2017), *Tunisia as a Revolutionized Space of Migration*, New York: Palgrave Macmillan.

Gay y Blasco, P. (2017), 'Doubts, Compromises, and Ideals: Attempting a Reciprocal Life Story', *Anthropology and Humanism*, 42 (1): 91–108.

Gay y Blasco, P. and L. De La Cruz Hernández (2012), 'Friendship, Anthropology', *Anthropology and Humanism*, 37 (1): 1–14.

Geertz, C. (1988), *Works and Lives: The Anthropologist as Author*, Stanford: Stanford University Press.

Geertz, C. (1993), *The Interpretation of Cultures: Selected Essays*, London: HarperCollins UK.

Ghazal, M. (2016), 'Population Stands at Around 9.5 Million, Including 2.9 Million Guests', *Jordan Times*, 30 January. Available online: www.jordantimes.com/news/local/population-stands-around-95-million-including-29-million-guests (accessed 1 January 2019).

Goffman, A. (2015), *On the Run: Fugitive Life in an American City*, London: Picador.

Goffman, E. (1959), *The Presentation of Self in Everyday Life*, New York: Doubleday & Company.

Golub, A. (2015), 'Committing Crimes during Fieldwork: Ethics, Ethnography, and "On The Run"', *Savage Minds*, 26 June. Available online: https://savageminds. org/2015/06/25/committing-crimes-during-fieldwork-ethics-ethnography-and-on-the-run/ (accessed 21 March 2019).

Gregson, N. (2007), *Living with Things: Ridding, Accommodation, Dwelling*, Wantage: Sean Kingston Publishers.

Gudeman, S. and A. Rivera (1990), *Conversations in Colombia*, Cambridge: Cambridge University Press.

Gudeman, S. and C. Hann (2015), 'Introduction: Self-Sufficiency as Reality and as Myth', in S. Gudeman and C. Hann (eds), *Oikos and Market: Explorations in Self-Sufficiency after Socialism*, 1–24, Oxford: Berghahn.

Hall, T. (2003), *Better Times Than This: Youth Homelessness in Britain*, London: Pluto Press.

Han, C. (2012), *Life in Debt: Times of Care and Violence in Neoliberal Chile*, London: University of Calgary Press.

Handelman, D. (1994), 'Critiques of Anthropology: Literary Turns, Slippery Bends', *Poetics Today*, 15 (3): 341–81.

Hanson, R. and P. Richards (2017), 'Sexual Harassment and the Construction of Ethnographic Knowledge', *Sociological Forum*, 32 (3): 587–609.

Haraway, D. (1988), 'Situated Knowledges: The Science Question in Feminism and the Privilege of Partial Perspective', *Feminist Studies*, 14 (3): 575–99.

Haraway, D. (1994), 'A Game of Cat's Cradle: Science Studies, Feminist Theory, Cultural Studies', *Configurations*, 2 (1): 59–71.

Haraway, D. (2016), *Staying with the Trouble: Making Kin in the Chthulucene*, Durham and London: Duke University Press.

Hart, K., J.-L. Laville and A. David Cattani (2010), *Human Economy: A Citizen's Guide*. Cambridge: Polity Press.

Hart, K., J. L. Laville and A. D. Cattani (2016), *Human Economy: A Citizen's Guide*, Cambridge: Polity Press.

Hearn, J. (2012), 'The Sociological Significance of Domestic Violence: Tensions, Paradoxes and Implications', *Current Sociology*, 61 (2): 152–70.

Hecht, T. (1998), *At Home in the Street: Street Children of Northeast Brazil*, Cambridge: Cambridge University Press.

Heidegger, M. (1977), *The Question Concerning Technology, and Other Essays*, New York: Harper Collins.

Herzfeld, M. (2016), *Cultural Intimacy: Social Poetics in the Nation-State, Third Edition*. London: Routledge.

Hillyard, S. (2010), *New Frontiers in Ethnography*, Bingley: Emerald Group Publishing.

Hobsbawm, E. (1991), 'Exile', *Social Research*, 58 (1): 65–8.

Hughes, G. F. (2016), 'The Proliferation of Men: Markets, Property, and Seizure in Jordan', *Anthropological Quarterly*, 89 (4): 1081–108.

Human Rights Watch (2017), 'I Have No Idea Why They Sent Us Back', *Jordanian Deportations and Expulsions of Syrian Refugees*, Human Rights Watch, 2 October. Available online: www.hrw.org/report/2017/10/02/i-have-no-idea-why-they-sent-us-back/jordanian-deportations-and-expulsions-syrian (accessed 1 January 2019).

Humphrey, C. (1988), 'No Place like Home: The Neglect of Architecture', *Anthropology Today*, 4 (1): 16–18.

Humphrey, C. (2005), 'Ideology in Infrastructure: Architecture and Soviet Imagination', *Journal of the Royal Anthropological Institute*, 11 (1): 39–58.

INSEE (2013), 'L'hébergement Des sans-Domicile En 2012', *L'Institut National de la Statistique et des Études Économiques*, July. Available online: www.insee.fr/fr/ffc/ipweb/ip1455/ip1455.pdf (accessed 31 March 2019).

Iphofen, R. (2011), *Ethical Decision-Making in Social Research: A Practical Guide*, London: Palgrave Macmillan.

Irwin, K. (2006), 'Into the Dark Heart of Ethnography: The Lived Ethics and Inequality of Intimate Field Relationships', *Qualitative Sociology*, 29 (2): 155–75.

Jaafari, S. (2017), 'This refugee camp in Jordan has turned into a frontier town for Syrians escaping war', *PRI*, 5 April. Available online: www.pri.org/stories/2017-04-05/refugee-camp-jordan-has-turned-frontier-town-syrians-escaping-war (accessed 31 March 2019).

Jackson, M. (2005), *At Home in the World*, Durham and London: Duke University Press.

Jacobs, J. M., S. Cairns and I. Strebel (2007), '"A Tall Storey … but, a Fact Just the Same": The Red Road Highrise as a Black Box', *Urban Studies*, 44 (3): 609–29.

Jansen, S. (2009), 'Hope and the State in the Anthropology of Home: Preliminary Notes', *Ethnologia Europaea*, 39 (1): 54–61.

Jansen, S. and S. Löfving (2011), *Struggles for Home: Violence, Hope and the Movement of People*, London: Berghahn Books.

Johnsen, S., P. Cloke and J. May (2005), 'Day Centres for Homeless People: Spaces of Care or Fear?', *Social & Cultural Geography*, 6 (6): 787–811.

Kaspar, H. and S. Landolt (2015), 'Flirting in the Field: Shifting Positionalities and Power Relations in Innocuous Sexualisations of Research Encounters', *Gender, Place & Culture*, 23 (1): 107–19.

Keane, W. (2005), 'Signs Are Not the Garb of Meaning: On the Social Analysis of Material Things', in D. Miller (eds), *Materiality*, Durham and London: Duke University Press.

Keane, W. (2015), *Ethical Life: Its Natural and Social Histories*, Princeton and Oxford: Princeton University Press.

Kellett, P. and J. Moore (2003), 'Routes to Home: Homelessness and Home-Making in Contrasting Societies', *Habitat International*, 27 (1): 123–41.

Kenyon, L. (1999), 'A Home from Home: Students' Transitional Experience of Home', in T. Chapman and J. Hockey (eds), *Ideal Homes? Social Change and Domestic Life*, London: Routledge.

Kulick, D. (1995), 'Introduction. The Sexual Life of Anthropologists: Erotic Subjectivity and Ethnographic Work', in D. Kulick and M. Wilson (eds), *Taboo: Sex, Identity and Erotic Subjectivity in Anthropological Fieldwork*, 1–29, London: Routledge.

Kusumadinata, K. (1979), *Data Dasar Adeunungapi Indonesia*, Bandung: Volcanological Survey of Indonesia.

Laplantine, F. (2015), *The Life of the Senses: Introduction to a Modal Anthropology*, London and New York: Bloomsbury Academic.

Latour, B. (2007), *Reassembling the Social: An Introduction to Actor-Network-Theory*, Oxford: Oxford University Press.

Latour, B. and A. Yaneva (2008), 'Give Me a Gun and I Will Make All Buildings Move', in R. Geiser (ed.), *Explorations in Architecture: Teaching, Design, Research*, 80–9, Basel: Birkhäuser.

Levi-Strauss, C. (1983), *The Way of the Masks*, London: Jonathan Cape.

Laing, O. (2016), *The Lonely City: Adventures in the Art of Being Alone*, Edinburgh: Canongate.

Lila, A. L. (1990), 'The Romance of Resistance: Tracing Transformations of Power Through Bedouin Women', *American Ethnologist*, 17 (1): 41–55.

Lindley, A. (2010), *The Early Morning Phone Call: Somali Refugees' Remittances*, London: Berghahn Books.

Lofland, J. (2009), *Analyzing Social Settings: A Guide to Qualitative Observation and Analysis*, Belmont: Wadsworth.

Long, K. and J. Crisp (2010), 'Migration, Mobility and Solutions: An Evolving Perspective', *Forced Migration Review*, 35: 56–7.

Low, S. (2004), *Behind the Gates: Life, Security, and the Pursuit of Happiness in Fortress America*, London and New York: Routledge.

Lubet, S. (2015), 'Ethics On The Run', *The New Rambler*. Available online: https://newramblerreview.com/book-reviews/law/ethics-on-the-run (accessed 31 April 2019).

Madigan, R., M. Munro and S. J. Smith (1990), 'Gender and the Meaning of the Home', *International Journal of Urban and Regional Research*, 14 (4): 625–47.

Mallett, S. (2004), 'Understanding Home: A Critical Review of the Literature', *The Sociological Review*, 52 (1): 62–89.

Marcus, G. E. (2007), 'Ethnography Two Decades after Writing Culture: From the Experimental to the Baroque', *Anthropological Quarterly*, 80 (4): 1127–45.

Martens, L. and S. Scott (2006), 'Under the Kitchen Surface: Domestic Products and Conflicting Constructions of Home', *Home Cultures: The Journal of Architecture, Design and Domestic Space*, 3 (1): 39–62.

Mascia-Lees, F. E., P. Sharpe and C. B. Cohen (1989), 'The Postmodernist Turn in Anthropology: Cautions from a Feminist Perspective', *Signs*, 15 (1): 7–33.

Mason, V. (2011), 'The Im/mobilities of Iraqi Refugees in Jordan: Pan-Arabism, "Hospitality" and the Figure of the "Refugee"', *Mobilities*, 6 (3): 353–73.

Maynard, M. and J. Hanmer (1987), *Women, Violence and Social Control*, London: Palgrave Macmillan.

Mazzocchetti, J. and E. Piccoli (2016), 'Défis méthodologiques, éthiques et émotionnels d'une ethnographie de l'intime, des silences et des situations de violences', *Parcours Anthropologiques*. Available online: https://journals.openedition.org/pa/471 (accessed 31 March 2019).

Miller, D. (1988), 'Appropriating the State on the Council Estate', *Man*, 23 (2): 353–72.

Miller, D., ed. (1998), *Material Cultures: Why Some Things Matter*, London: University College London Press.

Miller, D. (2001), *Home Possessions: Material Culture Behind Closed Doors*, London: Berg Publishers.

Miller, D. (2009), *The Comfort of Things*, London: Polity Press.

Miller, R. J. (2011), 'American Indians, the Doctrine of Discovery, and Manifest Destiny', *Wyoming Law Review*, 11 (2): 329–49.

Mitchell, J. (1984), *Women: The Longest Revolution*, New York: Pantheon Books.

Monsutti, A. (2008), 'Afghan Migratory Strategies and the Three Solutions to the Refugee Problem', *Refugee Survey Quarterly*, 27 (1): 58–73.

Moore, H. (2011), *Still Life: Hopes, Desires and Satisfactions*, Cambridge and Malden: Polity Press.

Morgan, L. H. (1981), *Houses and House-Life of the American Aborigines*, Chicago: University of Chicago Press.

Narayan, K. (2012), *Alive in the Writing*, Chicago: University of Chicago Press.

Newton, E. (1993), 'My Best Informant's Dress: The Erotic Equation in Fieldwork', *Cultural Anthropology*, 8 (1): 3–23.

Nowicka, M. (2007), 'Mobile Locations: Construction of Home in a Group of Mobile Transnational Professionals', *Global Networks*, 7 (1): 69–86.

O'Mahony, L. F. (2013), 'The Meaning of Home: From Theory to Practice', *International Journal of Law in the Built Environment*, 5 (2): 156–71. doi:10.1108/IJLBE-11-2012-0024.

Okely, J. (2013), *Anthropological Practice: Fieldwork and the Ethnographic Method*, London and New York: Berg.

Omari, R. (2014), 'Syrians Build Houses on Donated Land in Zaatari Village', *The Jordan Times*, 21 August. Available online: www.jordantimes.com/news/local/syrians-build-houses-donated-land-zaatari-village (accessed 31 March 2019).

Ortner, S. B. (1995), 'Resistance and the Problem of Ethnographic Refusal', *Comparative Studies in Society and History*, 37 (1): 173–93.

Oxford Dictionaries (2019), 'Homing', *Oxford Dictionaries*. Available online: https://en.oxforddictionaries.com/definition/homing (accessed 31 March 2019).

Peake, L. and M. Rieker (2013), *Rethinking Feminist Interventions into the Urban*, Oxford: Routledge.

Perrin, J., N. Bühler, M. A. Berthod, J. Forney, S. Kradolfer and L. Ossipow (2018), 'Searching for Ethics: Legal Requirements and Empirical Issues for Anthropology', *Tsantsa*, 23: 138–53.

Petridou, E. (2001), 'The Taste of Home', in D. Miller (ed.), *Home Possessions: Material Culture Behind Closed Doors*, 87–104, Oxford and New York: Berg Publishers.

Pina-Cabral, J. de (1986). *Sons of Adam, Daughters of Eve: The Peasant Worldview of the Alto Minho*, Oxford: Clarendon Press.

Pollard, A. (2009), 'Field of Screams: Difficulty and Ethnographic Fieldwork', *Anthropology Matters*, 11 (2). https://www.anthropologymatters.com/index.php/anth_matters/article/view/10

Pollner, M. and R. M. Emerson (2001), 'Ethnomethodology and Ethnography', in P. Atkinson, A. Coffey, S. Delamont, L. Lofland and L. U. Lofland (eds), *Handbook of Ethnography*, 118–35, London: Sage.

Pow, C. P. and L. Kong (2007), 'Marketing the Chinese Dream Home: Gated Communities and Representations of the Good Life in (Post-) Socialist Shanghai', *Urban Geography*, 28 (2): 37–41.

Powell, M. H. (1997), *Calliandra Calothyrsus Production and Use – A Field Manual*, Morrilton: Winrock International. Available online: www.nzdl.org (accessed 25 February 2019).

Ralph, D. and L. Staeheli (2010), 'Home and Migration: Mobilities, Belongings and Identities', *Geography Compass*, 5 (7): 517–30.

Rapport, N. and A. Dawson, eds. (1998), *Migrants of Identity: Perceptions of Home in a World of Movement*, Oxford: Berg.

Richie, B. E. (2000), 'A Black Feminist Reflection on the Antiviolence Movement', *Signs*, 25 (4): 1133–7.

Ring, L. A. (2006), *Zenana: Everyday Peace in a Karachi Apartment Building*, Bloomington and Indianapolis: Indiana University Press.

Royal Society for the Conservation of Nature (RSCN) (2015), 'Azraq Wetland Reserve', *Royal Society for the Conservation of Nature*. Available online: www.rscn.org.jo/content/azraq-wetland-reserve-0 (accessed 31 March 2019).

Salzman, P. C. (2002), 'On Reflexivity', *American Anthropologist*, 104 (3): 805–11.

Scalettaris, G. (2009), 'Refugees and Mobility', *Forced Migration Review*, 33: 58–9.

Shah, A. (2017), 'Ethnography? Participant Observation, a Potentially Revolutionary Practice', *Hau: Journal of Ethnographic Theory*, 7 (1): 45–59.

Shryock, A. (2004), 'The New Jordanian Hospitality: House, Host, and Guest in the Culture of Public Display', *Comparative Studies in Society and History*, 46 (1): 35–62.

Siegelbaum, L. H. (2008), *Cars for Comrades: The Life of the Soviet Automobile*, Ithaca: Cornell University Press.

Simpson, A. (2007), 'On Ethnographic Refusal: Indigeneity, 'Voice' and Colonial Citizenship', *Junctures: The Journal for Thematic Dialogue*, 9: 67–80.

Simpson, A. (2014), *Mohawk Interruptus: Political Life Across the Borders of Settler States*, Durham and London: Duke University Press.

Smith, Z. (2012), *NW*, London: Penguin UK.

Spronk, R. (2015), 'Sexuality and Subjectivity: Erotic Practices and the Question of Bodily Sensations', *Social Anthropology*, 22 (1): 3–22.

Stacey, J. (1988), 'Can There Be a Feminist Ethnography?' *Women's Studies International Forum*, 11 (1): 21–27.

Steglich, U. (2015), 'Teilräumung des TeePeeLands. TLG lässt Zelte räumen und einen Zaun am Spreeufer ziehen', ecke köpenicker – *Zeitung für das Sanierungsgebiet Nördliche Luisenstadt*, 2 (4). Available online: www.luisenstadt-mitte.de/download/pdf/akteure/ecke/150331_Ecke_02_April_2015.pdf (accessed 27 February 2019).

Strathern, M. (1988), *The Gender of the Gift: Problems with Women and Problems with Society in Melanesia*, Berkeley: University of California Press.

Taussig, M. (2011), *I Swear I Saw This: Drawings in Fieldwork Notebooks, Namely My Own*, Chicago and London: University of Chicago Press.

Thiollet, H. (2017), 'Managing Transnational Labour in the Arab Gulf: External and Internal Dynamics of Migration Politics since the 1950s', in L. Vignal (ed.), *The Transnational Middle East*, 21–43, London: Routledge.

Tiltnes, A. A., H. Zhang and J. Pedersen (2019), *The Living Conditions of Syrian Refugees in Jordan, Results from the 2017–2018 Survey of Syrian Refugees Inside and Outside Camps*, Oslo: Fafo. Available online: www.fafo.no/index.php/zoo-publikasjoner/fafo-rapporter/item/the-living-conditions-of-syrian-refugees-in-jordan (accessed 31 March 2019).

UN HABITAT (2014), *City Profile Homs. Multi Sector Assessment*, May 2014, UN Habitat. Available online: https://unhabitat.org/city-profile-homs-multi-sector-assessment/ (accessed 31 March 2019).

UNHCR (2018), 'Total persons of concern. Mafraq', *UNHCR Syria Regional Refugee Response*, 9 December. Available online: https://data2.unhcr.org/en/situations/syria/location/52 (accessed 1 January 2019).

UNHCR (2019), 'Jordan, Total Persons of Concern', *UNHCR Syria Regional Refugee Response*, 11 March. Available online: https://data2.unhcr.org/en/situations/syria/location/36 (accessed 31 March 2019).

Valentine, D. (2007), *Imagining Transgender: An Ethnography of a Category*, Durham and London: Duke University Press.

Van Aken, M. (2005), 'Values at Work: A Case of Labourers in Agribusiness (Jordan)', *Revue des mondes musulmans et de la Méditerranée*, 104–5: 109–31.

Van Gennep, A. (1960), *The Rites of Passage*, Chicago: The University of Chicago Press.

Vertovec, S. (2007), 'Super-Diversity and Its Implications', *Ethnic and Racial Studies*, 30 (6): 1024–54.

Vogel, L. (1973), 'The Earthly Family', *Radical America*, 7 (4–5): 9–44.

Voight, B. E. (2000), 'Historical Eruptions of Merapi Volcano, Central Java, Indonesia, 1768–1998', *Journal of Volcanology and Adeeothermal Research*, 100 (1): 69–138.

Wacquant, L. (2004), *Body and Soul: Notebooks of an Apprentice Boxer*, New York: Oxford University Press.

Wagner, A. C. (2019), *Transnational Mobilities during the Syrian War – An Ethnography of Rural Refugees and Evangelical Humanitarians in Mafraq, Jordan*, PhD dissertation, International Development, University of Edinburgh, Edinburgh.

Watson, C. W. (1999), *Being There: Fieldwork in Anthropology*, London: Pluto Press.

Wekker, G. (2006), *The Politics of Passion*, New York: Columbia University Press.

Wolch, J. R. and S. Rowe (1992), 'On the Streets: Mobility Paths of the Urban Homeless', *City and Society*, 6 (4): 115–40.

Yahya, M., J. Kassir and K. El-Hariri (2018), *Unheard Voices: What Syrian Refugees Need to Return Home*', Carnegie Middle East Center, 16 April. Available online: https://carnegie-mec.org/2018/04/16/unheard-voices-what-syrian-refugees-need-to-return-home-pub-76050 (accessed 1 March 2019).

Zigon, J. (2014), 'An Ethics of Dwelling and a Politics of World-Building: A Critical Response to Ordinary Ethics', *Journal of the Royal Anthropological Institute*, 20 (4): 746–64.

Index